Paradise
to Prison

Paradise to Prison

Studies in Genesis

John J. Davis

BAKER BOOK HOUSE
Grand Rapids, Michigan 49516

First printing, July 1975
Second printing, August 1976
Third printing, July 1978
Fourth printing, February 1980
Fifth printing, March 1982
Sixth printing, April 1983
Seventh printing, August 1984
Eighth printing, November 1985
Ninth printing, February 1986
Tenth printing, April 1987
Eleventh printing, September 1988
Twelfth printing, October 1988
Thirteenth printing, November 1989

To
my wife Carolyn
faithful companion and loving mother
and
our daughter Debbie
the joy of our lives

Contents

Tables of Transliteration

Whenever possible, these rules for transliteration are followed.

Hebrew

Consonants			Vowels	
א -'	ט -ṭ	פ -p,p̄	‍ָ -ā,ŏ	‍ֱ -ĕ
ב -b,b̲	י -y	צ -ṣ	‍ַ -a	‍ִ -i
ג -g,g̲	כ -k,k̲	ק -q	‍ֲ -ă	‍ִי -î
ד -d,d̲	ל -l	ר -r	הָ -â	וֹ -ô
ה -h	מ -m	שׂ -ś	‍ֶ -e	‍ֳ -ŏ
ו -w	נ -n	שׁ -š	‍ֵ -ē	וֹ -ō
ז -z	ס -s	ת -t,t̲	‍ֵי -ê	וּ -û
ח -ḥ	ע -'		‍ֶ -e	‍ֻ -u

Greek

α,ɑ -a	ζ -z	λ -l	π -p	φ -ph
β -b	η -ē	μ -m	ρ -r	χ -ch
γ -g	θ -th	ν -n	σ,ς -s	ψ -ps
δ -d	ι -i	ξ -x	τ -t	ω -ō
ε -e	κ -k	ο -o	υ -u	' -h

List of Illustrations

I. Charts

II. Maps

III. Photographs and line drawings

Foreword

The cosmic scope of its themes, the majestic imagery of its poetry, and the warm drama of its narrative only partially account for the enduring worth of the Book of Genesis. Its surpassing achievement is the communication of truth from God to man. When one acknowledges this fact, as Dr. John Davis does, the real beauty of this book unfolds and it becomes comprehensible to the reader.

It becomes even more understandable as the 3,800-year cultural, linguistic, and geographical gaps are bridged. This is just one task at which the present volume succeeds admirably. As few other writers have been able to do, Dr. Davis has drawn together a body of data usually regarded as the bailiwick of scholars and made it not only tolerable but eminently useful to the layman. Time after time selections from ancient literature, geographical phenomena, and archaeological artifacts are marshalled to illuminate the biblical text.

Readers familiar with Dr. Davis' earlier contributions to Old Testament studies will find more of what they have come to expect from his pen: a generous bibliography for the ambitious student; pointed spiritual applications for the pastor and Sunday school teacher; and an occasional touch of humor so well known to those of us who have sat under his classroom ministry.

From *Paradise to Prison* sounds like a downhill slide and, indeed, that is the story of man. But Genesis is preeminently a book of hope because it is the beginning of the story of redemption. The God who wrought the mighty works of creation is the same God who can unshackle the human heart from the bondage of sin.

Robert Ibach, Jr.

Preface

In spite of changing trends and shifting theological interests, the Book of Genesis continues to command the attention of scholars throughout the world. The simplicity of its narratives and the inexhaustibility of its spiritual truth make its charm and value enduring.

Moses takes the reader from an awesome, sinless paradise to death and burial in Egypt. In between are his grand descriptions of the origin and fall of man, the destruction of the world by water, the judgment of Babel, and the exciting adventures of the Hebrew patriarchs.

Any modern study of Genesis must consider the vast array of material unearthed by archaeologists in the Near East. Where appropriate we have also discussed the Hebrew text, geography, and ancient cultures. Comparisons between Genesis and its cultural background will not alone yield proper interpretations, however; the text still must be compared with other portions of Scripture.

Because space is limited, the biblical text is not quoted to any extent; we recommend that the reader have a Bible at hand while working through this volume.

Finally, we have attempted to make the study of Genesis practical and spiritually rewarding as well as intellectually informative. It is my hope that all who read this book will be drawn closer to the God of whom Moses spoke so eloquently.

We wish to express special appreciation to Mrs. Linda Dollar, who typed the first and final drafts; Mrs. Janice Jenkins, who assisted Mrs. Dollar in typing the final draft; Dr. John C. Whitcomb, James R. Battenfield, and Mrs. Laura Davis, all of whom read the entire manuscript for content and style; Robert Ibach, who also read the manuscript and who prepared the maps and charts; Dr. Benjamin A. Hamilton, who prepared the Scripture index; and Arthur W. Davis, who drew the line sketches. The contributions of all were invaluable and of the highest caliber.

Paradise
to Prison

1

Introduction to Genesis

No other piece of ancient Near Eastern literature that has survived the ravages of time compares favorably with the Book of Genesis. Its theological perspectives and historical profiles of early man are unique. It is important not because it is old—other collections antedate it by many years—but because it completely transcends the primitive mythology of the ancient world.

Reading and studying Genesis are not burdensome tasks. Its themes are varied and its personal portraits unparalleled. It immediately tackles one of man's most basic questions: What is the origin of all things? Its answer is as credible as it is captivating. From the origin of man the writer shifts attention to the fall of man and the human dilemma. These chapters are strategic because they resolve that dilemma. The problem of evil is rarely discussed in such a manner by other ancient writers. From this point the writer concentrates on the spiritual, moral, and practical consequences of sin. Great catastrophes, such as the flood and the confusion of tongues at Babel, demonstrate God's response to human rebellion.

Where in the annals of history can we find more imaginative and frank portraits than those of Abraham and his descendants?

Abraham's moments of great triumph and ecstasy are not reported to the exclusion of his hours of humility and disgrace; this balanced description is quite distinct from the idealism of ancient Near Eastern historiography. The detailed descriptions of Abraham's failures, therefore, constitute a remarkable proof for the inspiration of this book.

The sensitive reader cannot help but be struck by this book's great contrasting emphases: on one hand majestic, cosmological truth; on the other hand personal, intimate, and individualistic narratives of a man, a wife, and their family. While theological abstractions are common, they do not exclude personal warmth and historical objectivity. There are also great contrasts between personalities; the most significant is between God and Satan, and based on this contrast is the one between good and evil and their practical effects.

The Book of Genesis, therefore, is of utmost value to the scientist, the historian, and the theologian: to the scientist for its cosmology, to the historian for its early history of Israel, and to the theologian for its basic philosophical implications. But one must approach the book properly; only then can one hope to understand it, not to mention the rest of the Bible and Jesus Himself. Jesus told His hostile contemporaries that "had ye believed Moses, ye would have believed me: for he wrote of me. But if ye believe not his writings, how shall ye believe my words?" (John 5:46, 47)

I. The Title

The Hebrew title of the first book of Moses, $B^e r \bar{e}$ '$\check{s}it$, is also the first word of the book, translated "in the beginning." The Hebrew title for the third book of Moses, $Wayyiqr\bar{a}$', translated "and he [the Lord] called," is similarly derived. This was a common practice in the ancient Near East. Another example of it is the Babylonian creation story, which is entitled *Enūma Eliš* (meaning "when on high") and which begins, *Enūma eliš*.

The English title for the first book of Moses, like the title for the third book, comes from the Septuagint. The translators of this Greek version of the Old Testament named the first book *Genesis* because it described the genesis, or beginning, of the universe, and the Latin Vulgate retained that title. They named the third book *Leviticus* because it discussed the Levitical priesthood.

20

II. Authorship and Date

A. History of Pentateuchal Criticism

Until the nineteenth century both Jewish and Christian scholars generally agreed that Moses was the author of Genesis. There were, of course, a few dissenting voices of note. For example, Jerome found it difficult to decide whether Moses or Ezra had written the Pentateuch. The Gnostics denied Mosaic authorship completely. In the twelfth century Abraham ibn-Ezra felt that the post-Mosaic editions of the Pentateuch required a modification of Mosaic authorship. In the seventeenth century the philosopher Spinoza raised serious doubts about direct Mosaic authorship and launched what is now known as "higher criticism" of the Bible—that is, internal analysis as opposed to "lower criticism," or textual analysis. Since then the concept of multiple authorship from later periods of time has been extremely popular. French physician Jean Astruc was the first to isolate documentary sources for the Pentateuch. He found two, one preferring the divine name *ĕlōhîm*, the other preferring *YHWH*. The two-document theory was popularized and expanded by J. G. Eichhorn, a German scholar at the University of Jena. To the criterion of divine names Eichhorn added those of style and content, and unlike Astruc he gave up Mosaic authorship. He is designated by many the "father of higher criticism."

By the middle of the nineteenth century, the most popular version of the documentary hypothesis identified four sources. Opinions differed concerning their exact date and sequence, but the following pattern was typical: J (ca. 850 B.C.), E (ca. 750 B.C.), D (621 B.C.), and P (570 B.C.). This theory has been gradually revised until each of the four sources has been subdivided—J, for example, is commonly divided into J^1, J^2, and J^3—and additional sources have been postulated—S (Seir-Edom), L (Lay), and K (Kenite). These additional sources have been carefully defended but not widely accepted.

The traditional documentary theory began to change once Scandinavian scholars stressed the role of oral tradition in the origin of Scripture. In view of this and recent archaeological discoveries, some theorists conceded that some of the material had to be early, concluding that the documents merely represent streams of tradition and may be chronologically parallel. Most modern commentators, however, adhere to the traditional documentary analysis. They may disagree on the dates of sources or traditions, but they generally agree on a multiplicity of authors.[1] The major sources of Genesis are, they say, J, E, and P; "it shows no trace, whatever, of source D," according to E. A. Speiser.[2] P (priestly) shows decided preference for the divine names Elohim and El Shaddai. He was "forever concerned with such other statistics as the total life span of the given individual, the age of a father at the birth of his oldest son . . . , and the names of other members of the family, and the like."[3] J, on the other hand, used Yahweh exclusively. He was not given to stereotypes in either vocabulary or style; he was the literary genius behind the Book of Genesis. His writings are warmer and more intimate than P's, making freer use of anthropomorphisms. He probably belongs to the tenth century, which is about one hundred years earlier than scholars of the nineteenth century dated him. "In general, E lacks the directness of J where man's relations with God are concerned. . . . The center of E's world has not shifted all the way to heaven, as it has with P; neither is it earthbound, on the other hand, as in the case of J. E has a tendency, furthermore, to justify and explain rather than let actions speak for themselves. . . . Basically, however, E is interested in events, whereas J is concerned with people."[4] There are also other minor sources in the Book of Genesis; certain sections do not fit into the above categories, so there must have been a redactor or redactors—R.[5]

While this approach is widely circulated and defended, it does not, in this writer's opinion, solve the problem of Genesis' origin. A brief consideration of difficulties raised by traditional and modified documentary theories is in order.

1. The divine names. Isolating documents or traditions on the basis of divine names is a tenuous procedure indeed. In fact it must be ruled invalid since evidently no other religious document from the ancient Near East was compiled in such a manner; a documentary analysis of the *Gilgameš Epic* or *Enūma Eliš* would be complete folly. The author of Genesis may well have selected

---

1. See, for example, E. A. Speiser, *Genesis*, pp. xxii–xliii; and G. Henton Davies, *Genesis*, pp. 109–16.
2. *Genesis*, p. xxii.
3. Ibid., pp. xxiv–xxv.
4. Ibid., xxv–xxxi.
5. For a more extended discussion of these sources see R. K. Harrison, *Introduction to the Old Testament*, pp. 497–541.

divine names on the basis of theological emphasis rather than dogmatic preference. Many divine names were probably interchangeable; *Baal* and *Hadad* were used interchangeably in the Hadad Tablet from Ugarit,[6] and similar examples could be cited from Egyptian texts.[7]

2. Style and vocabulary. To conclude that differences in style or vocabulary unmistakably indicate different authors is invalid for any body of literature. It is well known that a single author may vary his style and select his vocabulary to fit the themes he is developing and the people he is addressing. It goes without saying that a young graduate student's love letter will vary significantly in vocabulary and style from his research paper.

3. The documents. Extensive criticisms of documentary analysis, as well as archaeological discoveries, have largely refuted its results when applied to the Pentateuch in general and Genesis in particular. Recent studies have demonstrated that dating the various documents is nearly impossible; at best it is rather subjective and arbitrary.[8] Samuel R. Külling, for example, has revealed the inherent weaknesses in assigning to P a postexilic date.[9] Another significant evaluation of source analysis is that of Kenneth A. Kitchen.[10] Since he and others have more than adequately dealt with all other aspects of literary criticism, it will not be discussed further.

B. Evidence for Mosaic Authorship

The concept of Mosaic authorship is not as simple as it may first appear. Did Moses personally write every word of the Pentateuch? Hardly, since sections like the one that describes his own death (Deut. 34:1-8) must have been written after he died. The amount of material added by inspired scribes, however, appears to be quite

---

6. G. R. Driver, *Canaanite Myths and Legends*, pp. 70–72.
7. For example, see the "Stele of Ikhernofret" in James B. Pritchard, ed., *Ancient Near Eastern Texts*, 2nd ed. (Princeton: Princeton University Press, 1955), pp. 329, 330 (hereafter cited as *ANET*).
8. Harrison, *Introduction to the Old Testament*, pp. 505ff.; Gleason Archer, *A Survey of Old Testament Introduction*, pp. 86–95; Oswald T. Allis, *The Five Books of Moses*.
9. *Zur Datierung de "Genesis-P-Stucke" Namentlich des Kapitels Genesis XVII.* Külling summarizes his book in "The Dating of the So-Called 'P-Sections' in Genesis."
10. *Ancient Orient and Old Testament*, pp. 112–38.

limited. Much evidence points to Mosaic authorship, and a summary of the most important evidence follows.

1. External evidence. This consists primarily of the testimony of the Bible to the authorship of the Pentateuch. The Pentateuch itself contains a number of references to Mosaic authorship of large portions (cf. Exod. 17:14; 24:4; 34:27; Num. 33:1, 2; Deut. 31:9).[11] But other Old Testament books also ascribe the Pentateuch to Moses. The most important reference is Joshua 1:7, 8, in which the law is associated with Moses and the phrase "the book of the law" appears. This phrase indicates that the Torah had already appeared in literary form and was accepted as the Word of God revealed. For that reason Joshua was commanded to meditate on it and obey it, and was promised that this would insure success. From this passage and many others like it, one can conclude that shortly after Moses' death the Torah appeared in written form and was recognized as a message from God and therefore fully authoritative. This gives some clue to the process by which biblical revelation received canonical status, a process superintended by the Holy Spirit.[12]

Numerous references in the New Testament also allude to Mosaic authorship, and many are direct quotes from Christ Himself. For example, Jesus asked the Sadducees, "Have ye not read in the book of Moses, how in the bush God spake unto him, saying, I am the God of Abraham, and the God of Isaac, and the God of Jacob?" (Mark 12:26).[13] The assertion implicit in the question is of utmost importance. The Lord is either clearly affirming Mosaic authorship of the Pentateuch or He is merely accommodating Himself to a historical error current in His day; these are the only alternatives. If one concedes that Christ practiced accommodation to error, how does one distinguish between what is truth and what is accommodation? And how can the Lord ever accommodate Himself to error, anyway? This writer contends that Jesus' words must have been historically true, and that therefore Moses must have written the Pentateuch.

The Jews of Palestine and the dispersion were unanimous on the matter, as is reflected in the Samaritan Pentateuch, the Palestinian

11. Additional evidence is provided by the expression in Lev. 1:1 and Num. 1:1, "God spoke to Moses."
12. Cf. also Josh. 8:31, 32; 22:5, Judg. 3:4; I Kings 2:3; II Kings 18:6; 12; 21:8; 23:25; Ezra 6:18; Neh. 31:1; Dan. 9:11–13; Mal. 4:4.
13. See also John 5:46, 47; 7:19; Acts 3:22; Rom. 10:5.

Talmud, the Babylonian Talmud, the Apocrypha (cf. Ecclus. 45:5; II Macc. 7:30), and the writings of both Philo (*Life of Moses*, 3:39) and Josephus (*Antiquities*, 4:8:45). The church fathers, with very few exceptions, concurred.

2. Internal evidence. This consists primarily in evidence within the Pentateuch concerning the author; the second millennium customs, literary forms, and language expressed or used in the Pentateuch; and the obvious unity of Genesis.

present

The author must have been thoroughly familiar with the desert and must, in fact, have written while in that environment (cf. Lev. 18:3; Deut. 12:9; 15:4, 7; 17:14; Num. 2:1ff.; Lev. 14:8; 16:21; 17:3, 9). He must have been an eyewitness since innumerable

eyewitness

details in the Pentateuch would have been lost to any but an eyewitness; they are incidental to the main story and reflect careful observation (cf. Exod. 15:27; 25:5). And the author knew Egypt well. He was familiar with Egyptian names such as *On*, a designation for the city of Heliopolis; *Pithom*, meaning "the house of Atum"; *Potiphera*, meaning "the gift of Ra"; *Asenath*; and

Egyptian Names

Moses, possibly a shortened form of Thutmose or Ahmose. He used Egyptian words freely (cf. Gen. 41:43 where the expression " . . . '*abrēk*" apparently refers to the Egyptian form '*b rk*—"O heart bow down!").[14] He referred to flora and fauna that are typically Egyptian or Sinaitic. For example, the Shittim, or Acacia tree, is indigenous to Egypt and the Sinai peninsula but not to Palestine. He also alluded to a number of animals that are typically Egyptian or Sinaitic (cf. Deut. 14:5; Lev. 11:16). The geographic references of the author are extensive, detailed, and extremely accurate.

Studies revolving around the Nuzi Tablets of the fifteenth century B.C. indicate that a number of customs in the patriarchal period were also common among the Hurrians in the northeast. Of more significance, however, are the covenant forms which are found in the Pentateuch and which appear to be distinctly second millennium in form and style. "If these works first took fixed literary forms only in the ninth to the sixth centuries B.C. and onward, why and how should their writers (or redactors) so easily be able to reproduce covenant forms that have fallen out of customary use 300 to 600 years earlier . . . , and entirely fail to reflect the first millennium covenant forms that were commonly

25

---

14. Archer, *Old Testament Introduction*, p. 102.

used in their own day?"[15] Of course it might be argued that the priest from the fifth century B.C. conducted archaeological expeditions to important sites which contained literary remains of the second millennium B.C. But even if that were true (and it is rather unlikely), it does not explain why he would have utilized such early covenant forms instead of the ones common in his own day.

2nd millennium

The Pentateuch's archaisms also put it in the second millennium. The most widely recognized example is the pronoun *she*, which appears as *hiw'* instead of the usual *hî'*. Another example is the word *young girl*, spelled *na'ar* instead of *na'ᵃrâ*, the feminine form.[16]

The unified content and style of Genesis can hardly be accounted for by the genius of a late redactor or redactors. Every indication is that it was organized and produced by one man. Notice, for example, the constant use of the refrain, "these are the generations" (cf. 2:4; 5:1; 6:9; 10:1; 11:20, 27; 25:12, 19; 36:1, 9; 37:2).

Intellectual capacity

Since "Moses was learned in all the wisdom of the Egyptians and was mighty in words and in deeds" (Acts 7:22), it is not unreasonable to assume that he had the intellectual capacity and training to be the primary author of Genesis. Archaeological light on Egyptian education indicates that as Moses grew in the royal court, he would have received much formal training in reading and writing the hieroglyphic and hieratic scripts, in copying texts, and in writing letters and other formal documents. He probably had opportunity to learn something of the languages of Canaan, for some Egyptian officials knew both the geography and languages of that land. Therefore, while it may be conceded that small portions were written later, we must conclude that Genesis was essentially written by Moses himself or a scribe under his immediate control. Whatever was added, was added by a scribe fully inspired by the Holy Spirit (II Tim. 3:16).

III. Primary Theological Themes

It is rather amazing that from a world completely saturated with polytheism should come a unique document advocating ethical monotheism. From the very outset Genesis confronts us with a

---

15. Kitchen, *Ancient Orient and Old Testament*, p. 100.
16. For other examples see Archer, *Old Testament Introduction*, p. 107.

An alphabetic inscription in Sinaitic script, dating from the fifteenth century B.C.

living, personal God. The writer makes no attempt to provide philosophical or scientific evidence for God's existence; he assumes it and views everything in the light of it. He presents God as sovereign and holy. God's majestic power is expressed in the beauty of creation and the awesomeness of divine judgment. The writer quite clearly asserts that what he says about God was revealed to him. He makes no attempt to glorify himself for his knowledge; he did not discover God through natural revelation alone.

Also important is the doctrine of man. Man was created by God, bears His image, and enjoys a unique relationship with Him. The Book of Genesis is extremely important for modern man's understanding of anthropology. Man's natural tendency toward evil can only be understood in the light of Genesis 3. Not only is the predicament of man fully described but the divine solution is highlighted. The exercise of the grace of God is an unmistakable feature of the book. Man in his darkest hour, condemned by the greatest of failures, first is approached by God. It was God who called Abraham and gave to him those things which were unearned. And Genesis is the book which informs us that the Savior

27

Savior

would be bruised for the redemption of man and that Satan would be crushed by Christ (Gen. 3:15).

Genesis also introduces the concept of a covenant relationship between God and His people. An understanding of that unique covenant between Abraham and God is essential to an understanding of the rest of the Old Testament and of the New as well.

Covenant Relation

Cosmology

Another of the book's important themes is cosmology. It explains the origin of the universe and its essential functions in simple yet scientifically accurate terms.

IV. Chronological Framework

A. Adam to Abraham

The chronology of events from the time of creation to the early years of Abraham is extremely difficult to determine for two fundamental reasons: (1) the Bible provides no controllable statistical data that apply to the problem of absolute chronology; (2) most of the events took place in the preliterate period for which we have no extrabiblical written documents. The term *prehistoric* has usually been applied to that period before written documents, a period ending at approximately 3000 B.C. The one thousand years preceding Abraham is documented with written materials in both Egypt and Mesopotamia. Prior to about 3000 B.C., however, the situation is quite different. Conclusions concerning chronological sequences must be drawn from archaeological data and typological interpretations.

Pre-historic pre 3000 B.C.

Archbishop James Ussher, working from the genealogical tables of Genesis 5 and 11, determined the date of creation as 4004 B.C. and the date of Abraham as a little after 2000 B.C. Ussher's date for Abraham is relatively close, but modern scholarship has properly rejected his dates for creation and the Noahic flood.

Problems of Chronology

The problem of pre-Abrahamic chronology usually revolves around the genealogies in Genesis 5 and 11. They have been regarded by many as sufficient to establish an absolute chronology. This assumption, however, has proved to be a tenuous one because the genealogies in the Bible are not designed to provide this type of statistical information. William H. Green correctly observes: "It can scarcely be necessary to adduce proof to one who has even a superficial acquaintance with the genealogies of the Bible, that these are frequently abbreviated by the omission of unimportant names. In fact, abridgement is the general rule, in-

28

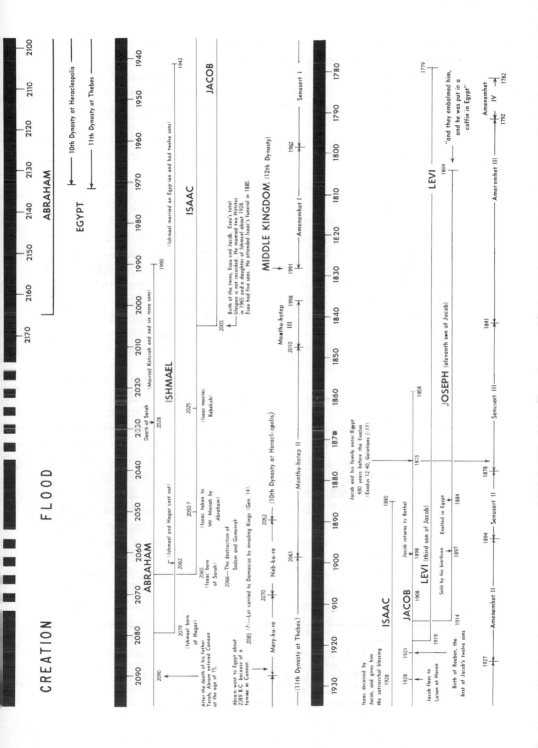

duced by the indisposition of the sacred writers to incumber their pages with more names than were necessary for their immediate purpose. This is so constantly the case, and the reason for it is so obvious, that the occurrence of it need create no surprise anywhere, and we are at liberty to suppose it whenever anything in the circumstances of the case favors that belief."[17] Had the author of Genesis intended these genealogies to be used for chronological purposes, he probably would have provided a numerical summation at the end of each list. Also noteworthy is that neither Moses nor any other inspired writer deduces from these genealogies a chronology. Scripture nowhere computes the time that elapsed from the creation to the flood or from the flood to the descent into Egypt; it does, however, for the period from the descent into Egypt to the exodus (Exod. 12:40) and the period from the exodus to the building of the temple (I Kings 6:1). Furthermore, if these lists were intended for chronological purposes, why are numbers introduced which have little relation to these purposes? The ages recorded are extremely significant in understanding longevity in the preflood era, but they do not provide sufficient information on which to construct an absolute chronology.

It should also be observed that not all the postdiluvian patriarchs are listed in the present Hebrew text of Genesis 11. In Luke's genealogy of Mary, the name *Cainan* appears between *Sala* and *Arphaxad* (3:36). This one omission makes it impossible to fix the date of the great flood. It should also be observed that if the genealogy of Genesis 11 is complete, only 292 years separate the flood from the birth of Abraham. Shem, the son of Noah, lived for 502 years after the flood and on this calculation would have outlived Abraham. Genesis 11, then, must have gaps of considerable magnitude, and it is equally probable that the genealogy of Genesis 5 is incomplete. Therefore, it is impossible to establish a firm date for creation or the flood.

This does not mean, however, that we have no framework whatever for this lengthy period of time. Stratified mounds in Mesopotamia and Palestine show an unbroken sequence of occupation as far back as 7000 B.C. Archaeologists base their calculations

---

17. "Primeval Chronology" in Walter C. Kaiser, ed., *Classical Evangelical Essays in Old Testament Interpretation*, pp. 13, 14. See also Kitchen, *Ancient Orient and Old Testament*, p. 37; R. Laird Harris, *Man: God's Eternal Creation*, pp. 68–71; John C. Whitcomb and Henry M. Morris, *The Genesis Flood*, p. 474; and Allis, *The Five Books of Moses*, pp. 295–98.

on stratigraphy, pottery typology, carbon 14, and other technical methods of dating. Thousands of carbon 14 dates from various sites, crosschecked with other information, seem of considerable magnitude.[18] The occupational sequences at Jericho go back to prepottery, Neolithic periods and indicate that the flood must be dated before about 6000 B.C.[19] —assuming, of course, that the flood was universal. Even if it was not, sites in the Mesopotamian valley still require a date earlier than 6000 B.C.[20] Those who insist on dating the flood later than this have the very delicate and difficult problem of how animal and human life became redistributed across the face of the earth in such an extremely short period of time. No solution to this problem does justice to the overwhelmingly abundant archaeological evidence.

Since primitive cultures apparently appeared worldwide approximately 12,000 to 10,000 B.C., the flood might have occurred sometime prior to that. It could have occurred anywhere from 18,000 to 15,000 B.C. although it may have been slightly later, depending on the accuracy of the dates assigned to Mesolithic and Neolithic sites.

The amount of time which elapsed between Adam and Noah is even more difficult to calculate.

Where then does all of this leave the student of Scripture with respect to the time when life appeared on earth? On one hand are the extravagant estimates of evolutionary geologists, ranging anywhere from 100,000,000[21] to 24,000,000 years,[22] and on the other are far lower ones which range from 100,000[23] to 4,974 years.[24] This wide range of figures makes it evident that at the present time a specific date for the origin of either the earth or man cannot be fixed with certainty. The only way it could, would be to agree, without qualification, to one of two rather arbitrary presuppositions. The first is that on which uniformitarian geology is based, that all natural processes have remained essentially un-

---

18. Recent studies of radiometric dating have raised some serious questions concerning its accuracy, however. See Harold S. Slusher, *Critique of Radiometric Dating*.

19. Kathleen Kenyon, *Archaeology in the Holy Land*. One of the addenda to the third edition, however, pushes back the date to 9000 B.C. because of carbon 14 tests.

20. See G. Ernest Wright, *The Bible and the Ancient Near East*, pp. 77–80.

21. George C. Simpson, "The Nonprevalence of Humanoids," p. 772.

22. G. Frederick Wright, *Origin and Antiquity of Man*, p. 6.

23. Robert W. Wood, "The Age of Man," p. 27.

24. Letter to the editor in *School Science and Mathematics* 70 (1970): 846.

changed. If this assumption is not granted, then all modern chemical and radiological dating techniques are suspect, and the scientist must seek other means of establishing a time sequence for earth history. The second presupposition is that the genealogies of Genesis 5 and 11 are sequential and unbroken, providing a fully dependable basis for a chronological scheme. This writer's view is that, given the objective data currently available, neither presupposition can be granted. The geological record of earth history points to major catastrophes which have sufficiently interrupted natural processes to render any general, unbroken uniformitarianism untenable. And because genealogies in Scripture are notorious for their schematic arrangement and omissions,[25] the second presupposition is equally untenable.

B. Abraham to Joseph

There is considerable disagreement among scholars with respect to the date of Abraham and his descendants. Cyrus H. Gordon has described Abraham as a "merchant prince" and places him and his family in the second half of the second millennium B.C. He argues that according to Genesis 47:11 Jacob came to Egypt an old man in the Ramesside age (late fourteenth century B.C.). Moses accordingly left Egypt during the third quarter of the thirteenth century. This would leave 125 years for the bondage. If Jacob was an aged man in the late fourteenth century, his grandfather must have lived in the fifteenth century B.C.[26] John Bright, on the other hand, sets the limits of the patriarchal period between the twentieth and sixteenth centuries B.C.[27] Nelson Glueck[28] and many others seem to agree with Bright.

The chronological framework of the biblical period from Abraham to Joseph rests upon two pivotal texts of Scripture. The first is I Kings 6:1, which dates the exodus 480 years before the fourth year of Solomon's reign. If one accepts Edwin R. Thiele's date of 930 B.C. for the end of Solomon's forty-year reign,[29] then the exodus occurred in 1445 B.C. The time gap between the exodus

---

25. For an extended discussion of this see Green, "Primeval Chronology," pp. 13–27.
26. "Abraham and the Merchants of Ura," p. 31; and *The Ancient Near East*, pp. 115ff.
27. *A History of Israel*, p. 76.
28. *Rivers in the Desert*, p. 68.
29. *The Mysterious Numbers of the Hebrew Kings*, p. 56.

and the arrival of Jacob's family in Egypt is determined by Exodus 12:40. It states that Jacob arrived in Egypt 430 years before the exodus. The date for Joseph, then, would be approximately 1875 B.C.[30] Since Jacob was 130 years old when he entered Egypt (Gen. 47:9, 28) and Joseph was 39 (Gen. 41:46, 47; 45:6), Jacob must have been 91 when Joseph was born. Jacob was probably born in 2005 B.C. (130 years before he entered Egypt). Isaac was 60 when Jacob was born (Gen. 25:26), and Abraham was 100 when Isaac was born (Gen. 21:5). Therefore, Abraham was born in 2165 B.C. This date is widely accepted by conservative scholars and would place Abraham in the Palestinian Middle Bronze I period. The archaeological and cultural implications of this will be discussed later.[31]

Abraham 2165 BC

V. Literary Style and Text

The literary style of the Book of Genesis is quite distinct from that of Exodus. The first book of the Torah emphasizes narrative arrangements, focusing primarily on personalities (e.g., Adam, Abel, Noah, Abraham, Isaac, Jacob, and Joseph) and the events associated with them; in the Book of Exodus the only individual to receive such detailed treatment is Moses himself. Genesis is an example of classical Hebrew prose and generally reads with considerable consistency and smoothness. It is apparent at some points that additions were made, probably by Joshua, Eleazar, or perhaps one of the priests closely associated with Moses.

Gen. primar[y] narrative

The original text of Genesis, unlike that of some other Old Testament books, is quite free from transcriptional errors. The errors that are present are of little consequence to the meaning and significance of the text as a whole. The six manuscripts of Genesis that are part of the Dead Sea Scroll collection generally follow the traditional readings of the Masoretic text.[32]

VI. Outline

A. The Creation (1:1–2:25)
   1. The beginning (1:1)

---

30. See my discussion of this verse in *Moses and the Gods of Egypt*, pp. 148–50.
31. See chapter 11.
32. Millar Burrows, *More Light on the Dead Sea Scrolls*, p. 135; William S. LaSor, *Amazing Dead Sea Scrolls and the Christian Faith*, pp. 40, 41.

H. Covenant Renewal (15:1-17:27)
1. The convenant reaffirmed (15:1-21)
2. The birth of Ishmael (16:1-16)
3. Sign of the covenant (17:1-27)

I. The Destruction of Sodom (18:1-19:38)
1. Abraham's fellowship (18:1-22)
2. Abraham's intercession (18:23-33)
3. The wickedness of Sodom (19:1-14)
4. The destruction of Sodom (19:15-29)
5. Lot and his daughters (19:30-38)

J. Life and Death (20:1-23:20)
1. Abraham in Gerar (20:1-18)
2. The birth of Isaac (21:1-21)
3. Abraham at Beersheba (21:22-34)
4. Abraham tested (22:1-24)
5. Sarah's death and burial (23:1-20)

K. The Last Days of Abraham (24:1-27:46)
1. A bride sought for Isaac (24:1-67)
2. Abraham's death and burial (25:1-34)
3. Isaac and Abimelech (26:1-35)
4. Blessing by deception (27:1-46)

L. A Dream and a Vow (28:1-22)
1. Jacob sent to Mesopotamia (28:1-9)
2. Jacob dreams at Bethel (28:10-22)

M. Jacob and the Daughters of Laban (29:1-30:43)
1. Jacob meets Rachel and her family (29:1-14)
2. Jacob marries Rachel and Leah (29:15-30)
3. Jacob's family grows (29:31-30:24)
4. Jacob's possessions grow (30:25-43)

N. The Return to Canaan (31:1-33:20)
1. Separation from Laban (31:1-55)
2. Reconciliation with Esau (32:1-33:20)

O. Jacob and His Family (34:1-36:43)
1. The massacre at Shechem (34:1-31)
2. Worship at Bethel (35:1-15)
3. The deaths of Rachel and Isaac (35:16-29)
4. The descendants of Esau (36:1-43)

P. From a Pit to a Palace (37:1-45:28)
1. The problems of a dreamer (37:1-36)
2. Judah and Tamar (38:1-30)
3. Joseph in Potiphar's house (39:1-23)
4. Joseph: interpreter of dreams (40:1-41:36)

2

The Origin of the Universe

Genesis 1:1–5

It has long been recognized that a necessary category of human thought is that of origins. The interest in origins is so universal and so consistent that one is tempted to consider it innate. Modern philosophers are deeply committed to defining the meaning of life, but they cannot succeed until they settle the matter of origins. A balanced discussion of the destiny of man must also include the origin of man.

The first chapter of Genesis has been the focal point of heated controversy. Modern science and scientism have confronted biblical theology with sophisticated theories which deny the historical and scientific value of the Genesis cosmology. In the last three decades the pressure of "scientific opinion" has increased to the point that some biblical scholars have made sweeping concessions, abandoning a literal interpretation of the text in favor of a mythical or poetic interpretation. The latter hermeneutic permits the interpreter to make the Genesis material fit the current theory. This procedure is not particularly new. In fact it was advocated by the old liberalism, which stated with some confidence that "the opening section of Genesis is not a scientific account of the actual process through which the universe originated. It is a world unknown to science whose origin is here described,—the world of antique imagination, composed of a solid expanse of earth, surrounded by and resting on a world-ocean, and surrounded by a vault called the 'firmament,' above which again are the waters of a heavenly ocean from which the rain descends on the earth. . . ."[1]

To many scholars Genesis represents a prescientific cosmology, a rather uncritical series of ideas. This viewpoint, with various modifications, was at the heart of Hermann Gunkel's *Classical Researches into the Book of Genesis*. For him the debate over the historical or legendary character of the Genesis narratives was settled; their legendary character had been substantiated.[2] Commentators since Gunkel have agreed with his conclusion and assumed its validity in their works.

Rightly understood, however, the text does not represent a scientific impossibility and, therefore, can be accepted on literal grounds. Quite often interpreters reject it on these grounds because they have read the text only superficially or because they are influenced by a priori assumptions. That the text is prose and not poetry is evidenced by the frequent use of the *wāw* consecutive; this is the grammatical device normally employed to describe sequential acts.[3]

Some would dismiss this controversy as irrelevant and unimportant. They might even suggest that Genesis 1 has no significant soteriological implications. This, however, is a gross underestimation of this material's importance. One only needs to examine the frequency of creative affirmations in both the Old and New Testaments to realize how important this subject is to biblical writers. God's power as well as His authority in human history are predicated upon His creative acts. His providence is best understood in the light of His creative work. Furthermore, the authority and deity of Christ are related to creation (cf. Col. 1:15-19). Therefore, since the Genesis cosmology is repeated so often and since vital theological truths are interwoven with it, it must be extremely important and foundational to the rest of Scripture. Only with such a sober attitude toward it can one fully appreciate

---

1. John Skinner, *A Critical and Exegetical Commentary on Genesis*, p. 5.
2. See his *Schöpfung und Chaos in Urzeit und Endzeit* (Göttingen: Vandenhoeck und Ruprecht, 1895), p. 1. The preface to his commentary on Genesis appears in English as *The Legends of Genesis*.
3. For a study of the literary problems of Genesis 1–11 see Walter C. Kaiser, "The Literary Form of Genesis 1–11," in J. Barton Payne, ed., *New Perspectives on the Old Testament*, pp. 48–65.

the text of Genesis and, perhaps, only with this disposition can one seriously attempt to reconcile apparent discrepancies between natural science and revealed truth.

I. The Beginning (v. 1)

A. Grammatical Construction

If the first verse of the Bible is to be regarded as historical, then its grammatical construction is of some importance. Indeed, the verse cannot be understood apart from a careful analysis of its literary features.

Two constructions of the first clause are possible. Recent interpreters have considered it a dependent clause: "when God created the heaven and the earth," or as Speiser suggests, "when God set about to create the heaven and earth."[4] This approach is not a new one; it was followed by two well-known medieval Jewish commentators, Rashi and ibn-Ezra. Ibn-Ezra translated the first verse and the first clause of the second verse, "When God began to create the heaven and the earth, the earth was without form and void." Speiser suggests that verse 2 is a parenthesis and verse 3 expresses the main thought.[5] The implications of this approach to verse 1 are quite significant. If, indeed, the first clause of the Bible is a temporal clause, then material (*hā'āres*) already exists and is not created from nothing. God's creative activity is merely the alteration of preexisting material.

While this construction is grammatically possible, its validity is extremely doubtful. Those who adopt it construe the first word, *bᵉrēʾšiṯ*, as a construct form and emend the principal verb, *bārāʾ* ("created"), to read *bᵉrōʾ*, an infinitive construct rather than a qal perfect, third masculine singular. This results in the translation, "when God began to create." An emendation, however, is unnecessary, for "the construct followed by a finite verb is a genuine Semitic usage."[6] Because *bᵉrēʾšiṯ* does not have the article, many deny that it can be in the absolute state. But

---

4. *Genesis*, p. 3. See also William R. Lane, "The Initiation of Creation," pp. 63–73.
5. *Genesis*, p. 3.
6. E. J. Young, *Studies in Genesis One*, p. 3. He cites numerous examples of this construction: e.g., Lev. 14:46; I Sam. 5:9; 25:15; Ps. 16:3; 58:9; 81:6; Isa. 29:1; Hos. 1:2. See also Alexander Heidel, *The Babylonian Genesis*, pp. 89–95.

Alexander Heidel argues that when terms like *rē'šît* ("beginning"), *rō'š* ("beginning, head"), *qedem* ("olden times"), and *'ôlām* ("eternity")[7] are used adverbially, they almost invariably lack the article, and that in the absolute state.[8] Two examples of *rē'šît* in the absolute state are Leviticus 2:12 and Nehemiah 12:44.

Further evidence for the first clause being an absolute statement is the accent mark which the Masoretes placed on the first word. The accent is the disjunctive *tiphā'*, indicating that the word is independent and therefore absolute. Furthermore, without exception the ancient versions translated *berē'šît* as an absolute statement. Finally, as E. J. Young notes, "In the Old Testament when a construct precedes a finite verb, that fact is apparent either from the form of the word in construct or from the fact that the context demands that that word be taken as a construct."[9]

B. The Nature of God's Work

The verb *bārā'* ("to create") expresses better than any other verb the idea of an absolute creation, or creation *ex nihilo*. The qal stem of this verb is employed exclusively in the Old Testament for God's activity; the subject of the verb is never man. God is said to create "the wind" (Amos 4:13), "a clean heart" (Ps. 51:10), and "new heavens and a new earth" (Isa. 65:17). Genesis 1 emphasizes three great beginnings, each initiated by God (cf. 1:21, 27).

Two other verbs figure prominently in the creation narratives. One is *'āśâ*, meaning essentially "to do or make."[10] This verb appears to be interchangeable with *bārā'*, a conclusion which many writers reject but for which the evidence is overwhelming. For example, Genesis 1:1 states that God *created* (*bārā'*) the heavens and the earth, while Exodus 20:11 and Nehemiah 9:6 note that He *made* (*'āśâ*) the heavens and the earth.[11] An even clearer example is found in verses 21 and 25 of Genesis 1. In spite of this evidence, some writers continue to maintain that *'āśâ* can refer

---

7. A. T. Pearson, "An Exegetical Study of Genesis 1:1–3," *Bethel Seminary Quarterly* 2 (1953): 14.

8. Heidel, *Babylonian Genesis*, p. 92.

9. *Studies in Genesis One*, p. 6. Additional evidence for translating v. 1 as an independent clause is in Gerhard F. Hasel, "Recent Translations of Genesis 1:1: A Critical Look," pp. 154–67; and G. Douglas Young, "Further Light on the Translation of Genesis 1:1," pp. 2, 3.

10. Francis Brown, S. R. Driver, and Charles Briggs, *A Hebrew and English Lexicon of the Old Testament*, p. 793.

11. See also Gen. 2:2, 3, 4; Exod. 34:10; Job 9:9; Prov. 8:26; Ps. 95:5; 100:3 (cf. Gen. 1:26, 27); Isa. 41:20; 43:7; 45:7.

only to the reforming of previously existing material.[12] Proponents of the gap theory have a special interest in maintaining the distinction between this verb and *bārā'*; the gap theory will be discussed later in this chapter.[13] The third verb employed in the creation narratives is *yāsar*, meaning basically "to form or fashion."[14] This verb is absent from Genesis 1, appearing for the first time in Genesis 2:7, where God *formed* man from the dust of the earth.

The creative act of God reflected in verse 1, therefore, involved no preexisting material; a sovereign, all-powerful God created the heavens and the earth from nothing. This happened "in the beginning," and the gnawing question remains: When was the beginning? As noted earlier, we are in no position to establish an absolute date, whether using current scientific dating techniques or the genealogies of Genesis 5 and 11. We are, therefore, caught between Ussher's 4004 B.C. and the evolutionist's 4,500,000,000 B.C. That nearly infinite gulf is one of both time and philosophy. We are not, however, completely in the dark. Recent, sober calculations, made in the light of new scientific evidence, find the earth to be relatively recent in origin. This does not commit one to 4004 B.C. or even to 7000 B.C., but it does exclude the possibility of the earth being millions of years old. In any event, scholars continue to discuss the age and origin of the earth with great enthusiasm.[15]

C. The Nature of God

The theological importance of Genesis 1:1 cannot be overemphasized. The verse identifies God as *'elōhîm*, a masculine

---

12. Donald G. Barnhouse, *The Invisible War*, p. 65; *The New Scofield Reference Bible* (New York: Oxford University Press, 1967), pp. 1, 2. This problem is further discussed in John C. Whitcomb, *The Early Earth*, pp. 127–31; and Weston W. Fields, "Unformed and Unfilled: A Critique of the Gap Theory of Genesis 1:1, 2" (monograph, Grace Theological Seminary, 1973), pp. 73–90.
13. See pp. 42–47.
14. Brown, Driver, and Briggs, *Lexicon of the Old Testament*, p. 427.
15. See, for example, Harold W. Clark, "When Was the Earth Created?"; Otto Struve, "Finding the Age of the Earth," in Thornton Page and Lou W. Page, eds., *The Origin of the Solar System*; H. R. Woltzer, "The Age of the Earth"; Roy M. Allen, "The Evaluation of Radioactive Evidence on the Age of the Earth"; Melvin A. Cook, "Radiological Dating and Some Pertinent Applications of Historical Interest"; Robert V. Gentry, "Cosmological Implications of Extinct Radioactivity from Pleochroic Halos"; D. O. Acrey, "Problems in Absolute Age Determination"; and Whitcomb, *The Early Earth*, pp. 29–38.

eldm

plural noun which emphasizes His majestic power and glory. That the noun's plural form does not reflect polytheism is evident from the form of the verb of which the noun is the subject: third masculine singular. It is generally agreed that the noun's root meaning is "power, strength, glory."

Implicit in this verse are important statements concerning God's nature and character, statements which refute at least six fundamental heresies. The first is atheism, the view that God does not exist. The Bible offers no philosophical argument for the existence of God; it assumes His existence and views everything in the light of that assumption. The second is polytheism. The singular form of the key verb indicates that the Hebrews believed in one God and not many. There is no evidence that Israel's religion evolved from animism through polytheism and henotheism before it reached ethical monotheism. Such a suggestion is quite arbitrary and in obvious conflict with statements of Scripture. Third, this verse opposes a radical materialism which holds matter to be eternal. Without preexisting material God brought the earth—that is, matter—into existence. Fourth, since God is clearly distinguished from His creation, this verse clearly denies pantheism. Fifth, the supernatural origin of the earth and the universe refutes naturalism; God is the Architect and Creator of all that exists. Finally, the uniqueness of this concept of origins in ancient literature makes untenable the position that special revelation is nonexistent or impossible. Human reason and inquiry, while valid, are seriously limited; the problem of origins, therefore, is best solved in the light of biblical truth.

II. Chaos or Cosmos? (v. 2)

The interpretation and significance of the second verse has been the object of no small controversy. Generally speaking, there are two theories.

A. The Gap Theory

The gap theory, more accurately described as the ruin-reconstruction theory, sees an indefinite time gap between verses 1 and 2. This theory, in one form or another, has been advocated for centuries,[16] but its modern form originated with Thomas Chal-

16. See Arthur C. Custance, *Without Form and Void*, pp. 10–40. This historical evidence is evaluated in Fields, "A Critique of the Gap Theory," pp. 17–42.

mers of Edinburgh University. He proposed it in 1814 to accom- Chalmers
modate Georges Cuvier's theory that the earth's fossiliferous strata
are the product of a series of catastrophes. Chalmers made room
for these catastrophes between verses 1 and 2 of Genesis 1.[17] The
gap theory was given wide circulation early in the twentieth
century by George H. Pember, whose *Earth's Earliest Ages* appeared in 1907,[18] and by the *Scofield Reference Bible*, which
appeared in 1909. C. I. Scofield advocated the gap theory in a
note on Genesis 1, but in a later edition of his reference Bible the
note was relegated to Isaiah 45. Pember argued that the traditional
interpretation of Genesis 1:1, 2 had been deeply influenced by the
pagan concept of creation out of chaos.[19] In the third edition of
his book, however, Pember revealed his real motive in advocating
the gap theory: "the solution of geological difficulties connected
with the Bible. . . . Critical care in translating the original is all that
it [the gap theory] needs for its support; and while it absolutely
disables the attacks of geology upon the book of Genesis, it casts
no discredit upon science itself for, when rightly understood, the
Bible is found to have left an interval of undefined magnitude
between creation and the post-tertiary period, and men may bridge
it as they can with their discoveries without fear of impugning the
revelations of God."[20] The most scholarly and lengthy defense of
the gap theory to date is Arthur C. Custance's *Without Form and* Custance
Void, published in 1970.[21]

The gap theory, as generally taught today, asserts that in the
dateless past God created a perfect heaven and earth. The earth
was inhabited by a pre-Adamic race and ruled by Satan, who dwelt
in the Garden of Eden. Satan desired to become like God and
eventually rebelled (Isa. 14). Thus sin entered the universe, and
God's judgment came in the form of first a great flood and then,
when the light and heat from the sun ended, a global ice age. All
plant, animal, and human fossils date from this great flood and
are genetically unrelated to plants, animals, and humans on the
earth today.

The argument for this theory is: (1) "The earth *was* [$h\bar{a}y^e t\hat{a}$]

17. See *The Works of Thomas Chalmers on Natural Theology* (Glasgow:
Collins, n.d.); and *Select Works of Thomas Chalmers*, ed. W. Hanna (Edinburgh: Constable, 1855), 5:149ff. Compare Bernard Ramm, *The Christian
View of Science and Scripture*, pp. 195ff.
18. (London: Hodder and Stoughton, 1907).
19. Ibid., p. 20.
20. Ibid., p. vii.
21. Reviewed by Whitcomb and Charles Smith in *Creation Research Society
Quarterly* 8 (1971): 130–34.

became

without form" should be translated "the earth (became) without form" or "*had become* without form." The early chaotic condition of the earth, then, was not the direct result of divine creation.

without form (waste)

(2) "Without form [*tōhû*, "waste"], and void [*wābōhû*]" represents an evil condition, the result of divine judgment and not of divine creation. Isaiah said that God did not make the earth "in vain [*tōhû*]" (45:18). (3) The two primary Hebrew verbs meaning "create," as has already been noted, must be carefully distinguished. (4) Because "darkness was upon the face of the deep"

Darkness evil

and because "God is light, and in him is no darkness at all" (I John 1:5), verse 2 cannot be describing the original state of creation. Darkness is a symbol in Scripture for evil. (5) God told Adam to

replenish.

replenish the earth (Gen. 1:28), so the earth must have been filled during an earlier period.

While the motive of gap theorists—the harmonization of the Bible with current geological theory—is commendable, the validity of their argument is extremely doubtful. Modern geology knows

Geolg. disprove

nothing of the theory's two global catastrophes with two distinct geologic periods. Hebrew usage does not permit the distinction in meaning and function between the two principal verbs meaning

create ∈

"create." While (*bārā'*) refers more specifically and exclusively to God's activity in special creation, (*'āsâ*) often refers to the same activity.[22] Furthermore, Hebrew grammar will not allow for a chronological gap between verses 1 and 2. This is the point at which the theory either stands or falls. The following observations regarding the construction of the verse are critical. First, the second verse begins not with a *wāw* consecutive, which indicates a sequential narrative, but with a disjunctive *wāw*, which introduces a circumstantial clause. It should be translated here, "*now* the

Now...the earth was

earth was ... " The Septuagint supports this conclusion by translating the *wāw* with *de*.[23] F. F. Bruce states that if a gap separated the two verses, one would expect to find "waw consecutive with the imperfect tense instead of 'waw copulative.'"[24] Speiser correctly observes that "a normal consecutive statement would have begun with *watt*^{e}*hî hā'āres*, not *w*^{e}*hā'āres hāy*^{e}*tā*."[25] The purpose

22. See pp. 40, 41.
23. Other *wāw* disjunctives are recognized by the Septuagint in Gen. 2:6, 10, 12.
24. "And the Earth Was Without Form and Void: An Enquiry into the Exact Meaning of Gen. 1:2," p. 21.
25. *Genesis*, p. 5. See also E. Kautzsch and A. E. Cowley, *Gesenius' Hebrew Grammar* (Oxford: The Clarendon Press, 1949), p. 453; and Derek Kidner, *Genesis*, p. 44.

of a *wāw* disjunctive is to describe something in a preceding clause, not something which happened subsequently.[26]

Custance makes much of the point that on the basis of Old Testament usage, the correct rendering of *hāy*ᵉ*tâ* is "had become."[27] His argument is apparently statistical.[28] Because the verb's active meaning ("become") is more common than its stative ("is"), the active meaning must be intended in Genesis 1:2. But this is reckless exegesis. The fact is, the verb is used as a simple copulative in circumstantial clauses: Jonah "went unto Nineveh. . . . *Now* Nineveh *was* an exceeding great city. . . ." (Jonah 3:3); "He shewed me Joshua. . . . *Now* Joshua *was* clothed with filthy garments. . . ." (Zech. 3:1-3).

Also essential to the gap theory is its view that *tōhû* and *bōhû* ("waste" and "void") indicate divine judgment; that is what they describe the only other times they appear together in the Bible (Isa. 24:1 and Jer. 4:23). However, *tōhû* does not always refer in Scripture to something evil. For example, Job said that God "stretched out the north over empty space [*tōhû*] and hangeth the earth upon nothing" (26:7 ASV). Obviously this empty space is not something evil. In many passages the word simply refers to the wilderness or desert where life is conspicuously absent (cf. Deut. 32:10; Job 6:18; 12:24; Ps. 107:40).[29]

Another major argument for the gap theory is that (as in John 3:19 or Jude 13, for example) darkness always symbolizes sin and judgment. The theory's proponents note that God called the light "good" but not the darkness (Gen. 1:4). They insist that God originally created the world in light (cf. Ps. 104:2; I Tim. 6:16), and that darkness resulted from God's judgment of Satan and his angels. But Young observes that even in Genesis 1 "darkness is recognized as a positive good for man. Whatever the precise connotation of the *'ereb* ["evening"] of each day, it certainly included darkness, and that darkness was for man's good. At times, therefore, darkness may typify evil and death; at other times it is to be looked upon as a positive blessing."[30] Psalm 104:19-24 also makes it quite clear that physical darkness is not inherently evil.

---

26. Kautzsch and Cowley, *Gesenius' Hebrew Grammar*, p. 453.
27. *Without Form and Void*, pp. 41ff.
28. Ibid., p. 54.
29. The point is discussed more thoroughly in Whitcomb, *The Early Earth*, pp. 122–25; and Fields, "A Critique of the Gap Theory," pp. 112–33.
30. *Studies in Genesis One*, p. 35.

The argument based on the English rendering, "replenish the earth," is extremely weak. The Hebrew verb simply means "fill," not "*re*fill." The gap theory postulates a pre-Adamic population that was violently destroyed, but this is neither described nor alluded to in the Bible. Such a theory lends itself too easily to uncontrolled subjectivism and imagination. Almost anything can be postulated for this mysterious gap of indefinite duration.[31]

B. The No-Gap Theory

The more commonly accepted view of Genesis 1:1, 2 is that these verses describe the first day of creation. Verse 1 is an independent clause describing the creation *ex nihilo* of the universe "in the beginning," and verse 2 is a series of three circumstantial clauses describing the condition of the earth before God completed His work of creation. The earth was still uninhabitable, so succeeding days God prepared it to sustain life forms which would reproduce in accordance with laws which He established. The earth was also dark: " . . . darkness was upon the face of the deep [$t^e h \hat{o} m$]." As observed above, darkness cannot be construed as evidence for judicial destruction or sin; on the contrary it represents one phase of God's creative activity.

$T^e h \hat{o} m$ has been the subject of considerable discussion. It appears to be etymologically akin to, but not derived from, *Ti-'āmat*, the Babylonian monster from whose body Marduk, the god of Babylon, made the heavens and the earth, an event described in *Enūma Eliš*.[32] R. Laird Harris writes: "Tiamat, an Accadian noun, has no guttural letter 'h' in the middle. Hebrew maintains the gutturals in Hebrew words, but would not have one in 'Tehom' if it were borrowed from the Babylonian. Rather obviously the influence is vice versa. 'Tehom' is probably old Semitic for 'ocean'. The Babylonians personified the ocean into Tiamat. The Hebrew creation account uses the word 'ocean' for the primeval cosmic stuff."[33] Gerhard von Rad argues that while

---

31. Additional evaluation of the gap theory can be found in Henry M. Morris, *Biblical Cosmology and Modern Science*, pp. 62–65.
32. Pritchard, *ANET*, pp. 61–63. Also see D. F. Payne, *Genesis One Reconsidered*, pp. 10ff.
33. "The Bible and Cosmology," p. 14. This objection probably is invalid since the Hebrew *h* in $t^e h \hat{o} m$ is equivalent to the ' ("aleph 2") in *ti-'āmat*. *Ti'āmtu, tāmtu,* and *tāmdu* indicate "saltwater" in Akkadian. C. Bezold, *Babylonisch-assyrisches Glossar* (Heidelberg: Carl Winter's Universitätsbuchhandlung, 1926), p. 289.

46

the term is, etymologically speaking, of mythological origin, it retains no mythological significance: "The terms used in verse 2 are freed from every mythological context; in Israel they had long since become cosmological catchwords, which belonged to the inalienable requisite of Priestly learning."[34] $T^{e}hôm$ is used about thirty-six times in the Old Testament, and the majority of times it refers to the sea or lakes.[35] A few obscure passages such as Psalm 78:15 and Deuteronomy 8:7 may refer to subterranean waters, but the Hebrews, unlike the Babylonians, had no mythological system or subterranean gods. Moses, therefore, is merely indicating that the earth was at this time completely covered or surrounded with water, upon which was complete darkness.

According to the last clause of verse 2, "the Spirit of God moved upon the face of the waters." Recent interpreters have suggested that it ought to be translated, "an awesome wind sweeping over the water."[36] While it is true that the Hebrew word *rûaḥ* can mean "wind" or "breeze," it appears in this context to refer to the third person of the Godhead (cf. Job 26:13; Ps. 104:30). The verb of which Spirit is the subject is an active participle and means, essentially, "hovering over" (cf. Deut. 32:11).[37] The latter part of verse 2, therefore, describes the Spirit hovering over, protecting, and participating in the creative activity. The same verb in Deuteronomy 32:11 is used of an eagle hovering over its young, and this seems to be the imagery suggested in Genesis 1:2. Other passages (cf. John 1:1 3; Col. 1:16) make it quite clear that more than one person of the Godhead was intricately involved in creation.

III. Light and Darkness (vv. 3–5)

The third verse begins with the simple clause, "and God said," which is pregnant with significant implications. It immediately suggests divine plan and purpose, precluding the concepts that the earth originated by accident or chance and that it is self-existent

---

34. *Genesis*, p. 48. A helpful summary of this problem is found in Hasel, "The Significance of the Cosmology in Genesis 1 in Relation to Ancient Near Eastern Parallels," pp. 4–7.
35. Cf. Exod. 15:5, 8; Job 28:14; 38:16, 30; 41:32; Ps. 107:26; Jonah 2:5; Ezek. 26:19; 31:4, 15.
36. Speiser, *Genesis*, pp. 3, 5 (n.). Also see Harry M. Orlinsky, "The Plain Meaning of $Rû^{a}ḥ$ in Gen. 1:2," pp. 174–82.
37. This word also appears in Jer. 23:9, where it means "to tremble."

or self-sustaining. Each of the six days begins with this announcement. The psalmist declares, "He spake, and it was done; He commanded, and it stood fast" (33:9). The writer of Hebrews similarly affirms that "through faith we understand that the worlds were framed by the word of God. . . ." (11:3). These proclamations demand creation by the fiat of God, a concept which is reasonable and probable only if one accepts the God of the Bible. The words that begin the third verse mark the beginning of earth history. The believer who accepts the biblical revelation of earth's origin is satisfied not only with the mechanism of creation but also with the purpose of creation. It is in God through Christ that earth history really has meaning (cf. Col. 1:16).

Whether creation by fiat is unique to Israel in the ancient Near East is a matter of debate. Some scholars find the concept of creation by spoken word in the cosmologies of Mesopotamia and Egypt.[38] They point, for example, to the Mesopotamian *Enūma Eliš*, in which the lesser gods tell Marduk:

> "Lord, truly thy decree is first among the gods.
> Say but to wreck or create; it shall be.
> Open thy mouth: the cloth will vanish!
> Speak again, and the cloth shall be whole!"
> At the word of his mouth the cloth vanished.
> He spoke again, and the cloth was restored.[39]

Other scholars disagree. They contend that particularly in Egypt the spoken word is more a magical formula and, therefore, does not carry the same significance as the spoken word in Genesis.[40] However that issue is settled, the contrast between the mythological gods and the God of Genesis is stark. The Babylonian deities, for example, are brutal and sadistic, while God is perfectly holy.

The fact that God's words were a means of creation may imply that His creative works occurred suddenly. Our Lord wrought miracles on earth through His words, and in almost every instance

---

38. Hasel, "The Cosmology in Genesis 1," pp. 9–12; D. J. Frame, "Creation by the Word" (Ph.D. diss., Drew University, 1969); and von Rad, *Old Testament Theology*, 2 vols. (New York: Harper and Row Publishers, 1962), 1:143.
39. IV: 20–27. Translated by Speiser in Pritchard, *ANET*, p. 66.
40. S. G. F. Brandon, *Creation Legends of the Ancient Near East* (London: S.P.C.K., 1963), p. 38; and E. D. James, "The Conception of Creation in Cosmology," pp. 99–102.

Miracle & spoken word immediate

the miracle occurred instantaneously after He spoke; the only recorded exception is Mark 8:25.

When God spoke, He called for light. The result was not sunlight—the sun was created on the fourth day (1:16)—but light from a fixed source outside the earth, instituting the light-darkness cycle called "day" (cf. v. 5). According to verse 5, "God called the light Day, and the darkness he called Night," a statement which, when coupled with the last clause of the verse, seems to imply the beginning of the earth's rotation.

The last clause, literally translated, is, "And there was evening and there was morning, day one." This expression, taken most simply and naturally, refers to an astronomical day of twenty-four hours. An equivalent expression in Daniel 8:14 (ASV) has been referred to traditionally as the twenty-four-hour, day-night cycle. The length of the Genesis days, however, will be discussed in more detail in the next chapter.

3

Days or Ages?

Genesis 1:5

The length and nature of the days of Genesis has occupied no small place in current discussions of biblical cosmology. To initiate the liveliest of debates one need only raise this issue, but far too often the discussion will produce more heat than light. This issue is so highly contested because of its multitude of ramifications—scientific, theological, and philosophical. Without considering these, one cannot arrive at an adequate conclusion.

Apart from the use of the Hebrew word *yôm,* "day," in verses 5, 8, 13, 19, 23, and 31, where it describes the days of creation, it is used in at least four ways in the first two chapters of Genesis: the twelve-hour period of daylight as opposed to night (vv. 14, 16, 18); a solar day of twenty-four hours (v. 14); the period of light that began with the creation of light on the first creative day (v. 5); and the entire, six-day creative period (2:4).[1]

I. Biblical Evidence

How long were the days of creation? Advocates of the literal day theory argue that they were approximately twenty-four hours

51

1. Franklin L. Gruber, *The Six Creative Days*, p. 72. See also Bernard Ramm, *The Christian View of Science and Scripture*, p. 213; and Francis A. Schaeffer, *Genesis in Space and Time*, p. 57.

long; advocates for the day-age theory, that they were long periods of indefinite duration; advocates of the literal-day-with-gaps theory, that they were twenty-four hours long but were separated by long periods of indefinite duration; and advocates of the revelatory day theory, that they were not days of creation at all but days of revelation.

A. The Literal Day Theory

Supporters of the literal day theory interpret the text in the most obvious way. Specialized expressions such as light and darkness, day and night, evening and morning, appear to require this interpretation, as does the use of numerical adjectives with *yôm* throughout the account. And Exodus 20:11 buttresses this theory, asserting that within "six days the Lord made the heaven and earth, the sea, and all that in them is."

B. The Day-Age Theory

The day-age theory, also called the geologic day theory because it attempts to correlate the geological ages with the seven days in Genesis 1, interprets these "days" metaphorically rather than literally. Its backers contend that the expression "evening and morning" is a figure for "beginning and ending." "Evening presents the picture of the gradual completion of the work of each creative period, succeeded by a morning of renewed activity."[2] And Exodus 20:11, they say, "simply means that the human week of seven days takes its rise from the divine week of seven creative epochs."[3]

Proponents of the day-age theory point to two strands of evidence within Genesis 1 itself. First, the creative works of the six days seem to require more than twenty-four-hour days. For example, on the third day "the earth brought forth grass, herbs yielding seed after their kind, and trees bearing fruit" (v. 12). Second, the law of the limitation of solar measure was not established until the fourth day, so days of creation could well have been much longer than twenty-four hours. (But could not the earth, before the fourth day, have rotated in relation to a light source, warranting the day-night distinction that is made in verse

52

---

2. Glen G. Cole, *Creation and Science*, p. 92.
3. Ramm, *Science and Scripture*, p. 214.

5?) The theory's advocates also cite other Scripture passages for support. Hebrews 4:1-11 appears to refer to the seventh day of creation as a period of indefinite length. If the seventh day was an age, the first six days must also be ages. "The mention of the creation Sabbath is proof of the symbolic character of the creation day."[4] Some Old Testament passages, they argue, ascribe to the earth an antiquity (Prov. 8:22ff.; Mic. 5:1; Ps. 104; 90; 49:15) that requires the days of creation to be ages. (But they admit that the Jewish concept of antiquity may be quite different from that of modern geologists.) Bernard Ramm mentions the "great array of geologists and theologians [who] accept the metaphorical interpretation of the word day" and concludes that "the case for the literal day cannot be conclusive nor the objections to the metaphorical interpretation too serious."[5]

This conclusion is unwarranted. The Hebrew word *yôm* can be used metaphorically, but those who argue for the day-age theory have not demonstrated that the days of creation are metaphorical days. Even when *yôm* does designate something other than a literal, twenty-four-hour day, it nonetheless refers to a period of specified duration. And it is doubtful that *yôm* ever signified a period of time extending into millions of years, which the day-age theory generally requires. These are serious hermeneutical difficulties.

C. The Literal-Day-with-Gaps Theory

This theory contends that the days of creation "need not be taken consecutively but may be understood as separated by long ages. Each day would then indicate a normal, twenty-four hour period, by the time of the arrival of which, the major phenomena which God had been creating since the previously mentioned day, had at length come into being. . . ."[6] John Urquhart pointed out that, with the exception of the sixth day, *yôm* has the indefinite form. He concluded that the days were not consecutive but were separated by long ages.[7] Each creative day "came" when the events previously described were completed.

This viewpoint has very few adherents because it severely strains

---

4. Sir Robert Anderson, *Bible and Modern Criticism*, p. 124.
5. *Science and Scripture*, p. 213.
6. J. Barton Payne, "Theistic Evolution and the Hebrew of Genesis 1–2," p. 87.
7. *The Bible: Its Structure and Purpose*, 2:69, 70.

the Hebrew text. If Moses had intended to describe noncon-secutive days, it would seem he could have done so with more clarity. Also, this theory regards the days as times only of comple-tion of divine creation, while the writer of Genesis appears to describe the beginning of creative activity as well as the comple-tion of it on each day.

D. The Revelatory Day Theory

This theory contends "that creation was *revealed* in six days, not *performed* in six days. . . . that the six days are pictorial-revelatory days, not literal days nor age days. The days are means of communicating to man the great fact that God is creator, and that He is creator of all."[8] Advocates of the theory point out that God reveals the unknown future by visions, so it is logical that He reveal the unknown past by visions.

This theory has not gained wide acceptance, probably because its assertions are somewhat arbitrary; no linguistic evidence has been produced to indicate that Genesis 1 is a series of visions rather than a historical narrative. Exodus 20:11 seems explicitly to contradict this theory, saying that "in six days the Lord *made* heaven and earth, the sea, and all that in them is," not that "in six days the Lord *revealed His creation of* heaven and earth. . . ." Furthermore, the use of visions to reveal the past is rare indeed. The only possible example of it is Daniel 7:1ff. Past events are normally revealed in literal, historical narratives, not in series of visions which can be manipulated and interpreted as indefinite time periods.

II. Scientific Evidence

Analysis of the alternatives to the literal day theory makes it apparent that the major criticism of that theory is not linguistic or philological. These alternatives have been formed in response to the pressure of scientific opinion.

It is quite true that the literal day theory conflicts with current scientific opinion. This theory does not limit the history of the earth to 6,000 years, but none of its advocates argue for a history longer than 100,000 years. Modern scientists, on the other hand, almost unanimously agree that the earth is millions of years old.

---

8. Ramm, *Science and Scripture*, p. 222. See also P. J. Wiseman, *Creation Revealed in Six Days*.

But the alternative theories also conflict with current scientific opinion. For one thing, they cannot harmonize perfectly the geological ages with the days of Genesis. According to the Bible, all plants were made on the third day, whereas fish and other marine organisms were created on the fifth day; geology normally reverses this order. In the Bible birds were created on the same day as fish and other marine creatures; most paleontologists argue that birds evolved from reptiles long after fish originated and probably after mammals appeared. The Bible says the sun was created on the fourth day, making the very survival of vegetation, created on the third day, very difficult if "days" are ages. In all fairness, however, it must be admitted that a general harmony can be established between the geological column and the seven days of Genesis.[9] It should also be noted that advocates of the revelatory day theory can argue that the order of creation in Genesis is topical rather than chronological. The creation narrative is intended, they say, to impart a sense of order in God's creative activity and to discourage the worship of anything other than the God who made all things.[10] A second way in which these theories fail to reconcile the Bible to modern science is this: the Bible repeatedly describes God's creative work as "good," but the geological ages are characterized by violence, upheaval, and death.

Furthermore, the prevailing scientific opinion is not without its problems. It argues that all forms of life evolved, but it has discovered no biological mechanism for evolution. This more than embarrasses the evolutionists, it cripples their theory. They must postulate lengthy periods of time for chance mutations to produce new species or families. But the laws of thermodynamics make it rather doubtful that vast increases in time really improve the probability of evolution by chance. Then, too, if life existed on earth for millions of years, there would be far more fossil evidence for it; and, if all living forms evolved, the fossil record would include millions of transitory forms. Scientific opinion itself, therefore, is suspect.

One must neither accept current scientific opinion uncritically nor develop an antiscientific posture which ignores empirical evidence. The specialist must examine all empirical evidence objec-

9. See Ramm, *Science and Scripture,* pp. 215–18; William F. Tanner, "Geology and the Days of Genesis"; and Allan A. MacRae, "The Scientific Approach to the Old Testament (Part II)," pp. 133–38.
10. Ramm, *Science and Scripture,* p. 223. See also Melvin G. Kyle, *Creation of Inanimate Things,* p. 307; and G. D. Boardman, *Studies in the Creative Week,* p. 71.

tively and evaluate it in the light of revelation and natural law. One must always keep in mind the limitations of both science and theology when it comes to origins. Nature, the province of science, is included in the curse of Eden, which makes the interpretation of nature difficult. And the Bible, the sourcebook of theology, provides no detailed and exhaustive treatment of the time of the world's origin. Unfortunately, many have deified scientific opinion to the point that the Bible is subject to it. This elevates modern science and the scientific method to a level of authority which cannot be justified. If the Bible is indeed inspired by God, then its authority supercedes that of a cursed creation. Scripture is unique. Even though heaven and earth will pass away, Scripture will not (Matt. 24:25). This is not to deny the validity of empirical evidence.

It is unfortunate that the lines in this battle are so tightly drawn that discussion has been reduced to caricatures and emotional charges. Opponents of the literal day theory usually present it in the worst light.[11] They constantly label the theory, which is based on the *prima facie* impression given by Genesis 1, naive. This objection is quite dangerous because it can be raised just as well against other crucial doctrines of Scripture. For example, the Gospels give the *prima facie* impression that Jesus physically rose from the dead, an impression at least as naive, according to modern scientific opinion and research, as that given by Genesis 1. Should we, then, reject the literal, physical resurrection of Jesus?

The tension between biblical revelation and scientific empiricism shows no sign of decreasing. Christian theologians and scientists are caught in a conflict. On one hand, one does not want to reject obvious empirical evidence, and on the other, one must never make all truth subject to the scientific method, which is incapable of verifying essential, supernatural events such as Christ's virgin birth, His death and resurrection, and His second coming. Incidentally, the most encouraging aspect of this conflict has been the active involvement of Christian men of science who hold a high view of the Scriptures and whose competence in their disciplines is unquestioned.

At this stage one is inclined to interpret Scripture in accordance with the best rules of hermeneutics and in the light of historical, grammatical research. When the resulting interpretation appears to conflict with empirical science, one might do well to

56

---

11. Ramm, *Science and Scripture*, pp. 173, 174.

assume the validity of the interpretation until irrefutable evidence is produced to disprove it. It is not easy to adhere to a position which is so unpopular in the scientific community. However, if biblical truth must be sacrificed at the altar of scientific acceptability, we are left with no hope whatsoever and are reduced to a world and life view of empty materialism. Perhaps in the years to come the problem of the age of the earth and the interpretation of the days of Genesis will be put in clearer perspective.[12]

---

12. This problem is further discussed in G. Douglas Young, "The Relevance of Scientific Thought to Scriptural Interpretation," pp. 117–20; James D. Bales, "The Relevance of Scriptural Interpretation to Scientific Thought," *Bulletin of the Evangelical Theological Society* 4 (1961): 121–28; and John C. Whitcomb, *The Early Earth.*

4

When Life Began

Genesis 1:6–25

Moses described the remaining days of creation, like the first, in the simple style characteristic of Hebrew literature. This does not mean that the narrative is not thoughtful, however; it reveals the great scientific and theological implications of the creative acts of God. The Genesis cosmology is characterized by both simplicity and majestic beauty.

This chapter will cover the history of creation up to its culmination in the creation of man. Before the beginning of human history is discussed, the relationship between the Genesis creation narrative and the Babylonian creation epic, *Enūma Eliš*, will be treated.

I. The Biblical Account

A. The Second Day: Firmament (vv. 6–8)

1. **The divine fiat (v. 6).** On the second day of God's creative activity, He divided horizontally the mass of waters in which the earth was situated. One body of water was suspended above a "firmament" (*rāqîa‘*) and another completely covered the earth

59

below the firmament. Once again the creative activity is quite clearly supernatural: " ... Let there be [$y^e h\hat{\imath}$]. ..." is unequivocally a divine fiat. The work of God is further described in verse 7: "And God made [$\bar{a}\dot{s}\hat{a}$]. ..."

2. The firmament (vv. 7, 8). The precise significance of *rāqîa'* has been widely disputed. Its essential meaning has been described as "an extended surface, (solid) expanse,"[1] and the Hebrews are said to have regarded *rāqîa'*, "the vault of heaven, ... as solid, and supporting 'waters' above it"[2] Von Rad suggests that they imagined it to be "a gigantic hemispherical and ponderous bell."[3] Some even have asserted that the writer of Genesis, influenced by contemporary mythology, saw in the universe three stories.[4] This suggestion, however, can only be maintained by the most strained exegesis.

Since the verb *rāqa'* means "to beat, stamp, beat out, and spread out,"[5] the noun can bear the figurative meaning of "an expanse," in this case a vast space. "Expanse" is a superior translation to "firmament," which is derived from the Vulgate's "*firmamentum*" and suggests something put firmly in place.

Students of biblical cosmology have developed the theory that above the pre-Noahic earth was suspended a vapor or ice crystalline canopy. The theory apparently appeared first in Isaac Newton Vail's books, *The Waters Above the Firmament* and *The Deluge and Its Cause*.[6] Howard W. Kellogg[7] and C. Theodore Schwarze[8] popularized it, and John C. Whitcomb and Henry M. Morris put it in its most scholarly, scientific form in *The Genesis Flood*. Whitcomb and Morris suggest that on the second day God suspended a vast body of water in vapor form over the earth, protecting it from

---

1. Brown, Driver, and Briggs, *Lexicon of the Old Testament*, p. 956.
2. Ibid. See also John Skinner, *A Critical and Exegetical Commentary on Genesis*, pp. 21, 22.
3. *Genesis*, p. 51.
4. Paul H. Seely, "The Three Storied Universe." See also the responses to this article in the following issues of the *Journal of the American Scientific Affiliation*.
5. Brown, Driver, and Briggs, *Lexicon of the Old Testament*, p. 955. Cf. Exod. 39:3; Isa. 40:19; Jer. 10:9; Ps. 136:6.
6. *The Waters Above the Firmament; or, The Earth's Annular System*, 2nd. ed. rev. (Philadelphia: Ferris & Leach, 1902); *The Deluge and Its Cause* (Chicago: Suggestion Publishing, 1905). A revised edition of the latter was published as *The Misread Record; or, The Deluge and Its Cause* (Seattle: Simplex Publishing, 1921).
7. *The Canopied Earth* (Los Angeles: American Prophetic League, n.d.), pp. 5, 6.
8. *The Marvel of Earth's Canopies*.

the destructive rays of the sun.[9] This might explain the longevity described in Genesis 5, and it provides a water source for the great, universal flood described in Genesis 6-9. The canopy theory also appears, with modifications, in Donald W. Patten's *The Biblical Flood and the Ice Age Epoch.*[10] He suggests that the earth's suspended canopy was similar to that of Venus.[11]

This theory is primarily an attempt to explain the tropical conditions that apparently characterized the early earth. Areas that are now arctic were inhabited by animals whose natural habitat is tropical or semitropical.[12] For example, large mastodons were present in arctic regions and elephants lived in the New Siberian Islands. Furthermore, many of these animals were frozen, suddenly, with undigested food still in their mouths. According to the canopy theory, the canopy distributed heat around the earth, making regions now arctic at least semitropical. During the great flood, the canopy broke up ("the windows of heaven . . . opened") and some regions previously tropical became arctic.[13]

The canopy theory helps explain several things, but it requires that the biblical term *firmament* (v. 8) include the area above the canopy, or suspended vapor body, as well as below it. In verse 17 God set the sun and moon "in the firmament of the heavens" (cf. v. 14). If "firmament of the heavens" includes that vast area above the canopy, then the theory has value (cf. II Cor 12:1-3).[14]

B. The Third Day: Land, Plants, and Seas (vv. 9–13)

1. Land and seas (vv. 9, 10). On the third day dry land, as distinguished from the *t^{e}hôm*, or the great seas, appeared. Again, this activity is initiated by the divinely spoken word (v. 9). At the Lord's command the waters were gathered and land masses arranged into continents, or literally "the dry" *(hayyabbāšâ)*. This

---

9. P. 229.
10. Patten's approach to this subject, however, is far more mechanistic than that of Whitcomb and Morris. He has too many uncritical historical assumptions and seems to rely too heavily on the catastrophism of Immanuel Velikovsky.
11. P. 198.
12. See Velikovsky, *Earth in Upheaval*, pp. 4–9, 16–18.
13. Whitcomb and Morris, *The Genesis Flood*, pp. 240–42; Patten, *The Biblical Flood*, pp. 198–204; Kellogg, *The Canopied Earth*, pp. 11–19.
14. Seely argues that the theory cannot stand because "this water, so far as the Bible is concerned, is on the far side of the sun, not between the sun and earth." "The Three Storied Universe," p. 20.

term commonly describes dry, solid ground (cf. Exod. 14:16, 22, 29; 15:19; Josh. 4:22; Jonah 1:9, 13; 2:11). It is interesting that God not only created the land masses but also gave both them and the seas names (v. 10). ". . . in the ancient oriental view the act of giving a name meant, above all, the exercise of a sovereign right (cf. II Kings 23:24; 24:17). Thus the naming of this and all subsequent creative works once more expresses graphically God's claim of lordship over the creatures."[15] The expression *yammîm* ("seas") is used in a very broad sense to include every body of water, even inland lakes and rivers. The psalmist describes this event very graphically:

> He gathereth the waters of the sea
> together as an heap:
> he layeth up the depth in storehouses.
> Let all the earth fear the Lord:
> let all the inhabitants of the world
> stand in awe of him.
> For he spake, and it was done;
> he commanded, and it stood fast.
> [Ps. 33:7–9]

When the work was complete, God called it "good" (*tôb*), probably in two senses. One would be aesthetic, indicating the perfection of His creative activity. The other sense of the word *good* would be that of purpose. "It corresponds, therefore, though with much more restraint, to the content of Psalm 104:31; Psalm 104 tells not so much of the beauty as of the marvelous purpose and order of creation."[16]

2. **Plants (vv. 11–13).** The second work of God on the third day was the creation of plant life. Again the process was initiated by the divinely spoken word: "And God said. . . ." (v. 11). What evolutionary biology has been unable to produce—a workable mechanism by which inorganic material becomes organic and self-producing—the Bible explains in terms of an all-powerful, personal God. In the simplest language the Bible states, "Let the earth bring forth grass, the herb yielding seed, and the fruit tree yielding fruit after his kind. . . ." (v. 11). The expression "let the earth bring forth" does not allow, as some have contended, for

62

---

15. Von Rad, *Genesis*, p. 51.
16. Ibid., p. 50.

evolution.[17] On the contrary, the biblical order of trees before marine organisms contradicts the concept of trees evolving from marine organisms.

The term *grass* translates the Hebrew word *deše'*, which seems to mean "that which is green, grows green or sprouts."[18] H. C. Leupold suggests that the term refers to that which is damp. "Whatever grows in a well-watered spot will be of a fresh green, therefore the word is rendered *frisches gruen*."[19] It designates the kind of green sprouts and tender herbs that animals commonly eat. There is some disagreement how *deše'* is related to the other two nouns in this verse which refer to plant life: *'eśeḇ* ("herb") and *ēṣ pᵉrî* ("fruit tree"). Some have suggested that *deše'* is a completely separate category of plant life, others that it is a larger category which includes the other two terms.[20] *Deše'* and *'eśeḇ* appear to be distinguished in II Kings 19:26 and Isaiah 37:27, and this discussion will assume that the three nouns describe separate orders of plant life. *'Eśeḇ* is a collective noun the general sense of which is "herbage."[21] This order of plants is seed-bearing and was one of two sources of food for human beings (cf. 1:29; 3:18) and cattle (Deut. 11:15). *'Eṣ pᵉrî* are trees which (1) bear fruit, (2) bear fruit that encloses the seed, and (3) bear fruit upon or above the earth. This fruit was also a source of food for man (cf. 1:29). *'Ēṣ pᵉrî*, literally translated "tree of fruit," probably includes, in addition to fruit-bearing trees, those yielding nuts and cones, and probably also includes bushes yielding berries.

Some have suggested on the basis of verse 12 that God produced a functioning and mature creation. Plants were created mature, self-reproducing biological units, containing their own seeds. They conclude that the original creation had the "appearance" of age; the plant, by empirical observation, would appear to have grown to such a height with seed-producing capacity when in fact God had created it instantaneously. The same is asserted of man.[22]

Each family of plant life could reproduce only "after his kind

---

17. Derek Kidner, *Genesis*, p. 48.
18. Brown, Driver, and Briggs, *Lexicon of the Old Testament*, pp. 205, 206.
19. *Exposition of Genesis*, 1:67.
20. See discussions in L. Koehler and W. Baumgartner, eds., *Lexicon in Veteris Testamenti Libros*, p. 220; and Leupold, *Exposition of Genesis*, 1:66, 67.
21. Brown, Driver, and Briggs, *Lexicon of the Old Testament*, p. 793.
22. Whitcomb and Morris, *The Genesis Flood*, pp. 232, 233.

mîn.

[*mîn*]." The significance of *mîn* has been widely discussed in recent years. It appears in the Old Testament thirty-one times. Interestingly enough, Moses accounts for thirty of these, Ezekiel for the other. J. Barton Payne concludes that, "while *mîn* does not . . . require the separate creation of God of each species, it does require at least the separate creation of families within orders."[23]

The third day is concluded when God again calls His creation "good" (v. 12).

C. The Fourth Day: Sun and Moon (vv. 14–19)

The sun and moon were created on the first day, according to those who insist that the verbs *bārā'* and *'āśâ* ("made" in v. 16) should be distinguished. They contend that on the fourth day God merely instituted the sun, moon, and stars in the firmament to function in a particular way relative to the earth. Others have felt that the material was created in the beginning but that it was not formed into heavenly bodies until the fourth day.[24] The most natural way to understand these verses is that on the fourth day God began and finished the creation of the sun and moon. The light source which existed previously may have been similiar to the sun, but there seems to be no reason to conclude that it was virtually identical to it. It already has been noted that *'āśâ* is commonly a synonym of *bārā'*. Furthermore, if Moses wanted to say that the heavenly bodies merely "appeared" on the fourth day, surely he would have used an expression similar to the one he used in verse 9 with respect to the dry land.

These lights were placed in the "firmament of heaven" (vv. 14, 15). According to verse 16 a greater light and a lesser light ruled the day and night, respectively. The writer's perspective is obviously geocentric rather than heliocentric, since the sun and moon could not be considered two of the greater lights in the universe. The language of appearance is common in the Old Testament and

---

23. "The Concept of 'Kinds' in Scripture," p. 18. For more recent studies of *mîn*, see Arthur J. Jones, "A General Analysis of the Biblical 'Kind' (*Min*)," pp. 53–57; Jones, "Boundaries of the Min: An Analysis of the Mosaic Lists of Clean and Unclean Animals," pp. 114–23; Whitcomb, *The Early Earth*, pp. 80–87; and Frank L. Marsh, "The Genesis Kinds in the Modern World," in Walter E. Lammerts, ed., *Scientific Studies in Special Creation*, pp. 136–55.
24. C.F. Keil and Franz Delitzsch, *Biblical Commentary on the Old Testament*, 25 vols. (Edinburgh: T. and T. Clark, 1864–1901), 1:58, 59. Reprinted in 1971 by Wm. B. Eerdmans Co.

is in no way unscientific or prescientific; even in the most advanced textbooks of science, words like *sunrise* and *sunset* still appear and are properly understood in their context. And while geocentrism is unwarranted on the basis of the earth's size, it is warranted on the basis of redemption; on this planet Jesus Christ gave His life to redeem men.

The purposes of the luminaries are:

1. *to distinguish day from night* ("to divide the day from the night"). The light-dark sequence on earth is now dependent upon the sun instead of "the light" created on the first day, when the earth began rotating. It may be assumed that, even when the sun superceded "the light," the earth's rate of rotation, and thus the duration of each light-dark sequence, remained the same.

2. *to provide signs* ("for signs"). Von Rad suggests that these signs might be the sights in the "heavenly vault which were not normal, as eclipses of the sun; in any case they were fixed astral points for regulating cult and work."[25] Many have mistakenly concluded from the phrase "for signs" that God designed the celestial bodies to determine the destinies of individual men. Modern astrologers have often appealed to verse 14 to justify their enterprise.[26] The signs of verse 14, however, relate to faith (Ps. 8, 19; Rom. 1:14-20), weather (Matt. 16:2, 3), prophecy (Matt. 2:2; Luke 21:25), and judgment (Joel 2:30, 31; Matt. 24:29). They are also a means of getting bearings for long journeys.

3. *to distinguish the seasons* ("for seasons, and for days, and years"). This concept seems consistent with the scientific understanding of seasonal change.

Interest in sun and moon has been increased immeasurably by space exploration. The exploits of American and Russian astronauts have once again confirmed the magnificence and awesome beauty of the universe. The very fact that Americans have been able to land on the moon is an indication of divine providence. If God were not in control of planetary movements, man hardly could have calculated moon landings with such precision; one need only observe the traffic jams in any of our large cities to discern immediately man's general inability to control moving bodies! Travel to the moon has increased speculation concerning life on other planets. Some firmly declare it possible and perhaps even

---

25. *Genesis*, p. 54.
26. For a study of modern astrology from a biblical perspective, see John J. Davis, *Contemporary Counterfeits*, pp. 7–11.

probable; others consider the planets with which we are familiar incapable of supporting life forms.[27] The debate is both lively and interesting and will continue for years to come. Many have felt that God never intended man to be on the moon. That the moon was not constructed for human habitation is quite evident from its surface and its lack of vegetation. However, it is extremely risky, if not embarrassing, to say without qualification that man will never live on the moon or reach another planet. When airplanes were beginning to make the headlines, some firmly asserted that, if God wanted man to fly, He would have given him wings; today biblical scholars, who may have made such statements years ago, enjoy the comforts of jet travel around the world. As the old Scotsman once said, "Make your words sweet today because tomorrow you might have to eat them!"

D. The Fifth Day: Marine Animals and Birds (vv. 20–25)

1. **Fish and fowl (vv. 20, 21).** The translation "Let the waters bring forth abundantly" (v. 20 AV) might be misleading. A literal translation is, "Let the waters swarm with swarms of living creatures." John Skinner wrote, "More probably . . . the sense is simply 'teem with,' indicating the place or element in which the swarming creatures abound. . . ."[28] This clearly precludes the conclusion that the waters themselves produced marine life. The text merely states that God, by His command, produced living creatures in the oceanic depths that had been separated from the land masses. The text also seems to imply that aquatic life and fowl appeared simultaneously. If it does imply this, then the evolutionary sequence of reptiles before birds must be rejected.

2. **Sea monsters (v. 21).** The selection of *whales* to translate *tannînim* in the Authorized Version was not the best. This word and its adjective are better translated "great sea monsters," which would include other great fish as well as whales. *Tannînim* is used elsewhere to describe the serpent (Exod. 7:9, 10, 12), the dragon (Isa. 51:9; Ezek. 29:3), and, of course, the sea monster (Ps. 148:7). The use of *bārā'* to describe God's creation of the whales or great sea monsters implies that He created them in a unique manner, perhaps without using any preexisting material.

66

---

27. See O. M. Erpenstein, "Could There Be Life on Other Planets of the Solar System?" pp. 58–63.
28. *Commentary on Genesis*, p. 27.

The organization and the reproductive limitations of these biological groups are indicated by the expressions "after their kind" and "after his kind" (v. 21). God gave to His newest creatures His special blessings and expressed His intention that they "be fruitful and multiply" (v. 22). As He did after the third and fourth days, God described the day's events as "good" (v. 21). This speaks of the absolute perfection of His creative work, including the ecological balance and exactness of function in the biological world. By the end of the fifth day, therefore, the earth was filled with luxuriant vegetation and swarming with wildlife in both sea and air, more perfectly balanced and more beautiful than we can ever imagine.

E. The Sixth Day: Terrestrial Animals (vv. 24, 25)

The work of God on the sixth day begins again with divine fiat. God commanded the earth to bring forth (*tōṣeʾ*), or cause to come forth, the living creature (*nepeš ḥayyâ*). God could, of course, have called these animals into existence without using previously existing material, but He apparently used inorganic substance. The Hebrew word translated "cattle" denotes generally the larger domesticated quadrupeds (cf. Gen. 47:18; Exod. 13:12) and occasionally other large animals (Prov. 30:30; Eccles. 3:19). The Hebrew term *remeś* ("creeping things") generally denotes that which moves either without feet or with feet that are scarcely noticeable: for example, worms, insects (cf. Lev. 11:20-23), and reptiles. Once again these biological forms are limited to reproducing after their own kind, and once again God declares His newest creation good (1:25).

These remarkable acts of God are described with utter simplicity, but the more one studies the nature and structure of biological life, the more one sees its intricacy and perfection. Perhaps science is, after all, watching God at work. If God's original creation can be so intricate and beautiful, and if, despite the fall of man, the original creation continues to be so awesome, how much greater is God's new creation in Christ to those who trust in Him.

II. The Babylonian Account

Enūma Eliš was one of the most popular epics among the Babylonians and Assyrians. It is written on seven clay tablets and contains more than one thousand lines. It is generally complete, the most notable exception being a large portion of tablet V.

The first portions of this epic were discovered between 1848 and 1876 at the great library of Ashurbanipal at Nineveh by Austen H. Layard, Jormuzd Rassam, and George Smith. In 1922-25 two almost complete tablets (I and VI) of a neo-Babylonian version were found at Kish by a joint expedition from Oxford University and Field Museum of Chicago. In 1928-29 the Germans found a large neo-Babylonian fragment of tablet VII at Uruk. Discoveries of various other versions also have helped compile this epic. The tablets from Nineveh belong to the seventh century B.C., those from Ashur to approximately 1000 B.C., and the fragments from Kish to the sixth century B.C. The exact date of composition is uncertain, although the weight of evidence seems to favor the period of the first Babylonian dynasty, especially the reign of the great Hammurabi.

Tablet IV of *Enūma Eliš* (Courtesy of the British Museum)

While *Enūma Eliš* is one of the more important witnesses to Babylonian cosmology, it is not primarily a creation epic.[29] Its purpose is obviously to honor Marduk as the greatest of all gods. It establishes his supremacy in part by telling of his creative power, but a careful reading of the epic clearly demonstrates that his creative acts are not the major emphasis of the epic.[30] Tablets II and III mention no creative acts at all, and tablets I and IV refer only incidentally to these acts. Another purpose of the epic may have been to exalt the city of Babylon; it does relate the origin of the city (VI:45-73).

According to the epic a male freshwater ocean, Apsu, and a female saltwater ocean, Tiamat, mated. The offspring were many lesser deities, which represented a variety of aspects of nature. Apsu became irritated with the noise of his offspring and decided to destroy them. He failed, however, and in fact was killed by one of them, the god of wisdom, who in turn fathered the great stone god, Marduk. This enraged Tiamat, who mothered a host of dragons to fight Marduk. During a great banquet Marduk was commissioned by other important gods to represent them and fight Tiamat. After a fierce battle, Marduk killed the dragon Tiamat and split her body in half. The upper half was made into the sky, and the lower half the earth. Out of this chaos came order, and the stars, moon, and calendar were created. Man was produced by mixing the blood of Kingu, Tiamat's field marshal, with some earth. Man was created to serve all the gods and goddesses.

The above survey sufficiently indicates that, while there are some general parallels between *Enūma Eliš* and the biblical account,[31] the differences are much greater. Since, however, similarities do exist, one must decide how the two accounts are related. Three answers have been offered.

The first is that the Genesis account was drawn from the Babylonian. This viewpoint has had widespread popularity, but it tends to generalize the similarities between the two accounts and either minimize or overlook very significant differences. Furthermore, it is questionable on purely philosophical grounds that structural similarity necessarily implies generic relationship. And Merrill F. Unger has noted that, "while the doctrine of biblical

---

29. Alexander Heidel, *Babylonian Genesis*, p. 10.
30. For translations of *Enūma Eliš* see E. A. Speiser, "The Creation Epic," in Pritchard, *ANET*, pp. 60–72; and Heidel, *Babylonian Genesis*, pp. 18–60.
31. See Heidel, *Babylonian Genesis*, p. 129.

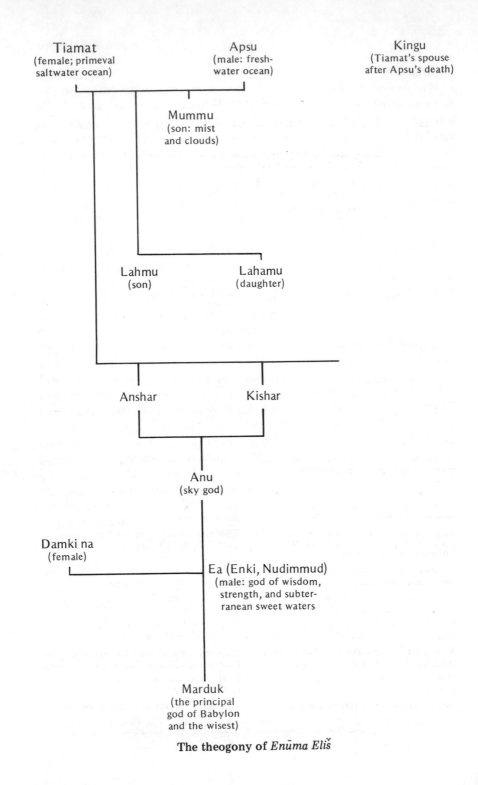

The theogony of Enūma Eliš

SIMILARITIES

I:1—10	Original mass of material was water.	1:2
IV:130—45	Two bodies of water separated by a firmament.	1:3

Narrative divided into seven parts, whether tablets (*Enūma Eliš*) or days (Genesis).

Narrative begins with living deity, whether many gods (*Enūma Eliš*) or one God (Genesis).

Heavens, earth, firmament created first; then celestial bodies; then man.

DIFFERENCES

Polytheistic (I).	Monotheistic (1:1).
Matter and spirit confounded (I: 1—10).	Matter and spirit clearly distinguished.
Matter is eternal.	Matter created by God from nothing (1:1).
Theogonic (I:1—II:20).	Not at all theogonic.
Primeval water animate (I).	Primeval water inanimate (1:2).
Primeval darkness referred to only in Berossus' interpretation of epic.	Primeval darkness referred to clearly (1:2).
Light (night and day) preexisted (I:38, 68, 102).	Light created by God: did not emanate from Him (1:3).
No systematic chronology; no days, etc.	Systematic chronology.
Firmament resulted from two acts: slaying of Apsu and Mummu (I:59—72), and slaying of Tiamat (IV:128—45).	Firmament resulted from single, creative act of God.
The earth and its water formed from preexisting matter (IV:128—45).	Both earth and its waters created from nothing (1:1, 2).
Stars and moon created as time dividers for the gods (V:1—20); no mention of the sun's creation.	Sun and moon created first, then the stars. No mythology (cf. Deut. 4:19; 17:3; Job 31:25, 27).
Suggests sun moved through east and west gates each day.	Nothing about the sun moving through east and west gates.
No record of the creation of vegetation, animals, birds, reptiles, fish.	Clear account of the creation of vegetation, animals, birds, reptiles, fish.
Man created by two gods, Marduk and Ea, from defeated god, Kingu.	Man created by one God in His image, after His likeness.
Man created to serve the gods, so that they might "be at ease" (VI:5—8).	Man created to rule the earth and its inhabitants (1:26—30; cf. Ps. 115:16).
Marduk's creative acts required great effort.	God's creative acts required only His spoken word.
Man created with evil tendency.	Man created without moral blemish.

A comparison between *Enūma Eliš* and Genesis

inspiration does not rule out the possibility of the dependence of the Genesis account, it renders such dependence wholly unnecessary. It seems inconceivable that the Holy Spirit would have used an epic so contaminated with heathen philosophy as a source of spiritual truth."[32]

A second approach is that the Babylonian epic was based on the Genesis narrative, but this is very unlikely. *Enuma Eliš* was probably written in the eighteenth or seventeenth centuries B.C., more than two hundred years before Genesis was written. Furthermore, this solution, like the first, has difficulty explaining the significant differences between the two.

The third possibility is that the two have a common source. Unger, who seems to favor this approach, summarizes it: "Early races of men wherever they wandered took with them these earliest traditions of mankind, and in varying latitudes and climes, have modified them according to their religions and mode of thought. Modifications, as time proceeded, resulted in the corruption of the original pure tradition. The Genesis account is not only the purest, but everywhere bears the unmistakable impress of divine inspiration when compared with the extravagances and corruptions of other accounts. The biblical narrative, we may conclude, represents the original form these traditions must have assumed."[33]

However one explains the similarities between ancient cosmologies and the Bible, one thing seems eminently clear: the Genesis account is without real parallel. Heidel leaves the question of relationships open and still concludes that "these exalted conceptions in the biblical account of creation give it a depth and dignity unparalleled in any cosmogony known to us from Babylonia or Assyria."[34] Genesis, therefore, is divinely inspired, and its ultimate origin is the Creator God Himself.

---

32. *Archeology and the Old Testament* (Grand Rapids: Zondervan Publishing House, 1954), p. 36.
33. Ibid., p. 37.
34. *Babylonian Genesis*, pp. 139, 140.

5

The First Man

Genesis 1:26–2:25

What did Adam look like? Did he have the same structural and facial characteristics we do? Did he have more hair and resemble the higher forms in the ape kingdom? How long ago did he live? Was he really the first man or were there others before him? These and many related questions continue to stir scholarly controversy. While the biblical material on this subject is tantalizingly brief, it is clear and precise and has important scientific implications. One's method of interpretation and locus of authority are once again crucial. This chapter offers a framework in which to understand the origin and nature of early man, a framework established by biblical truth in the light of verified scientific facts.

I. The Origin of Man (2:7, 21–25)

A. Major Theories

1. Evolution. Evolution, as represented in Darwinism and neo-Darwinism, simply asserts that all living organisms arose from one simple, living cell. The origin of that cell is traced to the accumulation of chemical and protein elements brought together over a long period of time by unknown chance factors.

The concept of spontaneous generation, which is widely accepted and on which evolutionary theory is based, is an a priori assumption that lacks controlled scientific proof. The concept that life evolved from the simple to the complex still lacks a biological mechanism and in fact runs counter to clearly defined and well-supported laws of biogenesis. Advocates of this school usually deny categorically biblical assertions concerning origins. Sir Julian Huxley argued, "After Darwin it was no longer necessary to deduce the existence of divine purpose for the facts of biological adaptation."[1] He later observed, "In the evolutionary pattern of thought there is no longer need or room for the supernatural. The earth was not created; it evolved. So did all the animals and plants that inhabit it, including our human selves, mind and soul as well as brain and body. So did religion."[2] Huxley may well not speak for all evolutionists, but he does speak for the vast majority. Since this theory is completely extrabiblical in nature and scope, we will analyze it no further. The postulates of Darwinism and neo-Darwinism have been adequately criticized by competent scholars.[3]

2. Theistic evolution. In recent years many Christian men of science, under tremendous pressure from prevailing scientific opinion, have acquiesced in some basic tenets of evolutionary geology and biology. Assuming that scientific speculation on this point is both valid and authoritative, as well as that the Holy Scriptures are the revealed Word of God, they have attempted to harmonize the two. Simply stated, theistic evolution asserts that God ordered and directed the evolutionary process. He may have directly produced the first life forms, but beyond that He merely superintended the process of evolution. God ordered and directed a creative process rather than performing a series of creative acts. Russell L. Mixter asserts, "Genesis 1 is designed to tell who is the creator, and not necessarily how the full process of creation was accomplished."[4]

---

1. *Rationalist Annual* (1946), p. 87. See also L.M. Davies, "The Present State of Teleology."
2. "Issues in Evolution," in Sol Tax, ed., *Evolution After Darwin*, 3 vols. (Chicago: University of Chicago Press, 1960), 3:252ff.
3. See, for example, A.E. Wilder-Smith, *Man's Origin, Man's Destiny;* Walter E. Lammerts, ed., *Why Not Creation?;* and Lammerts, *Scientific Studies in Special Creation.*
4. "Man in Creation," p. 25. See also his *The Story of Creation* (Grand Rapids: Zondervan Publishing House, 1955).

74

This statement has had wide appeal, but it does not come to grips with the text of Genesis. If the design of Genesis 1 were limited to that, the text would stop after the first verse. When the Christian scientist agrees that living organisms were the result of chance factors, he has abandoned *de facto* a biblical concept of origins. Even naturalisitic scientists do not consider the theory of theistic evolution to be a credible alternative to naturalistic evolution on the one hand, and biblical creation on the other. If, indeed, natural processes and chance factors adequately explain the origin of life, then what need is there for God? It appears that the acquiescence in major propositions of evolutionary thought can only lead one down a trail to antibiblical conclusions.[5]

3. Special creation. This viewpoint is biblically oriented. It asserts that God, through a series of supernatural acts, produced the world and all life forms in a relatively brief period of time. It interprets the biblical account of creation literally rather than parabolically or symbolically, historically rather than mythologically. It sees in the Bible specific statements concerning God's method for producing life, and it is based on these statements. It allows for variation in the form and structure of living animals. It also accommodates the existence of cave men and unusual ape forms. That skeletal evidence exists for unusual human forms or perhaps higher animal forms is beyond dispute; that cave men existed and widely inhabited the earth cannot be doubted. The issues are the *date* and the anthropological *implications*—social, economic, and religious—of their existence.

Dating Adam has been a serious bone of contention. Evolutionary paleontologists have argued for as ancient a date as one million years ago. Because their arguments are based largely on uniformitarian presuppositions and because it is rather doubtful that the gaps in the genealogies of Genesis 5 and 11 can be wide enough to stretch one million years, Christian scientists generally argue for a more recent date. James O. Buswell, feeling that Adam must antedate Neanderthal man and accepting the antiquity of Neanderthal man, considers Adam to have appeared at least forty to fifty thousand years ago.[6] Others, agreeing that Adam predated Neanderthal man but having serious reservations about the antiq-

---

5. Theistic evolution is further assessed in J. Barton Payne, "Theistic Evolution and the Hebrew of Genesis 1-2," pp. 85-90.
6. "Adam and Neolithic Man," pp. 49, 50. See also Mixter, *The Story of Creation*, p. 32.

uity of Neanderthal man, think Adam appeared from fifteen to ten thousand years ago.[7] The differences of opinion on the matter are obviously considerable. The Bible points to a relatively recent date, but how recent the date is, we will not know until science uncovers more conclusive evidence.

B. The Biblical Data (2:7, 21–25)

1. Creation of Adam (2:7). God "formed" (*yāṣar*) man. *Yāṣar* means to mold or shape a particular substance. It is used of the potter shaping pottery (Isa. 29:16; 49:5); the goldsmith making idols (Isa. 44:9; Hab. 2:18); and God fashioning things like the human eye (Ps. 94:9) and heart (Ps. 33:15), and the seasons (Ps. 74:17). God formed the human body from "dust" (*'āpār*) from the "ground" (*ᵃdāmâ*). This dust is not "dry, pulverized earth only," writes Leupold. "Here, without a doubt, a damp mass of the finest earth is under consideration. Luther's rendering is still unsurpassed, *Erdenkloss*, lit., 'lump of earth'. The term does not mean 'mud,' as the skeptics irreverently declare. Lest man form too high an estimate of the first man, it is here recorded that, in spite of the high station involved in being made in the image of God, man has a constituent part in his makeup, which forever forbids unseemly pride on his part. . . ."[8] After forming man's body, God "breathed into his nostrils the breath of life." The breath of God has special significance in Scripture. According to Psalm 33:6, God breathed the heavens into existence by His word. According to II Timothy 3:16, "all Scripture is given by inspiration of God," or is God-breathed. Only after God breathed life into the lifeless body did it become "a living soul" (*nepeš ḥayyâ*). This "living soul" is not uniquely human, however; the same Hebrew phrase is used in Genesis 1 of sea animals (vv. 20, 21) and land animals (v. 24). What is uniquely human is the divine "image" and "likeness" in man (1:26, 27).

The popular approach to this verse, as to all of Genesis 1-3, is the symbolical one advocated by theistic evolutionists. One writes that "Genesis 2 and 3 are not a literal account of a miracle. At the points where supernaturalism enters the narrative (2:7, 8, 15, 19, 21, 22; 3:8, 21, 24), the language is anthropomorphic. Literal

76

7. Henry M. Morris, *Evolution and the Modern Christian*, p. 64. See also Robert W. Wood, "The Age of Man," pp. 24–27.
8. *Exposition of Genesis*, 1:115.

interpretation would reduce the creator to a creature with hands, lungs, and legs. . . . Standard hermeneutics forces us to give up the naive literal interpretation of Genesis 2 and 3. Genesis 2 and 3 are purely symbolic."[9] Theistic evolutionists see "dust" in verse 7 as a symbol of an animal—an ape-like creature—and God's breathing life into His new creation's nostrils as a symbol of His transforming it from an animal to a man. Harold J. Ockenga writes that "God created man and at some point, regardless of whether God used dust of the ground or whether He used an animal whom He had already created, He bridged the gap by breathing into man the breath of life, thus making him in His own image."[10] Augustus H. Strong saw the creation of man as mediate in that God used "existing material in the shape of animal forms," and immediate in that "only a divine reinforcement of the process of life turned the animal into man. In other words, man came not from the brute, but through the brute, and the same immanent God who had previously created the brute created also the man."[11]

This view cannot be maintained in the light of the obvious meaning of the Hebrew text. *Dust* cannot be a symbol for animal life. It is the inanimate, inorganic material which we know as soil, or earth. Even after God had formed a human body from it, it was inanimate and lifeless, requiring God to breathe life into it. This same material, in Genesis 3, is cursed by God (v. 17), who promises that it will produce "thorns . . . and thistles" (v. 18); and this is the material to which man returns when he dies (v. 19). *Dust* cannot possibly be a symbol for animal life in Genesis 3:17-19 (Can animals bring forth thorns or thistles? Or do men return to animal life at death?), and there is no adequate reason for so understanding it in 2:7.

Needless to say, the interpretation of Genesis 2:7 is crucial to establishing a biblical anthropology. If it is interpreted incorrectly, the biblical view falls victim to anthropological speculation. To understand man's origin and fall is to understand his capacities and limitations. Theistic evolutionists contend that the Bible's symbolic history of man's origin is primarily concerned not with anthropology or science but with theology.[12] If this is true, then the Bible has very little to contribute to our understanding of man and to a resolution of the human dilemma.

9. Paul Seely, "Adam and Anthropology: A Proposed Solution," p. 89.
10. *Women Who Made Bible History*, p. 12.
11. *Systematic Theology*, 2:466.
12. Seely, "Adam and Anthropology," p. 90.

2. **Creation of Eve (2:21–25).** For the first time in the history of creation, God said, "It is not good. . . ." (2:18). Everything up to this point had been perfect in function and appearance. However, God had not designed Adam to be alone, and Adam realized his incompleteness when he named all the cattle, fowl, and beasts of the field; none was "a helper meet for him," a phrase better translated, "a helper corresponding to him." This was the situation God described as "not good."

A helper corresponding to him

The narrative of God's creation of Eve is one of the greatest beauty and intimacy. According to verse 21 God caused "a deep sleep [*tardēmâ*] to fall upon Adam." This "deep sleep" is so deep that all consciousness of the outer world and of one's own existence vanishes. This sleep is usually produced by a supernatural agency (cf. Gen. 15:12; Job 4:13; 33:15); the verb form of *tardēmâ*, however, also applies to sleep caused by something else, including complete exhaustion (cf. Jonah 1:5). After putting Adam in this deep sleep, God removed one of Adam's ribs and made from it a woman, giving her all the life qualities that He had given Adam. The Hebrew word *selāʿ* ("rib") refers elsewhere in the Bible to "side, wing of a building, and a panel." Many have felt it should be translated in verses 21 and 22 "side part," but the traditional translation is supported by the fact that the Akkadian word for "rib" is *ṣēlu*.

The creation of Adam and Eve teaches us much about the marriage relationship. First, marriage was instituted by God (vv. 22-24). Second, marriage is to be monogamous; God gave Adam just one wife. The Old Testament reports many polygamous relationships, but the Lord Jesus reminds us that "from the beginning it was not so" (Matt. 19:8). Third, marriage is to be heterosexual; the mate whom God created for Adam, a male, was Eve, a female. In spite of the persistence with which the "gay liberation movement" argues the case for legitimizing homosexuality, its case cannot stand in the light of biblical revelation. If God had intended marriages to be homosexual, Genesis 2 would say something about Adam and Bill. The first marriage that God performed is quite clearly a pattern. Those who attempt to mount a biblical case for homosexuality must completely abandon reasonable hermeneutics. Fourth, the husband and wife are to be unified physically and spiritually, knit together by love and mutual respect; the man is to "leave his father and mother, and . . . cleave unto his wife: and they shall be one flesh" (2:24; cf. Matt. 19:4, 5). This unity implies the permanency of marriage, an implication

78

which Jesus makes explicit in his exposition of verse 24 (Matt. 19:6). And fifth, the husband is to be the head of the wife. Adam was created before Eve (cf. I Cor. 11:8, 9; I Tim. 2:13), and Eve was created as a partner for Adam, one who complemented him and corresponded to him. Another liberation movement making appeals to the biblical text is that of women. Many of the movement's complaints are legitimate, but it is also guilty of extremism in trying to solve the problems that exist. Recent articles have attempted to demonstrate from Genesis the complete and unreserved equality of the sexes. Their authors aim, presumably, to restructure the home and society on this basis. In all fairness we must admit that there is an equality between husband and wife, but we must continue to maintain that there is also a well-defined chain of authority. This chain exists not because men are superior but because God instituted it.

II. The Creator and Nature of Man (1:26, 27)

The plural pronoun *us* in verse 26, used by God, has been the subject of no small debate over the years. Six of the more common explanations make it (1) a reference to the trinity, (2) a survival of early polytheism, (3) a plural of majesty, (4) a plural of the fullness of attributes and powers, (5) a plural of deliberation, and (6) God addressing angelic beings in heaven.[13] G. Henton Davies rejects all of them, concluding that "for the Hebrew, God speaks out of a plurality or singularity of being, and so a plural is as coherent as a singular."[14] Some scholars who have wrestled with this pronoun from the standpoint of mythological origins suggest that it might reflect (1) an unassimilated fragment of myth, (2) an address to creation, (3) a plural of majesty, (4) an address to the heavenly court, (5) self-deliberation or self-summons, or (6) duality within the Godhead.[15] They have also suggested that God is addressing His own Spirit, who appeared in verse 2.[16]

It is highly improbable that God was taking counsel with angelic beings on this occasion.[17] Many writers feel that this pronoun, along with the plural noun *'elōhîm*, suggest the fullness of the

---

13. Herbert E. Ryle, *The Book of Genesis*, pp. 18, 19.
14. *Genesis*, p. 130.
15. D. J. A. Clines, "The Image of God in Man," pp. 62–69.
16. Ibid., p. 69.
17. Leupold, *Exposition of Genesis*, 1:87.

divine personality and foreshadows the doctrine of the trinity.[18]
It is clear from the New Testament that the Son, the second
person of the Godhead, was associated with His Father in the
work of creation.[19] But from the standpoint of Hebrew grammar
and syntax, *us* is more likely a majestic/plural. This interpretation
"comprehends in its deepest and most intensive form (God speaking of Himself and with Himself in the plural number, not *rever-
entiae cause*, but with reference to the fullness of the divine
powers and essences which He possesses) the truth that lies at the
foundation of the Trinitarian view, *viz*. that the potencies concentrated in the absolute divine being are something more than
powers and attributes of God...."[20] To make *us* a plural of
majesty does not, then, eliminate altogether any reference to the
trinity. Oswald T. Allis contends that "this is the language of
soliloquy, God talking with Himself,... involving *in germ* the
doctrine of the trinity." He concludes that the plural pronoun
"should not be appealed to as a formal proof" of that doctrine.[21]

The church fathers rather uniformly distinguished between the
terms *image* and *likeness*. Irenaeus was probably the unconscious
originator of this distinction.[22] Catholic scholarship normally
asserts that the image consists not in dominion over the animal
kingdom but in a share of the divine wisdom, justice, virtue,
holiness, and truth, and that this "moral image" was completely
effaced by the fall.[23] Martin Luther suggested that the divine
image was man's original righteousness.[24] John Calvin, on the
other hand, considered the terms *image* and *likeness* similar and
stressed the importance of renewal in Christ. Calvin apparently
encompassed in *image* the idea of nature, thus suggesting that the
image was lost and finally restored in Christ.[25] Karl Barth suggests
that the image refers to the creation of man as male and female.

---

18. Thomas Whitelaw, *Genesis*, p. 29; Leupold, *Exposition of Genesis*, 1:
85–88.
19. Cf. John 1:1–3, 14; I Cor. 8:6; Col. 1:16, 17; Heb. 1:2.
20. C. F. Keil and Franz Delitzsch, *Biblical Commentary on the Old Testament*, 25 vols. (Edinburgh: T. and T. Clark, 1864–1901), 1:62.
21. *God Spake by Moses*, p. 13.
22. Helmut Thielicke, *Theological Ethics: Foundations*, p. 202.
23. This position is evaluated in Strong, *Systematic Theology*, 2:521; and
Gordon Clark, "The Image of God in Man," p. 221.
24. *Luther's Commentary on Genesis*, p. 30.
25. See Richard Prins, "The Image of God in Adam and the Restoration of
Man in Jesus Christ: A Study in Calvin," *Scottish Journal of Theology* 28
(1972): 32–44; and G. C. Berkouwer, *Man: The Image of God*, pp. 88, 89.

He sees an analogy between the sexes and the persons of the Godhead.[26]

The Hebrew terms *selem* ("image") and *d^emût* ("likeness") are best regarded as essentially synonymous. Differentiation between them has been rejected on both exegetical and theological grounds.[27] The use of these two terms in the Old Testament and the Septuagint's rendering of them provide more than adequate evidence that they are synonyms.[28] C.F. Keil and Franz Delitzsch strongly affirm that "there is no possibility of discovering a sharp or well defined difference."[29] Both terms, therefore, point to spiritual qualities shared by God and man. It is this image and likeness that completely distinguishes man from the animal kingdom. He alone has the capacity for self-consciousness, speech, and moral discernment. Even though man has fallen and the image of God is marred, man retains this image (cf. Gen. 9:6; James 3:9).[30]

III. The Dominion of Man (1:26–31)

God made man in His own image and likeness, and then immediately granted him dominion over the fish of the sea, the fowl of the air, cattle, and other creeping things (1:26). The dominion which man enjoyed in the Garden of Eden was a direct consequence of the image of God in him. Since man had been endowed with considerable intellectual faculties, he was commanded to "dress" the garden and "keep" it (2:15). Man was not only granted dominion over life, both in the sea and on the land, but commanded to "subdue" the earth (1:28). The term *subdue* implies a degree of sovereignty, control, and direction over nature. This call to rule is a call to advance civilization and regulate natural forces.[31] It is also a call to "be fruitful, and multiply, and replenish the earth" (v. 28). The gift of dominion and the effective exercise of power over nature was designed to enable man to enjoy his environment fully. However, with the fall into sin came a curse

---

26. *The Doctrine of Creation*, 1:214.
27. Charles Feinberg, "The Image of God," p. 237.
28. S. R. Driver, *The Book of Genesis*, pp. 14, 15.
29. *Biblical Commentary*, 1:63. Also see Regin Prenter, *Creation and Redemption*, p. 283.
30. A complete study of this problem is Phillip Taylor, "Man: His Image and Dominion" (Th.D. diss., Grace Theological Seminary, 1974).
31. Erich Sauer, *King of the Earth: The Nobility of Man According to the Bible and Science*. p. 83.

upon the ground and the animal kingdom. Man continues to exercise some control over nature, but his control is limited compared to Adam's before he sinned. I have been reminded more than once of this limitation when, on a fishing trip, I have been outsmarted by a fish. I do not intend, however, to excuse my poor craftsmanship on the basis of the Adamic fall!

Adam's intellectual capacity probably surpassed ours; he was able to name all the animals which inhabited that early environment (vv. 19, 20). This silences the argument that Adam was some type of primitive man groping for self-identity and self-consciousness. God created him with a complete, unhindered intellect. Early man was decidedly different from animals in both origin and intelligence. Similarities in structure between, for example, the chimpanzee and man furnish no evidence to the contrary. "God made the chimpanzee as well as the man, both of the dust, and He gave the same food to them. If they both eat the same carbohydrates, fats, proteins, vitamins, mineral salts, and water, why should not their bodies have the same general makeup and functions? Identical metabolic processes occur in both their bodies, their serological reactions are quite identical, and their blood groups are the same even though their bloods cannot be used in cross transfusions."[32]

IV. The Environment of Man (1:29–2:6; 2:8–20)

The same infinite care with which God created the universe and earthly vegetation and animals is apparent in His preparation of a home for man. God, according to 2:8, "planted a garden eastward in Eden." This is another special and particular act of God in behalf of man. The Creator desired man to have ideal living conditions in which to realize his potential. The garden, the beauty of which must have been unexcelled, provided an environment in which man was to examine, and to learn. Man's early diet was diversified and complete; God gave him and the animals "every green herb for meat" (1:30). The trees in the garden were designed especially for man (2:9). John Milton described this early paradise and Adam's introduction to it in *Paradise Lost:*

> . . . One came, methought, of shape Divine,
> And said, thy Mansion wants thee, Adam, arise,

---

32. Frank L. Marsh, *Life, Man and Time*, p. 78.

> First Man, of Men innumerable ordain'd
> First Father, call'd by thee I come thy Guide
> To the Garden of bliss, thy seat prepar'd.
> [8.295-99]

Genesis 2:15, 16 imply that God led Adam to the garden personally, and this is in keeping with the unspoiled, intimate relationship between Adam and his Creator.

The trees in the garden were designed especially for man (2:9). Two trees of particular significance were "the tree of life" and "the tree of knowlege of good and evil" (v. 9). Were these literal trees? Or is this, as is often asserted, merely symbolic language that need not be taken seriously? The simple reading of the text is that these were two literal trees. Their appearance was probably not unusual, and they possessed no magical power; they were set apart only by the divine designation.

This unusual garden was watered by "a mist ['ēḏ] from the earth" (2:5). The term 'ēḏ has been variously interpreted. Speiser relates it to the Akkadian edû ("flood, waves, swell").[33] Harris rejects Speiser's mythological interpretation of the passage but agrees that 'ēḏ means flooding rather than misting. He translates verses 5 and 6: "No plant of the field was yet in the land and no herb of the field had as yet sprung up, but an inundation went up from the country and it watered all the face of the ground."[34] Others retain the translation "mist."[35]

Running through the garden was a river (2:10), which upon leaving the garden divided into four rivers, two of which are the well-known Tigris (Hiddekel; cf. Dan. 10:4) and Euphrates (v. 14). The other two rivers, Pishon (v. 11) and Gihon (v. 13), were located further east. It is futile, however, to try to pinpoint the garden's location; the area was probably altered greatly first by God's curse upon the earth and then by the great flood of Noah.

Man's activity in that garden, unlike the type of toil associated with a cursed earth (3:17, 18), was rewarded by complete fruition and productivity. Earliest man had almost complete freedom; he was restricted only with regard to the tree of knowledge of good and evil. The penalty for eating fruit from that tree in defiance of God's command was death (2:17). Adam and Eve enjoyed a

---

33. "'*Ed* in the Story of Creation," pp. 9–11; *Genesis*, p. 16.
34. "The Mist, the Canopy and the Rivers of Eden," *Bulletin of the Evangelical Theological Society* 11 (1968): 178.
35. John C. Whitcomb and Morris, *The Genesis Flood*, pp. 241, 242.

perfect relationship—spiritually, mentally, and physically. They were both naked, but they were not ashamed (2:25). Nakedness did not result in sensuous impropriety and guilt; these are the tragic result of man's fall into sin. Adam and Eve were the capstone of God's creative activity.

6

Temptation and Fall

Genesis 3:1–24

It would be marvelous indeed if the same could be said of man throughout history that was said in the beginning: he was "not ashamed" (2:25). The Edenic paradise represented God's best for man; He had anticipated every human need and circumstance, and made adequate provision for it. All that God had created was good, and man enjoyed the closest, most intimate relationship with Him. How tragic that in Genesis 3 man's relationship with God was spoiled and the course of human history drastically altered.

Needless to say, it is impossible to understand the rest of the Bible without understanding Genesis 3. God's intricate plan of redemption fulfilled in Christ is meaningless if the events of Genesis 3 are not historical. If this narrative is a mere etiology, we are left with no record of the introduction of sin and violence into human history. Some have classified the story of man's fall a fable. They argue that a talking serpent makes a prosaic interpretation of Genesis 3 impossible, an argument with which we must disagree. While it is true that talking animals often appear in fables, this account, unlike a fable, emphasizes no particular moral, is utterly serious, and is obviously grounded in reality—the presence of sin and the dilemma of man.

I. The Tempter (v. 1)

The words which introduce the third chapter are ominous: "Now the serpent . . . " Was this a literal snake that spoke audibly to Eve, or was it, as ancient Jewish tradition has it, a mere symbol of the evil impulses lurking in the human heart? What did it look like? Was it Satan himself? These and many other questions of interpretation have been raised.

That the serpent was real seems beyond doubt. Moses called the serpent a divinely created "beast of the field." The contention that it is biologically impossible for a serpent to speak is irrelevant; Satan, the master deceiver, was certainly capable of making a serpent speak. The evidence is decisive that Satan, who had already been cast from the presence of God, used this "subtle" and beautiful animal, which apart from Satan was not evil. Satan is not mentioned in 3:1, but the serpent's words are in character for the one called by John the "father of lies" (John 8:44). When discussing the last days and Satan's activity during them, John refers to him as "that old serpent, called the Devil, and Satan, which deceiveth the whole world. . . ." (Rev. 12:9; cf. Rev. 20:2 and I John 3:8). Satan's arrogance and pride caused his humiliation and fall (Isa. 14:12-14). Not satisfied with being the foremost angel, he resolved to ascend into heaven and exalt his throne above the stars of God; He desired to be "like the most High" Himself. God immediately judged Lucifer, casting him from his position in the heavens. The fallen angel recognized that he was not powerful enough to contend with the Creator and settled for attacking the creation.

Moses described the serpent as "more subtil [$\bar{a}r\hat{u}m$] than any beast of the field." '$\bar{A}r\hat{u}m$ means essentially "crafty, shrewd, sensible,"[1] and this cleverness can be either good (Prov. 12:16, 23; 13:16; 14:8, 15, 18; 22:3; 27:12) or evil (Job 5:12; 15:5). Whether it is good or evil in the serpent is debatable. Young opts for the latter: "The word 'subtle' is evidently used with respect to what follows, where the words spoken by the serpent tempt the woman and lead her into moral evil. It is this fact which throws the light upon the meaning. And in the light of this fact it would

86

---

1. Brown, Driver, and Briggs, *Lexicon of the Old Testament*, p. 791.

seem that the subtlety is something which could belong only to a responsible being. No mere snake could of itself display the craftiness and cunning which manifest themselves in the subsequent discourse with Eve."[2] Leupold, however, chooses the former: "This was a purely harmless cleverness, after the pattern of Matthew 10:16. Such cleverness may well make this creature the most subtle vehicle of Satan's evil devices. From all this it dimly appears that the chief agent is a spirit of an unusual power and cleverness and clearly, too, a fallen spirit."[3] The serpent is often described in the Bible as a clever or wise animal. Jesus sent forth His twelve disciples "as sheep in the midst of wolves," exhorting them to be "wise as serpents, and harmless as doves" (Matt. 10:16). The writer of Proverbs identifies "three things which are too wonderful for me, yea, four which I know not: the way of an eagle in the air; the way of a serpent upon a rock; the way of a ship in the midst of the sea; and the way of a man with a maid" (30:18, 19). It would seem, then, that the description of the serpent in Genesis 3:1 as clever is not pejorative. It was probably because the serpent was more subtle than any other beast of the field that Satan decided to use it.

What this original serpent looked like is open to speculation. Some have inferred from God's subsequent curse on it that it had legs and was unusually beautiful: "Upon thy belly shalt thou go, and dust shalt eat all the days of thy life" (Gen 3:14). "If these words are not to be robbed of their meaning, they cannot be understood in any other way than as denoting that the form and movements of the serpent were altered...."[4] However, both Leupold and Derek Kidner contend that serpents had always lacked legs; the curse simply gave to their movements and characteristics a symbolic significance.[5]

In any event, the snake which tempted Eve was much more than a snake; it was Satan himself, who is the father of deception and lies, and who can appear as an angel of light—attractive, reasonable, and enticing.[6]

2. *Genesis 3*, p. 9. See also C. F. Keil and Franz Delitzsch, *Biblical Commentary on the Old Testament*, 25 vols. (Edinburgh: T. and T. Clark, 1864–1901), 1:94.
3. *Exposition of Genesis*, 1:142, 143. See also Francis D. Nichol, ed., *The Seventh-Day Adventist Bible Commentary*, 1:229.
4. Keil and Delitzsch, *Biblical Commentary*, 1:99.
5. Leupold, *Exposition of Genesis*, 1:162; Kidner, *Genesis*, p. 70.
6. Interestingly, Gerhard von Rad completely rejects the identification of the serpent with Satan. He regards the snake as "almost secondary" to the whole account. *Genesis*, p. 85.

II. The Temptation (vv. 1–5)

A. Doubt of God's Word (vv. 1–3)

The serpent approached Eve both cleverly and subtly, not with any brash denial or bitter denunciation, but with an apparently innocent inquiry: "Yea [*'ap kî*], hath God said, Ye shall not eat any of every [*mikkōl*] tree of the garden?" (v. 1). The tempter was probably wise enough to wait until Eve was alone and, therefore, without Adam's support. His question was carefully couched and apparently included an element of surprise or exclamation. *'Ap kî* is literally translated "indeed that" or "really that." The sense would be, "Is it really true that. . . . ?" The key word is *mikkōl* ("from all"). It suggests that perhaps God was not being completely fair with Adam and Eve, despite the fact that He had granted them access to all other trees. The question, designed to elicit a response, attacks the sanctity and appropriateness of God's word. The real tragedy is not that Eve was tempted, nor that she listened to the question and examined its implications, but that, as her response to her interrogator revealed, she was inclined to agree with his subtle attack on God. She admitted that God permitted man to eat fruit from the trees of the garden. But she failed to add that man could eat that fruit freely (cf. 2:16); she failed to *name* the one tree the fruit of which man was forbidden to eat; she apparently added to God's prohibition (2:17), saying that man could not even "touch" the fruit; and she weakened God's warning of punishment for disobedience. God had said: "Thou shalt not eat of it [the tree of the knowledge of good and evil] : for in the day that thou eatest thereof thou shalt surely die" (2:17). Eve's paraphrase was: "Ye shall not eat of it . . . lest [*pen*] ye die" (3:3). God promised that death *would* follow disobedience; Eve implied only that death *might* follow. Satan's question already seems to have aroused doubts in Eve concerning God's goodness toward her and Adam.

Did Eve know that she was being tempted? Since this was the first temptation, how could she have understood that her very relationship with God was being threatened? Eve was, according to the New Testament, deceived, but she was not totally naive. She knew well the goodness and care of God, whose beautiful creation surrounded her. She and Adam undoubtedly communed with God and recognized the glory of His presence. Certainly Eve recognized that snakes do not speak, knowing that man alone is capable of rational judgment and communication. But the animal's question was so enticing that she overlooked the unnaturalness of the situation. The result was the most disastrous dialogue in the history of the human race.

B. Denial of God's Word (vv. 4, 5)

Once the serpent had succeeded in securing a response from Eve, he was ready to openly criticize God and the condition which He had given the first human couple. Satan did not challenge the quality of the tree or God's right to restrict man from its fruit; he denied God's promise of punishment: "Ye shall not surely die" (v. 4). The Hebrew construction is extremely emphatic, just as emphatic as that of God's promise to punish disobedience.[7] It is instructive that the first doctrine to be denied was that of judgment.

The tempter then explained why God had issued the prohibition in the first place: "In the day ye eat thereof, then your eyes shall be opened. . . ." (v. 5). This part of Satan's statement was true, for after Adam and Eve ate the fruit their eyes were opened (vv. 7, 22). What the tempter did not say, however, was that their opened eyes would see all things in the light of their own wickedness and rebellion. Perhaps the tempter was charging that God envied His own creation's happiness, or that He had become jealous of those qualities which characterized His personal existence. But Satan further affirmed, ". . . and ye shall be as gods [$^{e}l\bar{o}h\hat{i}m$]" (v. 5). $^{e}l\bar{o}h\hat{i}m$ can legitimately be translated "gods" as well as "God," and the Authorized Version's translation agrees with the Septuagint's and the Vulgate's. But *God* appears preferable. Eve knew of no other gods so a reference to them would have been meaningless. Satan left several impressions: that the knowledge of good and evil was what made God, God; that Adam and Eve were capable of knowing good and evil as perfectly and completely as God knew them and thus could be like God; and that God was jealous of His knowledge of good and evil and of His unique place in the universe. The truth was that Adam and Eve could never attain God's knowledge of good and evil because, in part, to know evil they had to sin, something which God had never done and something which would be fatal to their experiential knowledge of good.

---

7. Cf. *môt t^{e}mutûn* with *môt tāmût* in 2:17.

89

III. The Fall (v. 6)

The steps to Eve's tragic fall are instructive, and they provide a grim warning to all who would take just the first one. She listened to Satan (v. 1), then responded to him (v. 2), and finally yielded by participating in sin (v. 6). What choice did she really have? James would reply, "Resist the devil and he will flee from you" (4:7). She sought no counsel from her husband Adam or from God. She made her decision on the basis of her own judgment and reasoning.

This sequence of temptation and fall, which has been repeated over and over again in human history, is outlined in three words in verse 6. The first is *saw*. Eve went to the center of the garden and gazed upon that tree, and this led to the "lust of the flesh" (I John 2:16). The second is *pleasant*: "It was pleasant to the eyes." John refers to this stage as the "lust of the eyes" (I John 2:16). The tree made her think not of the horrible consequence of death but of the possibility of knowledge. Looking at the pleasant tree was not enough; she had to eat its fruit and become wise. The third word is *took*. "The pride of life" resulted in rebellion against God.

It seems that the pattern for temptation and sin changes little over the ages. Recall, for example, the tragic story of Achan. According to Joshua 7:21 he "saw" among the spoils a beautiful garment from Shinar and other precious objects, then "coveted them," and finally "took them." There was the gaze, perhaps innocent enough at first, but then the desire, and then participation. Another example is recorded in II Samuel 11:2-4. David, during a time of leisure, gazed upon a woman washing herself (v. 2), then desired to meet her (v. 3), and finally took her, making the sin complete (v. 4). The Holy Spirit was most careful to record these examples to admonish and help us. What we look at is, after all, quite important. The proposition that an adult can gaze at anything is ludicrous and naive, for gazing is too often followed by desiring and sinning.

When Eve did not die immediately, she involved Adam in her sin (v. 6). She may have felt that the tempter was correct after all, and, elated by her keen judgment and discovery, asked her husband to eat as well; he did. According to I Timothy 2:14, Eve was deceived by Satan, but Adam was not. Adam, who chose permanent separation from God instead of from Eve, represented the entire human race. When he sinned, "death passed unto all men, for that all have sinned" (Rom. 5:12).

90

Some have speculated that "eating forbidden fruit" is a circumlocution for "having sexual intercourse." The knowledge of good and evil, then, is a knowledge of sex, and it is only natural that Adam and Eve, after committing the first sin, were ashamed of their nudity.[8] This view must be rejected for at least two reasons. First, the Bible clearly states that Eve sinned first and alone. Second, God had already sanctioned and even commanded sexual intercourse when He told the first husband and wife to be fruitful and multiply (1:28), and this sanction is repeated in the New Testament (e.g., Heb. 13:4); therefore, intercourse could not have been a sin for Adam and Eve.

Several scholars have attempted to trace the biblical story of the temptation and fall to Mesopotamia, citing some parallels between it and both the *Gilgameš Epic*[9] and the myth of Adapa.[10] The parallels cited, however, appear superficial when subjected to rigorous exegesis.[11]

How much time elapsed between creation and the fall? Jewish tradition suggests seven years, but this is pure speculation, lacking any biblical foundation.

IV. The Effects of the Fall (vv. 7–24)

A. Effects on the Entire Human Race (vv. 7–13, 22–24)

1. **Sense of guilt (v. 7).** The tempter promised that eating the fruit would open Adam's and Eve's eyes, but he did not say what they would see. They saw themselves as sinners devoid of their original beauty. They saw good and evil only from the standpoint of sinners, from the rock-bottom level of corruption. They became like God in that their natures were fixed, but God was confirmed in holiness while they were confirmed in sinfulness. They now experienced the dilemma which the apostle Paul described so eloquently: "For the good that I would, I do not: but the evil which I would not, that I do" (Rom. 7:19). In other words, they knew good but were unable to do it; they also knew evil but were unable to resist it. This is what depravity is all about; this is the human dilemma. Seeing their nakedness in a new light, they

---

8. Bo Reicke, "The Knowledge Hidden in the Tree of Paradise," pp. 193–201; E. A. Speiser, *Genesis*, p. 26.
9. Speiser, *Genesis*, pp. 26, 27.
10. Ibid., p. 27.
11. Merrill F. Unger, "Archaeology and Genesis 3–4," pp. 11–17.

experienced shame and disgrace. In a pitiful attempt to replace the radiant garments of their innocence, they sewed together fig leaves. Man has ever since attempted to cover his guilt and assuage his conscience. His efforts, however sophisticated and impressive, still fall far short of God's demands.

2. Separation from God (vv. 8–13). The Lord had evidently visited the garden and communed with Adam and Eve on many occasions prior to their fall. This time, however, the sound of God walking in the garden aroused fear rather than joyful anticipation. The description of God in verse 8, of course, is anthropomorphic, but it is the best way for the writer to describe the presence of God on this occasion: Adam and Eve "heard the voice of the Lord God walking [*mithallēk*] in the garden. . . ." It is highly probable that this was a theophany, especially since the verb *mithallēk* is employed. As do all sinners, Adam and Eve ran from God and hid. The natural inclination of the heart is not to seek God but to hide from Him. The apostle Paul assessed man perfectly: ". . . none . . . seeketh after God" (Rom. 3:11). Marvel of all marvels, however, God did not give up pursuit. He knew that Adam and Eve had sinned and still He made the approach. No clearer picture could be painted of God's concern for the lost human race.

Then God asked that penetrating question, "Where art thou?" (v. 9). God knew very well where Adam and Eve were; He was soliciting a response from His creation which was now separated from Him by sin. The effects of the fall were all too obvious. Adam and Eve became afraid when they sensed God's presence in the garden (vv. 8-10). And they refused to accept responsibility for their sins. When the Lord inquired who had told them they were naked, and when He further inquired if they had eaten the forbidden fruit, Adam blamed Eve for giving him the fruit and Eve blamed the serpent for beguiling her. God was silent. Adam and Eve knew they were fully responsible for what they had done; sin always blurs a man's perspective and prevents him from candidly assessing his guilt.

B. Effects on the Serpent (vv. 14, 15)

92

God next addressed the serpent. It is clear from Jeremiah 12:4 and Romans 8:20 that the whole animal kingdom was affected by the fall and the Edenic curse. The serpent, however, was cursed "above all cattle and above every beast of the field." He would go upon his belly and eat dust all the days of his life. This may well mean that the serpent's method of mobilization was changed. Some commentators have criticized the expression "dust shalt thou eat all the days of thy life" as typically prescientific. The problem disappears, however, when the clause is regarded as figurative. This same figure is found in other ancient Near Eastern literature; for example, in the myth "Descent of Ishtar to the Nether World" the cursed live in a place "where dust is their fare and clay is their food."[12] It is a figure, then, of being cursed, and it is used here to communicate that the serpent would be the most cursed of all creatures. The effects of this curse would remain even during the millennium (Isa. 65:25), providing a grim reminder of the fall and its continued effects.

Satan's ultimate defeat is described in verse 15, a passage that has been appropriately called the *protevangelium*—the first Gospel. In this verse God's attention is directed not so much to the serpent as to the one who was behind the whole affair—Satan himself. Interestingly enough, the ultimate victory of Messiah is given not as a promise to man but as a judgment upon Satan. Some commentators feel that the penalties in the verses surrounding verse 15 are to be understood etiologically and that verse 15 is not, therefore, a Messianic prophecy.[13] The traditional Christian interpretation, however, is that it is the first direct expression of the gospel. It recognizes the essential conflict between Satan and the Lord and indicates that this conflict also will involve the people of God and the followers of Satan (cf. John 8:44; Acts 13:10; I John 3:10). The seed of the woman is a clear reference to the Messiah, the Lord Jesus (cf. Rev. 12:1-5; Gal. 3:16, 19), who came "to destroy the works of the devil" (Heb. 2:14; I John 3:8). The *protevangelium* prophesied that Christ would deliver a death blow to Satan, but in so doing would suffer death Himself.

C. Effects on Women (v. 16)

At least three things are direct results of the fall. First, the Lord would multiply the woman's "sorrow of conception," a better translation than the Authorized Version's "thy sorrow and thy conception."[14] God originally commanded Adam and Eve to "be

12. Translated by Speiser in Pritchard, *ANET*, p. 107 (see obverse, line 8).
13. Von Rad, *Genesis*, pp. 89, 90.
14. This assumes that the Hebrew phrase is a hendiadys. See Speiser, *Genesis*, pp. lxx, 24.

93

fruitful and multiply" (1:28), making repeated conception a blessing. Sin, however, made it something of a curse since pregnancy and childbirth would be accompanied by '*iṣṣabôn*, ("sorrow"), a word which is usually translated "pain, sorrow, toil and labor" in the Old Testament (cf. 3:17; 5:29). This is exactly what a pregnant woman experiences during "labor" just prior to birth.[15] God said He would "multiply," or increase, that pain, implying that Eve could or did experience some pain prior to the fall.

Second, the wife would have a deep natural attraction to her husband: ". . . thy desire [the Hebrew noun comes from the verbal root *šûq*] shall be to thy husband." *Šûq* connotes a desire so strong for something that one would run after, or violently crave it. Some commentators have felt that this is not so much a curse as a compensation for the sorrow of childbirth: "It seems reasonable to conclude that this 'desire' was given to alleviate the sorrows of womanhood and to bind the hearts of husband and wife ever more closely together."[16]

Finally, the woman would be ruled by the man. God imposed this order on society because of sin; without a chain of authority, chaos would reign. According to the New Testament it is a sin for the wife to withhold obedience or for the husband to withhold love and kindness (cf. I Cor. 11:3; 14:34; Eph. 5:24, 25; Titus 2:3-5; I Peter 3:1, 5, 6; etc.).

D. Effects on Men (vv. 17–20)

Divine judgment on man focused on his environment. The curse was not upon Adam but was, because of him, upon the ground (v. 17). His "sorrow" would be his effort to farm. Thorns and thistles would greatly increase his work and, in a measure, frustrate his agriculture. How different from life in the garden! Keeping it had been enjoyable, and Adam's labor had resulted in complete and unhindered productivity. Centuries later, Lamech cried out for relief from the curse upon the ground and the difficulty of farming (Gen. 5:29). God concluded the curse with a reminder that men were now mortal; Adam had been created from the dust of the ground, and he would return to it (v. 19).

---

15. See W. W. Baur, ed., *Today's Health Guide* (American Medical Association, 1965), pp. 22, 23. Other biblical texts describe the pain and anguish of childbirth: Gen. 38:7; Ps. 48:6; Isa. 66:7; Jer. 4:31; 6:24; 13:21; 22:23; 30:6; 49:21; 50:43; John 16:21; Rev. 12:2.
16. Nichol, ed., *Bible Commentary*, 1:234.

Then it was that Adam named his wife, *Eve*, giving her the distinctive identity of "the mother of all living" (v. 20). Literally interpreted, this verse seems to preclude the existence of other *Homo sapiens* before the fall. This is the expression that has caused theologians to conclude that Adam and Eve were indeed parents of the whole human race. This also seems to be a necessary conclusion from Adam's role as head of the race (cf. Acts 17:26; Rom. 5:12-21).

Out of the blackness and tragedy of man's fall comes another glimmer of light and grace that supplements the *protevangelium*. God slew animals and made coats of skin to replace Adam's and Eve's inadequate fig leaves (v. 21). While it may be premature to read into this the introduction of animal sacrifice, it certainly illustrated to Adam and Eve, who may even have witnessed the death of these innocent animals, the high cost of their guilt. If the concept of sacrifice was not revealed to them at this time, it apparently was very soon thereafter (cf. Gen. 4:4). To punish sin appropriately and to prevent man from living eternally in his sinfulness, the Lord expelled the two from the garden (vv. 22-24). The expulsion was not merely geographical; it was spiritual. Fellowship between man and God was broken.

7

The Beginning of Civilization

Genesis 4, 5

Although Adam and Eve had been specifically commanded to multiply and fill the earth, not until after they fell and were expelled from the garden did they have any children. It is again appropriate to note that the account is couched in typical Hebrew prose and, therefore, should be understood historically. The New Testament refers to Cain and Abel, as it does to Adam and Eve, as real, historical characters (Matt. 25:35; I John 3:12; Jude 11; Heb. 11:4; 12:24). The story of Cain and Abel vividly illustrates man's depraved condition.

I. Cain and Abel (4:1–15)

A. The First Children (4:1, 2)

The conception of Cain is described in typical Hebrew idiom: "Adam knew [$y\bar{a}\underline{d}\hat{a}'$] Eve" (v. 1). *Knew* is a common euphemism for sexual union (cf. Gen. 19:5; Num. 31:17, 18, 35; Judg. 11:39; 19:22, 25; I Sam. 1:19; etc.). Eve "bare Cain [$qayin$], and said, I have gotten [the verb is $q\bar{a}n\hat{a}$] a man [$'\hat{i}\check{s}$]. . . ." (v. 1). Perhaps this is a play on the words $qayin$ and $q\bar{a}n\hat{a}$ ("to acquire, get"). Their similar sounds have led some to argue that they are

97

etymologically related, although no other evidence supports that argument. Von Rad suggests that *Cain* "means 'spear' (II Sam. 21:16) and is also attested in early Arabic as a personal name."[1] Why Eve used the verb *qānâ* instead of the usual *yālad* ("to bear, give birth to"), and why she used *'îš* for a newborn, are perplexing. Perhaps she intended to convey the general idea of "life."[2] Even more perplexing is the last phrase, "from the Lord" ('*et YHWH*). '*Et* can be understood as the sign of the direct object ("I have gotten a man with [the help of] the Lord"). According to the former interpretation, Eve was referring to the Deliverer promised in 3:15.[3] "Though Eve was mistaken in her hope, her words show that she was a pious woman who believed the promise of the coming salvation by the blessed Savior," wrote Luther.[4] According to the latter interpretation, Eve was emphasizing God's role in the birth of her child. We can safely conclude, whichever interpretation we adopt, that Eve saw her son as some kind of deliverer. She may have identified him with the deliverer of 3:15, but she could scarcely have understood that deliverer to be the divine Messiah.

A second son was named *Abel*. It has been suggested that the sons were twins, but this unnecessarily burdens the meaning of the Hebrew text. *Abel* means "vanity" or "breath," but if its meaning is significant to the story, that significance is not particularly clear.

Much has been made of the occupations of the two sons: Abel raised livestock and Cain cultivated crops. According to some, the literary theme of great conflicts between the pastoral and agricultural ways of life was common in the ancient Near East.[5] But this is not the theme of Genesis 4; the cultural and religious implications of these occupations are not the primary point of the story. God allows for both ways of life (Deut. 8: especially vv. 7, 8, 13), and accepts gifts from both shepherds and farmers.

B. The First Offering (4:3–7)

The story of the first offering raises a number of questions, such as, How old were Cain and Abel at the time? and, Were their offerings in response to a command from God to give offerings?

1. *Genesis*, p. 100.
2. E. A. Speiser, *Genesis*, p. 30.
3. Francis D. Nichol, *The Seventh-Day Adventist Bible Commentary*, 1:238.
4. *Luther's Commentary on Genesis*, p. 91. This view is evaluated in H. C. Leupold, *Exposition of Genesis*, 1:190.
5. Speiser, *Genesis*, p. 31. See, for example, "Dumuzi and Enkimdu: The

But the most important question is, Why did God reject Cain's offering? Many have contended that God had commanded Cain and Abel to give offerings, and that God had specified blood sacrifice. Cain's offering was rejected, then, because He refused to meet God's specifications. There can be no doubt that Cain's attitude was rebellious. When his offering was rejected, he "was very wroth [*wayyiḥar leqayin me'ōd*] and his countenance fell" (v. 5). The Hebrew words paint a vivid picture of extreme anger. The New Testament teaches that Abel's faith made his offering acceptable (Heb. 11:4). The Old Testament teaches that God will reject the most perfect sacrifice if that sacrifice is offered by an apostate heart (cf. Isa. 1:11-13; Hos. 6:6; Mic. 6:6-8). However, since Moses recorded no divine command to bring an offering, or specifications for that sacrifice, it is more likely that the *only* reason Cain's offering was rejected was his attitude in offering it. The term translated "offering" in this passage, *minḥâ*, is used in the Levitical laws for the bloodless thank offering, consisting either of flour and oil or of flour prepared with frankincense (2:1, 4, 14, 15); it is also used in the Old Testament in a broader sense, including both bloodless and bloody offerings. The broader sense is obviously intended here.

As was the case after the first sin (3:9), God came to the sinner, not the sinner to God. The Lord appropriately asked Cain to justify his anger; surely he had discerned no inequity or injustice on God's part. The Lord's approach to Cain is similar to His approach to Jonah when the prophet was angry (Jonah 4:4). What a marvelous exhibition of divine patience and grace! How far this is from the medieval representations of God as a tyrant ruler who would crush the sinner without mercy. With intimate tenderness and concern the Lord encouraged Cain to assess himself. God promised that if Cain should do well, he would be "accepted" (*se'ēt*). *Se'ēt* comes from the root *nāsā'*, the primary meaning of which is "lifting, lifting up." Cain's countenance would be lifted because he would be restored to favor. However, if Cain should resist the grace of God, then "sin [*haṭṭā't*] lieth at the door." Two basic interpretations have been offered for this clause. First, *haṭṭā't* should be translated here "sin offering," as it is in some other passages (e.g. Exod. 30:10; Lev. 4:32; Num. 7:16, 22).[6] Thus,

Dispute Between the Shepherd-God and the Farmer-God," in Pritchard, *ANET*, pp. 41, 42.
6. *The Scofield Reference Bible* (New York: Oxford University Press, 1909), p. 11.

God is exhorting Cain to offer a sin offering—presumably a bloody sacrifice. However, the concept of a sin offering may be premature at this point. The second and more likely interpretation is that "sin" refers to the effects of sin. Thus, God is warning Cain that if he sins, tragedy will follow. God might be suggesting the word picture of a wild beast couching at the door, waiting to attack the one who opens it. This would explain the masculine gender of *robēṣ* ("lieth"), which normally would be feminine to agree with *haṭṭā't*, its subject.

C. The First Murder (4:8—15)

In a rage of jealousy, rebellion, and unbelief, Cain devised a way to satisfy his anger. There is no indication that he responded to the gracious words of God; Cain saved his words for Abel. What he said is not recorded in the Hebrew text, but the Samaritan Pentateuch and the Septuagint attribute to him the words,"Let us go out into the field." When the opportunity presented itself, Cain slew his brother (v. 8), "because his own works were evil, and his brother's righteous" (I John 3:12). The Lord again approached and queried Cain: "Where is Abel thy brother?" (v. 9). Cain's response was twofold: an arrogant lie ("I know not") and a sarcastic question ("Am I my brother's keeper?"). With infinite patience the Lord continued: "What have you done?" (v. 10). Cain, like most murderers, thought he had successfully concealed his deed. He had overlooked, however, the voice of his brother's blood, which cried out for judgment and justice. God had created life and could not tolerate the indiscriminate, unjustified slaughter of a man. Premeditated murder in the history of the world's first family was no accident; sin distorts reason unbelievably and produces irrational acts. While the blood of Abel cried out for judgment, the blood of Jesus Christ "speaketh better than that of Abel" (Heb. 12:24), for it cries out to God for the sinner's redemption.

God responded to Cain's highhanded rebellion decisively (4:12). Up to then God's curse had fallen only upon the serpent (3:14) and the ground (3:17), but God cursed Cain. Because Cain had polluted the ground with his brother's blood, all future attempts at cultivation would be futile. He would be a fugitive, or vagabond, moving from one place to another. Cain confessed that the punishment was greater than he could bear (v. 13). He feared that "every one that findeth me shall slay me" (v. 14), a reference to

100

other people which has produced some interesting speculation. One need not postulate a pre-Adamic race; the people whom Cain feared could have been brothers or sisters, or perhaps his own children (v. 17). Considering pre-Noahic longevity, the human race could have multiplied quite rapidly.[7] The Lord guaranteed Cain protection: He "set a mark [*'ōt*] upon [*le*] Cain" (v. 15). It has been suggested on the basis of the Septuagint that the "mark" was ~~mark~~ paralysis; the targum of Jonathan ben-Uzziel suggested that it was the great and precious word *Yahweh*;[8] and Rabbi Joseph suggested that it was a long horn growing out of Cain's forehead.[9] The difficulty is that *'ōt* normally means "sign, pledge, or token"; of the seventy-five other times it occurs in the Old Testament, it is always translated "sign." An additional difficulty is that *le* does not mean "in" or "on" but "for." The best interpretation, therefore, is that God produced a sign for Cain. This could have been a verification of God's promise similar to those given Gideon (Judg. 6:36–40) and Elisha (II Kings 2:9–12). Why did God protect the first murderer and permit him to live? For that matter, why did God permit David to live after he committed adultery and murder (cf. II Sam. 12:13)? We can only answer that God is sovereign, His grace boundless.

II. The Family of Cain (4:16–26)

A. Settlement Patterns (4:16, 17)

Cain, who had said "From thy face shall I be hid" (v. 14), left the presence of the Lord. Cursed as a vagabond and fugitive, he dwelt in the land east of Eden called *Nôd*, a word which means "wandering, flight, or exile," and which probably refers to an area rather than a specific site.

Many have charged that the Bible contradicts itself, saying on the one hand that only Cain and his parents existed, and on the other that Cain found a woman to marry (v. 17). But this charge is groundless. According to Genesis 5:4 Cain had many sisters, and in all probability he married one of them. Such a relationship would

---

7. See speculation on this in Adam Clarke, *The Holy Bible Containing the Old and New Testament with Commentary and Critical Notes*, 6 vols. (New York: Eaton and Maines, n.d.), 1:59.
8. Samuel Shuckford, *The Sacred and Profane History of the World*, p. 4; cf. Louis Ginzberg, *The Legends of the Jews*, 1:111, 112.
9. Elwood Worcester, *The Book of Genesis in the Light of Modern Knowledge*, p. 276.

eventually be forbidden by Mosaic law, but at this stage of human development, it could not be considered wrong or unnatural.

Cain named his first son, as well as the city (*'îr*) he built, *Enoch.* The name has several connotations, including "dedication," "consecration," and "initiation," and Cain's choice of that name seems to represent a promise to himself of a new beginning in life. *'Îr* should not be pressed to mean anything more than a permanent settlement, or perhaps a fortified village. The excavations at Jericho indicate that urban societies appeared in the Neolithic period and constructed rather sophisticated defensive systems. Enoch is the first city mentioned in the Bible, but it may not be the world's first city; other, similar habitations may already have been constructed. It is significant, however, that Cain built such a site. Perhaps he was attempting to neutralize God's curse of banishment (vv. 11-15).

B. Occupations and Crafts (4:18–24)

Some of the names which appear in the list of Cain's descendants (4:18–22) also appear in the list of Seth's descendants (5:6–32), indicating to some scholars that both lists ultimately were derived from a single source; the dissimilarities between these lists they attribute to a long period of intervening oral transmission.[10] However, the differences are too significant to warrant this conclusion. These are two distinct genealogical lists, not one corrupted list.[11]

Early in the history of the human race, the original marriage pattern of God was violated: Lamech, the son of Methusael, took two wives. Both Adah and Zillah are named in the biblical text.

Rapid technological development may be attributed to the longevity of the pre-Noahic patriarchs. Jubal was considered "the father of all such as handle the harp and organ" (v. 21). The Hebrew word translated "harp" is more accurately translated "lyre," a musical instrument depicted in Egyptian, Palestinian, and Mesopotamian paintings, and consisting of a sounding board across which strings are stretched. The word translated "organ" probably refers to an early form of the flute, an instrument still used by

10. Speiser, *Genesis*, pp. 35, 36.
11. See discussions in C. F. Keil and Franz Delitzsch, *Biblical Commentary on the Old Testament*, 25 vols. (Edinburgh: T. and T. Clark, 1864–1901), 1:117, 119; and Nichol, ed., *Bible Commentary*, 1:242.

A relief of a musician, discovered in Khafajah, Mesopotamia, and dated ca. 2000 B.C.

shepherds throughout the Near East. Tubal-cain was a "forger [from *lāṭaš*] of every cutting instrument of brass [bronze] and iron" (v. 22 ASV). Verse 22 gives no indication of how widespread this technology was. Furthermore, this craft probably ceased in the great flood when the whole line of Cain was destroyed. Archaeological excavations in Anatolia, as well as other areas, have indicated a rather early use of iron; in Palestine the production of common implements did not become widespread until about the middle of the thirteenth century B.C. The earliest iron objects may have been meteoric. Objects would have been formed from this type of iron by hammering rather than smelting, and *lāṭaš* means "to hammer" or "to sharpen." What was the state of technology after the flood? The widespread Neolithic cultures which appeared approximately 10,000–7000 B.C. in the Near East

103

may reflect postflood technology. This does not imply an inferior intellect; it merely indicates that man's tools and bowls were limited to stoneware, a durable and easily accessible resource.

The first poetry in Genesis is the so-called "Song of Lamech." In it he told his two wives that he had slain a man who apparently had attempted to wound him (v. 23), and that, should he be threatened again, he would avenge himself again (v. 24).[12]

The introduction to cultural achievement in these verses is interesting and instructive. Kidner observes that the phrase in verse 21, " 'he was the father of all such' acknowledges the debt and prepares us to accept for ourselves a similar indebtedness to secular enterprise; for the Bible nowhere teaches that the godly should have all the gifts. At the same time we are saved from over-valuing these skills: the family of Lamech could handle its environment but not itself. The attempt to improve on God's marriage ordinance (19; cf. 2:24) set a disastrous precedent, on which the rest of Genesis is comment enough; and the immediate conversion of metal-working to weapon-making is equally ominous."[13]

The dismal story of the moral failures of the line of Cain is followed by the good news of the birth of Seth (v. 25). The name šēṯ can mean "the appointed one," "the compensation," or "the substitute." Apparently Eve thought of Seth as taking the place of Abel, who had been slain. The birth of Seth was crucial since Cain obviously could not fulfill the promise of the seed (Gen. 3:15), and the time came when Seth and his descendants began "to call upon the name of the Lord." This phrase frequently designates public worship (cf. Ps. 79:6; 116:17; Jer. 10:25; Zeph. 3:9); evidently, corporate and formal worship now supplemented individual, spontaneous worship.

III. The Descendants of Seth (5:1–32)

Reading Genesis 5, like walking through a cemetery, produces a solemnity of soul. The purpose of this chapter, and the source of its historical importance, is its testimony to the development of the human race from Adam to Noah. It does not list every antediluvian patriarch, but it does mention the key ones. Genesis 5

---

12. Note the RSV rendering, "I have slain a man for wounding me."
13. *Genesis*, pp. 77, 78.

also appears to be God's answer to Satan's blasphemous lie: "Ye shall not surely die. . . ." (3:4). Adam did not die physically the moment he ate the fruit—spiritual death, separation from God, was the immediate result—but according to 5:5, "he died." The same thing—"and he died"—is said of seven other patriarchs in this chapter. Death reigned, and God's word was fully vindicated.

The chapter begins with the formula, "This is the book of the generations of . . . " a formula which occurs frequently in Genesis. Moses also refers to the creation of man, and by calling both male and female, "Adam" (v. 2), emphasizes the unity of the race. Each reference to a patriarch follows a scheme, giving (1) his name, (2) his age at the birth of his first son, (3) the length of his remaining life (with a statement that he begat other children), and (4) his age at death. The only variations occur in the cases of Adam (v. 3), Enoch (vv. 22, 24), and Lamech (vv. 28, 29). The patriarchs' ages at the birth of their first sons present a textual problem. According to the Hebrew text, these ages (which span the period from creation to the birth of Noah's sons) total 1,556 years. But according to the Samaritan Pentateuch the total is only 1,207, and according to the Septuagint it is all of 2,142 years. The Septuagint adds 100 years to the ages of the first five patriarchs and of Enoch, and varies the ages of two other patriarchs less significantly. It appears, however, that the numbers in the Hebrew text of Genesis 5 are more reliable than variants appearing elsewhere.

The longevity of the ten patriarchs—seven of them lived more than 900 years—has convinced many scholars that the entire narrative is mythical. They see in it reflections of epic traditions whose source may be Sumer. The Sumerian antediluvian king list includes eight kings who reigned, according to that list, for a total of 241,200 years. That document probably dates from the third dynasty of Ur or earlier.[14] However, the many attempts to demonstrate philological parallels between this Sumerian list and Genesis 5[15] are strained and in many cases artificial.

Some have noted that the longevity of the antediluvian patriarchs listed in Genesis 5 is only apparent. They argue either that each name in the list is a dynasty rather than an individual, or that "year" means "month" (or some other period shorter than a year). But there is no indication in the text that dynasties rather

14. Jack Finegan, *Light from the Ancient Past*, p. 29.
15. George A. Barton, *Archaeology and the Bible*, pp. 317ff.

than individuals are in view. And there is no other example in the Old Testament of "year" meaning a period shorter than a year. Further, if "year" means "month" in Genesis 5, then Seth fathered Enos when Seth was just 105 months—or about nine years—old! And Enos, Cainan, Mahalaleel, and Enoch would have been fathers at even younger ages.

There seems to be no reason to regard the names and ages of the individuals in this chapter as other than fully historical. How do we explain the longevity of these men? Advocates of the canopy theory suggest that this antediluvian canopy arrested life-shortening solar rays,[16] but Leupold answers the question less speculatively: "He . . . who is duly impressed by the excellence of man's original state, will have no difficulty in accepting the common explanation that even under the curse of sin man's constitution displayed such vitality that it did not at first submit to the ravages of time until after many centuries had passed."[17]

A. The Translation of Enoch (5:21–24)

Not all the "tombstones" in Genesis 5 are engraved with epitaphs to the dead. One tells of a man who walked with God and who was translated so "that he should not see death" (Heb. 11:5). Only Enoch and Noah are said to have "walked with God," an expression which denotes intimate fellowship with the Lord. According to verses 14 and 15 of Jude, Enoch's walk was not an easy one. Instead of allowing him to die, God "took" Enoch. The verb, which is also used to describe Elijah's experience (II Kings 2:3, 5, 9, 10), was rendered "translated" in the Septuagint, and the writer of Hebrews followed suit (11:5). Because of this unusual experience, Enoch is remembered not only in the New Testament but also in Jewish tradition (cf. Ecclus. 44:16). The story of Enoch's life and his supernatural "translation" illustrates God's grace.

B. The Family of Noah (5:28–32)

The days preceding Noah's birth must have been extremely difficult ones. Lamech named his son *Noah*, a word which means

16. John C. Whitcomb and Henry M. Morris, *The Genesis Flood*, pp. 404, 405.
17. *Exposition of Genesis*, 1:234. These numbers are further discussed in John J. Davis, *Biblical Numerology*, pp. 56–58.

"to rest" or "to lie down," hoping that Noah "shall comfort us concerning our work and toil of our hands, because of the ground which the Lord hath cursed" (v. 29). Noah was about 500 years old when he fathered his three sons, "Shem, Ham, and Japheth" (v. 32). They are not named in chronological order; Ham was the youngest of the three (9:24) and Japheth the oldest (10:21). Shem is mentioned first because it was through him that God's Messiah would come. This narrative, then, illustrates God's faithfulness to His promise of a chosen seed.

Stop

8

The Degeneration of Man

Genesis 6:1–13

The moral degeneration of man apparent in Genesis 4, illustrated by Cain and Lamech, culminates in Genesis 6:1–13. As the fallen human race multiplied and expanded, so did evil. The imaginations of the human heart became so wicked that God had to judge them, and He did so in the great flood. The nature and extent of God's judicial acts always reflect the seriousness of the sin which is being judged, and with the exception of Noah's family the flood destroyed all of human life. God clearly considered the sins of the antediluvian race so wicked that nothing short of near total destruction would satisfy His holy demands.

I. The Provocation

When divine judgment falls in Scripture, the reasons or causes are always carefully delineated. Chapter 6 furnishes two fundamental reasons for the flood: the sins of the "sons of God," and the sins of mankind in general.

A. The Sons of God (vv. 1–4)

Exactly how much time elapsed between the creation and the events of Genesis 6 is unknown. What is clear, however, is that men were beginning to multiply at a rapid rate. Men lived to be over five hundred years old, and their procreative powers persisted over an extended number of years, from as young as sixty-five years of age (Mahalaleel and Enoch) to as old as five hundred (Noah). Their families must have been large. Population, it must be remembered, increases geometrically rather than arithmetically.[1] The human race, expanding as rapidly as it was, must have distributed itself over a wide geographical area.[2]

The text further indicates that the "sons of God" saw that the "daughters of men . . . were fair" and took them in marriage. This statement of fact is simple enough, even in the Hebrew, but interpreting it is another matter altogether.

1. Their identity. The lively controversy among evangelical interpreters over the identification of the sons of God has resulted in no consensus, probably because decisive evidence does not exist. Skinner sees in this passage an allusion to the mythological motif of marriage between gods and human beings, suggesting that in the earliest recension of this passage, the "sons of God" were simply called "gods" ($'^el\bar{o}h\hat{i}m$).[3] But the three identifications most prevalent among evangelicals are: angels, the line of Seth, and kings or nobles.

A wide variety of commentators regard the sons of God as fallen, wicked, angelic beings who cohabited with the fair "daughters of men" ($b^en\hat{o}\underline{t}$ $h\bar{a}'\bar{a}\underline{d}\bar{a}m$) in a most unnatural way. This interpretation is an ancient one. It is found in the Book of Enoch, a pseudepigraph dating from the last two centuries B.C.: "And it came to pass when the children of men had multiplied that in those days were born unto them beautiful and comely daughters. And the angels, the children of heaven, saw and lusted after them, and said to one another: 'Come, let us choose us wives from among the children of men and beget us children' " (6:1, 2).[4] This was also the view of Philo, Josephus, most of the rabbinical writers, and the oldest church fathers—Justin, Tertullian, Cyprian, Ambrose, and Lactantius.[5]

Arguments for this view follow. First, the expression "sons of

---

1. Leroy Birney, "An Exegetical Study of Genesis 6:1–4," p. 43.
2. John C. Whitcomb and Henry M. Morris, *The Genesis Flood*, pp. 23–33.
3. *A Critical and Exegetical Commentary on Genesis*, p. 142.
4. In R. H. Charles, ed., *The Apocrypha and Pseudepigrapha of the Old Testament*, 2:191.
5. Merrill F. Unger, *Biblical Demonology*, p. 46; Stewart Custer, "The Sons of God and the Daughters of Men," pp. 109–11.

God" is used exclusively in the Old Testament of angels (cf. Job 1:6; 2:1; 38:7). A similar phrase $b^e n\hat{e}$ ʾ $\bar{e}l\hat{\imath}m$ ("sons of God" or "sons of the Mighty One"), which appears in Psalms 29:1 and 89:7, may refer to angels as well. Another similar phrase in Daniel 3:25 also may refer to angels, although this has been disputed. Second, two New Testament passages appear to identify angels with the incident described in Genesis 6:1-4. In II Peter the sin of the angels is mentioned just before God's judgment upon the ancient world: ". . . God spared not the angels that sinned, but cast them down to hell, and delivered them into chains of darkness, to be reserved unto judgment; and spared not the old world, but saved Noah the eighth person, a preacher of righteousness, bringing in the flood upon the world of the ungodly. . . ." (2:4, 5). In Jude the sin of the angels is identified with the sexual sins of Sodom and Gomorrah: "And angels that kept not their own principality, but left their proper habitation [*oiketerion*] he hath kept in everlasting bonds under darkness unto the judgment of the great day. Even as Sodom and Gomorrah, and the cities about them, having in like manner with these [*toutois*] given themselves over to fornication and gone after strange flesh, are set forth as an example, suffering the punishment of eternal fire" (vv. 6, 7 ASV). Delitzsch argues that *toutois* must refer to angels.[6] The only other time that *oiketerion* appears in the New Testament, it refers to the spiritual body for which believers are longing (II Cor. 5:2). Stewart Custer concludes that the angels in Jude 6 "left their normal spiritual bodies to assume an abnormal physical form to cohabit with human women. Some expositors will object that this cannot be done. Such an objection begs the question because there is no proof that angels cannot assume another form."[7]

While this view has been widely circulated and defended, and while it is reinforced by the technical use of the expression "sons of God" in Job, it does present some difficult problems. Keil points out two: (1) there is no other reference to angels in the context; and (2) the combination of the verb *lāqah* ("take") and the ʾ $i\check{s}\check{s}\hat{a}$ ("wife") is "a standing expression throughout the whole of the Old Testament for the marriage relation established by God at the creation," and Christ specifically stated that angels cannot marry (Matt. 22:30; Mark 12:25; cf. Luke 20:34, 35).[8] In

---

6. *A New Commentary on Genesis*, 1:225.
7. "The Sons of God," p. 108.
8. C. F. Keil and Franz Delitzsch, *Biblical Commentary on the Old Testa-*

response to Keil's second point, Richard Wolff admits that "marriage is against the nature of angels in heaven" but insists that this "does not exclude of itself the unnatural action of fallen angels." He adds that "the expression 'they took them wives' does not always refer to God-ordained marriage, as is demonstrated by Leviticus 20:14, 17 and Judges 21:22."[9] However, it is difficult to believe that after angels rebelled against God and were cast from heaven, they acquired the capacity for human reproduction. After man fell, he experienced no essential biological transformation; the only change was represented by the introduction of pain and difficulty. An equally formidable problem is that judgment in Genesis 6:6ff. fell upon men alone. Since the sons of God were the real initiators of the evil that was judged, surely they were human rather than angelic.[10] Another problem, one cited by Leupold, is that angels are not mentioned in the first five chapters in Genesis; to introduce them in such a narrative and in connection with such a strange, unprecedented union is unnatural and foreign to the text.[11] As for the passage in Jude, Keil argues that it is not referring to Genesis 6:1–4: Jude 6, 7 are concerned with fornication, Genesis 6:2 with marriage.[12] Wolff replies: "That such a union deserved the name 'fornication' can hardly be doubted and that the relation was permanent is neither affirmed nor denied in the Scriptures."[13] It should be added that if angels were capable of committing fornication with human beings, they were capable of marrying them. Keil points out, however, that Jude 7 may not even say that *angels* had "given themselves over to fornication"; *toutois* can refer to Sodom and Gomorrah or to the inhabitants in them.[14]

The view that the "sons of God" were the godly line of Seth also has been widely circulated. According to this interpretation the sin of these men was not polygamy but marriage to unbelievers, resulting in an unholy alliance. Arguments advanced for it are: (1) the concept of a godly line has already been

---

ment, 25 vols. (Edinburgh: T. and T. Clark, 1864–1901), 1:130, 131. Delitzsch's attempt to relieve this problem by stating that angels were working through demoniacs (*Commentary on Genesis*, 1:226) is not adequate. This idea has no parallel elsewhere in Scripture.
9. *A Commentary on the Epistle of Jude*, p. 68.
10. H. C. Leupold, *Exposition of Genesis*, 1:253, 254; John Murray, *Principles of Conduct*, p. 245.
11. *Exposition of Genesis*, 1:251, 252.
12. Keil and Delitzsch, *Biblical Commentary*, 1:132.
13. *The Epistle of Jude*, p. 68.
14. Keil and Delitzsch, *Biblical Commentary*, 1:132, 133.

established (cf. 4:26); (2) the concept of sonship, based on God's election, is common in the Old Testament (cf. Exod. 4:22; Deut. 14:1; 32:5, 6, 18, 19; Hos. 1:10; Isa. 1:2; 11:1; 43:6; 45:11; Jer. 31:20; Ps. 73:15);[15] and (3) warnings against marriage between believers and unbelievers are a theme of the entire Pentateuch.[16] Two primary objections have been raised against this view. First, it does not come to grips with the technical use of the expression "sons of God" in the Old Testament. The concept of sonship based on God's election is indeed common in the Old Testament, but in none of the passages cited above does the phrase "sons of God" appear. Second, while the phrase "sons of God" can refer to a select group, the phrase "daughters of men" cannot. "What reasons have we to suppose that for all this length of time there had been maintained a sharp distinction between the two lines of descent, or that they had come to be called respectively, the 'sons of God' and the 'daughters of men'?"[17]

The third view, that the "sons of God" were dynastic rulers in the Cainite line, is suggested by both the Aramaic Targums and the Greek translation of Symmachus. Arguments for it are: (1) magistrates or administrators of justice are called *'elōhîm* in Exodus 21:6; 22:8, 9, 28, and in Psalm 82:1, 6; (2) a thematic parallelism exists between biblical motifs and the Sumero-Babylonian antediluvian traditions;[18] and (3) kings are often referred to in ancient Near Eastern literature as sons of deities, so this idiom might have been similarly understood in Genesis 6.[19] Objections to this view are: (1) there is no evidence that a monarchical system of rulers had been established in the line of Cain; (2) it is difficult to understand why something as familiar as kingship should be expressed so indirectly;[20] (3) there is no evidence that the expression "sons of God" was borrowed from contemporary literature; and (4) no writer of Scripture ever considered kings to be deities or sons of deities.

---

15. This point is discussed fully in Leupold, *Exposition of Genesis*, 1:250, 251.
16. Cf. Gen. 24:3, 4; 27:46; 28:1–3. Note the distress caused by Esau's marrying Canaanite women (26:34, 35; 29:6–8) and the difficulties between Dinah and the Shechemites (34:1ff.). This is discussed further in William H. Green, *The Unity of the Book of Genesis*, pp. 55, 56.
17. Albertus Pieters, *Notes on Genesis*, p. 115. Cf. Meredith G. Kline, "Divine Kingship and Genesis 6:1–4," *The Westminster Theological Journal* 24 (1962): 189, 190.
18. Kline, "Divine Kingship," p. 196.
19. Ivan Engell, *Studies in Divine Kingship in the Ancient Near East*, pp. 4, 6, 12, 14, 58, 80.
20. Derek Kidner, *Genesis*, p. 84 (n. 5).

It should be obvious that certain identification of the sons of God is impossible at this point. It seems to this author that the third view is the least likely, and that either of the first two is credible, given the evidence currently available. Albertus Pieters concludes a discussion of the matter with the observation: "What does he [Moses] mean? I do not know, and I do not believe anyone knows. So far as I am concerned, the passage is unintelligible."[21] This statement is perhaps too despairing, but the fact is, the interpretation of Genesis 6:1-4 has not been settled.

2. Their sin. If the sons of God were angels, they sinned by "taking" women. If they were men, they did not sin in taking wives, but in taking wives "of all which they chose" (*mikkōl* *$^{\textit{a}}$šer* *bāḥārû*). The preposition *min* (the prefix in *mikkōl*) can be interpreted in two ways, the generalizing and partitive or the explicative. According to the former, the sons of God took "whichever" women they chose,[22] without regard to their spiritual status (if the sons of God were Sethites) or to their royal status (if the sons of God were kings). According to the latter, the sons of God took "even all" the women they chose; that is, they committed polygamy.[23] This interpretation finds some support in the fact that Lamech had already practiced polygamy (4:19). Some propose that polygamy helps explain the rapid multiplication of man described in 6:1, but antediluvian man's longevity and reproductive capacity are a sufficient explanation in themselves.

There is also considerable difference of opinion over whether the "giants" (*n^{e}p̄ilîm*) who "were . . . in the earth in those days" (v. 4) existed before the marriages took place (v. 2) or were the offspring of those marriages. Meredith G. Kline and Delitzsch favor the latter, translating "were," "arose," as that verb can be translated in Genesis 7:6, 10 and 15:17.[24] Most interpreters, however, incline toward the former, and this seems to better suit the context.[25] *N^{e}p̄ilîm* occurs only here and in Numbers 13:33, where it is used of the Anakim, men who were of great stature. The translation "giants" in the Authorized Version was influenced

---

21. *Notes on Genesis*, p. 116.
22. Delitzsch, *Commentary on Genesis*, 1:225.
23. Kline, "Divine Kingship," p. 196 (n. 28). In support of his view he cites Gen. 7:22; 9:10; Lev. 11:32.
24. "Divine Kingship," p. 190; *Commentary on Genesis*, 1:232.
25. Francis D. Nichol, ed., *The Seventh-Day Adventist Commentary*, 1:251; Leupold, *Exposition of Genesis*, 1:257-60; Keil and Delitzsch, *Biblical Commentary*, 1:137, 138.

by the Septuagint's *gigantes*. Various meanings have been suggested for the root *npl*. One is "to be aborted," that is, to be unnaturally begotten by angels.[26] The one adopted by most is "to fall." Thus, it refers to angels who have fallen from heaven, or to tyrants or invaders who fall upon others. The one that best fits Numbers 13:33, however, is the idea of strength and prowess.

The children born to the sons of God and daughters of men, according to the last part of verse 4, became "mighty men" and "men of renown." The former expression is commonly used for military men; the latter is broader, extending to those well known for wealth or political power. In any event, the descendants of the sons of God and daughters of men became widely known for their prowess and strength, most likely as military men.

B. Men in General (vv. 5, 11–13)

God's assessment of the antediluvian race is one of the most dismal on record. According to verse 5 the wickedness of man was "great in the earth." But even more disheartening than that, "every imagination [*yēṣer*] of the thoughts of his heart was only evil continually." This is in striking contrast to the language of Genesis 1:31: " . . . God saw every thing that He had made, and . . . it was very good." When He looked upon the human race years after Adam and Eve had fallen, He saw its total depravity and corruption. *Yēṣer* means "device" or "formation" and is derived from the verb *yāṣar*, which in Genesis 2:7 describes God's formation of man's body. Evil imagination, therefore, is the product of a wicked heart, a corrupt nature.

The unbelievable corruption of the antediluvian world is described further in verses 11–13. The might of the men mentioned in verse 4 became famous through widespread violence and death; twice it is said that the earth was filled with violence (vv. 11, 13). God could tolerate the highhanded arrogance of a thoroughly wicked race no longer. Soon judgment would fall, and it would be most severe.

II. The Divine Response

A. An End to Mercy (v. 3)

God warned the contemporaries of Noah that "My spirit [*rûaḥ*] shall not always strive [*yāḏôn*]" with them and their unbridled

115

---

26. Delitzsch, *Commentary on Genesis*, 1:137.

wickedness. The etymological significance of *yāḏôn* has been widely debated. Most trace it to the verb *dîn*, "to judge" or "to execute judgment."[27] But many trace it to the root *dnn*, "to abide": "My spirit shall not abide in man forever."[28] This translation is supported by many of the ancient versions. The first derivation sees *rûaḥ* as God's spirit, a convicting agent and restraining force among men. Because of the unbridled wickedness and rebellion of man, God would cease to mercifully convict and restrain, and would bring judgment. The second derivation sees *rûaḥ* as the breath infused in the clay, the life principle of man. God warns He is about to remove it, and this points to impending death for a universally corrupt race. Either view, of course, is grammatically possible. The traditional one of the Spirit judging or striving with men fits the context well and is still fully acceptable.

Two interpretations have been offered for the clause, "Yet his days shall be an hundred and twenty years." One is that this is how long mankind would have after God's warning and before His judgment (cf. I Peter 3:20). The other is that this would become the approximate life span for men. While the latter has been accepted by some, it is improbable, especially because Noah's sons and many of the postdiluvian patriarchs lived longer.

B. Repentance and Grief (v. 6)

When the Lord viewed the wickedness of men, He "repented" (*nāḥam*) that He had made man and was grieved in His heart. The repentance of the Lord has long been a problem to commentators. Obviously it does not mean that God decided He had made a mistake or miscalculation, or that He was unsure of His own desires. It denotes instead a change in God's actions resulting from a significant change in the objects of His actions. It is "an anthropopathic description of the pain which is caused to the love of God by the destruction of His creatures."[29] *Nāḥam* means "to be sorry," "to be moved to pity," "to have compassion." It is used thirty times with God as its subject, and in each case it speaks of a change of mind or intention that accords with His righteous purposes and results in action commensurate with that purpose.[30]

27. Brown, Driver, and Briggs, *Lexicon of the Old Testament*, p. 192. See also Keil and Delitzsch, *Biblical Commentary*, 1:134; and Leupold, *Exposition of Genesis*, 1:254–56.
28. Kidner, *Genesis*, p. 84 (n. 7).
29. Keil and Delitzsch, *Biblical Commentary*, 2:225.
30. Roy L. Honeycutt, Jr., *Exodus*, p. 452.

C. Judgment and Destruction (vv. 6–13)

God's reaction to the violence that characterized society was one of grief and anger. The Lord promised to "destroy man" from the face of the earth (v. 7). The verb translated "destroy" is *māḥâ*, meaning "to wipe, wipe out, blot out,"[31] an excellent description of the impending destruction. Since the earth was filled with violence and "all flesh had corrupted his way," all flesh would have to die. Unless one is inclined to limit human occupation to the Mesopotamian valley, this clearly points to a flood of universal proportions.

III. The Man Noah (vv. 8–10)

Even though the antediluvian world was completely overcome with violence and wickedness, Noah refused to be part of that trend and found "grace in the eyes of the Lord" (v. 8). This is the first occurrence in Scripture of the word *grace;* in the midst of colossal human failure, which it seemed would result in total annihilation of the race, comes the expression of unmerited divine favor. Verse 8 concludes the story of the "generations of Adam" which began in 5:1. Verse 9 introduces the "generations of Noah."

According to verse 9 Noah was "a just [*ṣadîq*] man and perfect [*tāmîm*]" among his contemporaries. *Ṣadîq* usually means "righteous" and is so translated in the Revised, American Standard, and Revised Standard versions. *Tāmîm* signifies perfection not in the sense of flawlessness but in the sense of completeness or maturity. These two adjectives describe the qualities of Noah both manward and Godward. He, like his pious ancestor Enoch (5:22, 24), "walked with God." He separated himself from the wickedness of his contemporaries and followed the Lord. Apparently no other man achieved this stature during the years between Enoch's translation and Noah's birth; they were spiritual giants in a world that was thoroughly corrupt.

---

31. Brown, Driver, and Briggs, *Lexicon of the Old Testament*, p. 562.

9

The Great Flood

Genesis 6:14–9:29

The story of the great flood and Noah's ark is a captivating one, but it must never divert our attention completely from the reasons for the flood discussed in the previous chapter. Nor should it be abused, as many mockers have done who make it the brunt of jokes, caustic remarks, and outright denials. It is a warning to all who would lift the hand in rebellion against an infinitely holy God. It presents Noah as a champion of faith, a worthy candidate for the heroes of Hebrews 11; even though experience and observation made a flood very unlikely, Noah believed God when He promised a flood.

This chapter will cover, in addition to the biblical account of the flood, the account in the Babylonian *Gilgameš Epic* and the search for Noah's ark on Mt. Ararat.

I. The Biblical Account

The biblical account of the great deluge is usually regarded as having two sources, J and P. "The redactor has wonderfully worked both texts together in such a way that both flood stories have remained almost intact."[1] This contention is valid, however, only if the documentary hypothesis is. Further, the isolation of the two sources appears rather arbitrary and artificial at many points. The supposed contradictions in the flood account are easily resolved and do not furnish sufficient grounds for source analysis.[2]

A. Preparations for the Flood (6:14–7:16)

1. Constructing the ark (6:14–16). In order to save Noah and his family from the great judgment that was coming, the Lord commanded the patriarch to build an "ark" (*tēbâ*). *Tēbâ* appears only here and in Exodus 2:3, 5, where it is the small basket in which Moses was placed. It is probably a loan-word from the Egyptian *ṭeb(t)*, which designated "large sea-worthy ships used for the transport of obelisks, and . . . processional barks for carrying

---

1. Gerhard von Rad, *Genesis*, p. 115. See also E. A. Speiser, *Genesis*, pp. 44–56.
2. See discussions in Kenneth A. Kitchen, *Ancient Orient and Old Testament*, pp. 120, 121; and Derek Kidner, *Genesis*, pp. 97–100.

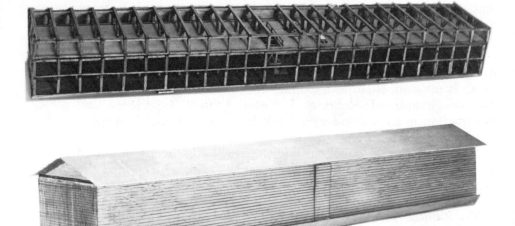

A scale model of the ark

sacred statues on the Nile."[3] The ark was to be made of "gopher wood," a type which has not been identified conclusively but which may be cedar or cypress. The ark was more of a barge than a ship. Using the small cubit of 17.5 inches, it was 437.5 feet long, 72.92 feet wide, and 43.75 feet high. According to verse 16 it had three decks, giving it approximately 95,700 square feet, 1,396,000 cubic feet, and gross tonnage of 13,960.[4] The biblical text does not give the precise thickness and weight of the beams, but the structure was solid enough to withstand the battering of both the storm and the turbulent flood waters. A vessel constructed in this manner uses space efficiently and becomes more stable as its cargo increases; when the ark was filled, the possibility of its capsizing was minimal.[5] To insure adequate light and air circulation, the ark was to have a "window" (*ṣōhar*): ". . . in a cubit shalt thou finish it above. . . ." This "can only signify that a hole or opening for light and air was to be so constructed as to reach within a cubit of the edge of the roof. A window only a cubit square could not possibly be intended; for *shr* is not synonymous with *hallon* (8:6), but signifies, generally, a space for light, or by which light could be admitted into the ark, and in which the window, or lattice for opening and shutting, could be fixed; though we can form no distinct idea of which the arrangement was."[6] The technology required for constructing such a barge may startle us at first, but it should not, especially in the light of the achievements of Cain's descendants (Gen. 4:16-24). The ark was well designed to protect Noah and his family, but one must remember that their survival was the result of the direct intervention of God, who promised before the flood that Noah would survive (6:18) and who during the flood "remembered Noah" (8:1).

2. Explaining the ark (6:17, 18). Before commanding Noah to build an ark, God promised to destroy the earth (v. 13) but said nothing about how He would destroy it. Now he explains that He

---

3. Francis D. Nichol, ed., *The Seventh-Day Adventist Commentary*, 1:253. See also James R. Battenfield, "Atra-Hasis: A Survey," *Grace Journal* 12 (1971): 21 (n. 88).
4. John C. Whitcomb and Henry M. Morris, *The Genesis Flood*, p. 10.
5. Further details on the size and construction of the ark are in Whitcomb and Morris, *The Genesis Flood*, pp. 11–14, 65–70; and John W. Montgomery, *The Quest for Noah's Ark*, pp. 41–54.
6. C. F. Keil and Franz Delitzsch, *Biblical Commentary on the Old Testament*, 25 vols. (Edinburgh: T. and T. Clark, 1864–1901), 1:143. Cf. Brown, Driver, and Briggs, *Lexicon of the Old Testament*, p. 844.

will bring a "flood [*hammabûl*] of waters upon the earth." *Hammabûl* refers in the Old Testament to the flood of Noah alone, the only possible exception being Psalm 29:10. The etymology of the word has not been clearly established, but some relate it to the Assyrian *nabālu*, meaning "to destroy."[7] "Flood of waters," then, might be literally translated "destruction of waters." Verse 17 emphasizes that everything on the earth would die in the impending flood. This implies a flood of universal scope—unless animal and human life was restricted to the Mesopotamian valley, a supposition that is out of harmony with the beauty and luxuriance of the earth before the fall. It is of interest that when God first promised this sweeping judgment, He also promised to Noah and his family a covenant (v. 18).

3. **Filling the ark (6:19–22; 7:1–9, 13–16).** In order to preserve the basic "kinds" of animal life, two—one male and one female—of every sort were to be taken into the ark (6:19, 20). This command, which is further spelled out in 7:2, has been criticized as a physical impossibility: the ark could never have held them all, it is alleged. One writer argues: "... of the clean animals and of the birds there were seven pairs, of the unclean one pair. There are known at present about 15,000 species of birds. This means that there were 210,000 birds in the ark."[8] However, this seems to misrepresent the Hebrew text. The Hebrew of 7:2 states that Noah was to take, literally, "seven seven" of every clean beast, and this can mean "seven each"—three pairs and one supernumerary.[9] "For all practical purposes, one could say that, at the outside, there was need for no more than 35,000 individual vertebrate animals on the ark."[10] In all probability the reptiles chosen for the ark were small, because reptiles attain sexual maturity long before they are fully grown. Perhaps the "extra" clean animal was designated for sacrifice at the end of the flood. Evidently there was some knowledge of the distinction between clean and unclean animals, but the extent to which this distinction was understood cannot be determined.

The precise method by which Noah gathered the required

7. Kyle M. Yates, "Genesis," in Charles F. Pfeiffer and Everett F. Harrison, eds., *The Wycliffe Bible Commentary* (Chicago: Moody Press, 1962), p. 13.
8. Jan Lever, *Creation and Evolution*, p. 17.
9. H. C. Leupold, *Exposition of Genesis*, 1:290.
10. Whitcomb and Morris, *The Genesis Flood*, p. 69.

number of animals is not given in Scripture; it contains mere summary statements. Supernatural intervention must have been necessary, however. And the Lord who would provide a great fish to save Jonah and another fish to supply tax money for Peter was certainly capable of helping Noah gather the animals. Noah also was responsible for stocking sufficient food for his family and the animals (v. 21). Providing food for so many creatures seems impossible, but the animals' food requirements were probably greatly reduced by their general inactivity and by the hibernation periods of some.[11]

The Lord further explained to Noah that He would cause it to rain for forty days and forty nights (7:4). Such a downpour presupposes a vast store of water suspended above the earth. Many have felt that a vapor canopy surrounding the earth would have more than provided enough water.

One gets the impression that the loading of the ark was well organized. Where the ark was built the text gives no indication, but it must have been on a site that made the ark easy and natural to enter. How long it took to gather the animals and food supply is also unknown. What is certain is that Noah did everything God commanded him to do, giving us a most impressive example of obedience.

B. Extent of the Flood (7:10–12, 17–24)

The extent of this great deluge has been the subject of considerable discussion among scholars in recent years. There are of course only two alternatives: it was universal or it was not. Because the catastrophism implicit in a universal flood is out of harmony with many current theories of the earth's origin and early history, many modern scholars have abandoned a global flood for a local one. Some argue for a flood confined to the Mesopotamian valley that nevertheless killed all animal and human life outside the ark; they assume that man and animals never migrated beyond that valley, an assumption seemingly impossible to defend. The more popular approach is that animal and human life was more widespread than the flood and it was eliminated only where the flood occurred. Ramm argues this in *The Christian*

123

---

11. My daughter once suggested that most of the animals were probably sea sick and did not eat much anyway!

View of Science and Scripture: "... the entire record must be interpreted phenomenally. If the flood is local, though spoken of in universal terms, so the destruction of man is local though spoken of in universal terms. The record neither affirms nor denies that man existed beyond the Mesopotamian valley. Noah certainly was not a preacher of righteousness to the peoples of Africa, of India, of China or of America, places where there is evidence for the existence of man many thousands of years before the flood (10,000 to 15,000 years in America)."[12] The terms in the account which seem to have universal implications Ramm regards as restrictive or local in extent.[13] He contends that the universality of flood traditions does not prove a universal flood; these may only be local and unrelated floods.[14] Finally he asserts that "there is no known geological data to support those who defend a universal flood."[15] The principal concern of those advocating a local flood is to escape the geological implications of a universal flood. That the language *could* apply to a universal deluge they readily admit. They contend, however, that since the terms need not be universally applied, the account should be conformed to geological opinion.

It is true that terms like *all*, *every*, and *whole* can be used in a restricted sense, as is *all* in Luke 2:1. But these terms are also used in their universal sense, as is *all* in Matthew 28:18–20. Their use depends on their context, and the general and immediate context of the flood narrative must be studied carefully to determine their use in the narrative. By and large, the tradition of the Christian church is that the context requires a universal flood, and many Christian scholars have maintained this position knowing well the geological difficulties it raises. We must remember that divine creation and our Lord's miracles also raise scientific difficulties, neither being verifiable at this time by empirical evidence. The matter of geological evidence for a universal flood, however, may be a problem more of interpretation than availability. Whitcomb's and Morris' *The Genesis Flood*, while significant primarily for its development of the geological implications of a universal flood, contains a good synopsis of the biblical arguments for a universal flood.[16]

---

12. Pp. 239, 240.
13. Ibid., p. 241.
14. Ibid., p. 242.
15. Ibid., p. 243.
16. Pp. 116ff. and 1–35, respectively.

1. **The depth of the flood.** According to Genesis 7:19 the flood waters covered "all the high hills, that were under the whole heaven." All the mountains of the earth were covered, and by at least fifteen cubits of water—about twenty-three feet—the approximate draft of the ark.

2. **The duration of the flood.** The Scriptures clearly state that flood waters prevailed for five months, and that it was seven more months before Noah could disembark in the mountains of Ararat. A flood which lasts 371 days cannot be anything short of universal.

3. **The geology of the flood.** Not only did it rain, but according to Genesis 7:11 "all the fountains of the great deep [$t^e h\hat{o}m$]" were "broken up." $T^e h\hat{o}m$ probably refers to the vast subterranean and suboceanic foundations upon which the antediluvian world rested. This geological phenomenon was not confined to one day; "the fountains . . . of the deep . . . were stopped" only after an extended period—probably 150 days (8:2).

4. **The size of the ark.** The ark, with 95,700 square feet of deck space, could hardly have been designed for a local flood.

5. **The need of an ark.** If the flood were local, why would an ark be necessary at all? God could have directed Noah, his family, and the animals, to a safe place before the flood came. The argument that the ark was merely a test of Noah's faith seems to beg the question.

6. **The testimony of the apostle Peter.** One of the most important biblical passages relating to the magnitude of the deluge is II Peter 3:3–7. The apostle Peter answered skeptics concerning the end times by pointing to two events which undeniably occurred and which could not be explained by naturalistic uniformitarianism: creation ("there were heavens from old, and an earth . . . by the word of God"—ASV) and the flood ("the world that then was, being overflowed with water, perished"—ASV). Peter specifically compared the flood with the second coming of Christ and the final destruction of the world. Since creation and the final destruction of the world are universal, the flood of Noah must also have been universal.

125

7. **The purpose of the flood.** The purpose of the flood was to judge the sinfulness of the entire antediluvian population (Gen.

6:5–7, 11–13). Anything less than a universal flood would not have fulfilled this purpose. Furthermore, God covenanted with Noah that such a flood would never happen again. If the flood were local, God has broken His covenant because there have been many local floods since that one; if the flood was universal, then God has not broken His covenant. Finally, the Lord Jesus clearly stated that all men were destroyed by the flood (Luke 17:26–30). But in the light of the longevity of antediluvian man and of human migration patterns under generally ideal conditions, it is inconceivable that men lived only in the Mesopotamian valley during the flood. Therefore, the flood must have been universal.

The flood narrative, understood in context, demands a universal flood, and such a flood has significant geological implications. The breaking up of the subterranean oceanic levels must have had catastrophic effects on the earth's surface. The isolation and identification of these effects has hardly begun because geology has been dominated by uniformitarian concepts. As experts have begun to analyze earth history, it has become more and more evident that uniformitarian presuppositions are inadequate. Perhaps as times goes on, Christian scientists will become more involved in field research and will help formulate a legitimate earth history, one that includes a universal flood.

C. Termination of the Flood (8:1–9:19)

1. Subsidence of flood waters (8:1–19). This section of the flood account begins with a very intimate and significant expression: "And God remembered Noah and every living thing." The term *remembered* refers not to God's mercy but to His activity. It always emphasizes God's faithful love and intervention on behalf of His own. This was the sense in which Samson (Judg. 16:28), Hannah (I Sam. 1:11), and the thief on the cross (Luke 23:42) desired to be remembered by God. God supernaturally protected and cared for the animals on the ark just as He did the representatives of the human race.

According to verse 2 the fountains of the deep and the windows of heaven were stopped. How long had it been since they had opened? (7:11). Presumably 150 days (7:24), although the text is not entirely clear at this point; the second verse may be parenthetical. In any event, after 150 days the waters began to decrease and Noah's ark rested on the mountains of Ararat (8:4). Seventy-four days later the tops of the mountains could be seen

126

(v. 5). After another forty days Noah opened the window of the ark and released the raven (vv. 6, 7). Evidently the raven returned to the ark because it could find no resting place, indicating that there was too little dry land for debarkation. Shortly thereafter a dove was released the first time; the third time it found a resting place and did not return to the ark (vv. 8–12). God finally commanded Noah, fifty-seven days after Noah had opened the window and released the raven, to exit from the ark (vv. 13–19). God also renewed the command He had given to Adam (1:22, 28): ". . . be fruitful and multiply upon the earth" (8:17; cf. 9:1).

2. Sacrifice and covenant (8:20–9:19). It was no accident that the first deed of Noah in the new world was to build an altar to the Lord and to make burnt offerings of "clean beasts" and "clean fowl" (v. 20). Noah's devotion was not at all surprising; he had already distinguished himself as a man who walked with God and whose faith was unwavering. The Lord regarded this sacrifice as a "sweet savor," or more literally, "a smell of satisfaction." He promised never again to curse the ground (v. 21), which is significant in the light of Genesis 3:14 and 5:29. The cursing of the earth in 8:21, however, referred to universal destruction of the land by flooding (v. 22; cf. 9:9–17). As has been pointed out, if the flood of Noah's day were merely local, the Lord has violated His promise.

God's covenant with Noah and his descendants is further described in 9:1–19. God blessed Noah, commanded him to "be fruitful, and multiply" (v. 2), reaffirmed man's dominion over the animal kingdom (v. 2), and for the first time encouraged man to utilize animals, in addition to vegetation, for food (v. 3), warning only that man should not eat blood (v. 4).

God's assessment of life in verses 5 and 6 is vital to a philosophy of governmental authority. The bearing of these verses on capital punishment has been widely debated in recent years. Two things are clear: human life is sacred and premeditated murder is utterly evil. The meaning of "whoso sheddeth man's blood" is obvious; the meaning of the next clause, "by man [*bā'ādām*] shall his blood be shed," has been the subject of very heated debate. To exactly what man does this refer? According to Leupold, John Benson, and others, it is the civil government or magistrates.[17]

127

---

17. *Exposition of Genesis*, pp. 333ff.; *Benson's Commentary*, 1:43.

Quite often it is assumed that human government did not exist prior to the Noachian flood. "By man" means "by legally constituted authorities," and this is understood to be the chartering of human government. The argument, of course, is based on silence. According to other scholars the man in this clause is the "avenger of blood."[18] Another interpretation is that *bā'ādām* should be translated "for man" rather than "by man."[19] This passage is admittedly difficult to interpret, but it is not impossible. With all the evidence in view, the best approach is to regard *'ādām* as a reference to man generally but to civil authority in particular. That God has established government to punish evil is clear not only from Old Testament law but from the New Testament as well (Rom. 13:1-4).

In the remaining verses of this section, God reaffirms His covenant with Noah and his descendants, and makes the sign of the covenant the "bow in the cloud" (v. 13). It is possible that rainbows had appeared before and that now they were merely given covenantal significance.

D. Noah's Final Years (9:20-29)

1. Drunkenness and shame (9:20-27). How much time elapsed between Noah's exit from the ark and the events of 9:20-23 is unknown, although a grandson (Canaan) had been born to him during the interim. Noah was a husbandman engaged in planting vineyards. It should not be assumed that this is all he planted; only vineyards are mentioned because of the events that follow. Under conditions which are not explained, Noah became drunk and was found "uncovered" within his tent (v. 21). No details are given, but quite evidently his grandson Canaan was involved in the debauchery. Perhaps Habakkuk's observation is appropriate: "Woe unto him that giveth his neighbor drink, that puttest thy bottle to him, and makest him drunken also, that thou mayest look on their nakedness!" (2:15). Wine is indeed a "mocker" (Prov. 20:1). When Noah awoke, he cursed Canaan, making Canaan the third being to be cursed: the first was the serpent (3:14); the second, Cain (4:11). It must be emphasized that Noah cursed Canaan, not Ham. Popular (although totally misguided) exposition of the

18. John P. Lange, *Genesis*, p. 327.
19. Ibid., pp. 324, 332, 334. See also John H. Yoder, "Capital Punishment and the Bible," pp. 348, 349.

passage has applied the curse to the descendants of Ham and ultimately to black peoples, and concluded that the latter are inferior and doomed to servitude. This unsubstantiated interpretation, however, is utterly foreign to the text. The curse upon Canaan was basically fulfilled when Israel, led by Joshua, conquered the inhabitants of Canaan and made them subject.[20] Noah also blessed Shem and Japheth (v. 27). Note in verse 26 that Noah blessed the Lord God of Shem, implying that the descendants of Shem would be blessed only to the extent that they honored the Lord as their God and Savior. The blessing on Japheth (whose name means "enlargement") was that he be "enlarged," a play upon words which meant his descendants would inhabit much of the earth and would prosper.

2. **Death (9:28, 29).** Except for the sad event described in 9:20–27, Scripture records nothing of the 350 years that Noah lived after the flood. It is somewhat tragic that this man's life should be marred during his last years, but it serves as a grim reminder that even the greatest of biblical heroes was subject to the temptation of Satan. In the words of the apostle Paul, "All these things happened unto them for examples: and they are written for our admonition. . . ." (I Cor. 10:11). Noah died at the age of 950.

II. The Babylonian Account

Excavators at Nineveh discovered in the library of Ashurbanipal and the temple library of the god Nabu twelve tablets which contain the now-famous *Gilgameš Epic.* This discovery created quite a stir among biblical scholars, and rightly so; the description of a great flood in tablet XI exhibits numerous significant parallels to the description in Genesis. Since that day numerous other accounts of this story have been found, some at places as far away as Boghazkoy, one of the key cities of the old Hittite empire.

The central figure of the twelve tablets is a young ruler named Gilgamesh, whom the Sumerian king list assigned to the first dynasty of Uruk. According to the epic Gilgamesh was the son of the goddess Ninsun. Ninsun's husband was the god Lugalbanda,

---

20. Other studies of the curse are G. Rice, "The Curse That Never Was"; F. W. Bassett, "Noah's Nakedness and the Curse of Canaan"; L. Richard Bradley, "The Curse of Canaan and the American Negro"; and Thomas O. Figart, *A Biblical Perspective on the Race Problem* (Grand Rapids: Baker Book House, 1973).

Tablet XI of the *Gilgameš Epic* (Courtesy of the British Museum)

but Gilgamesh's father was an unknown man. Gilgamesh, therefore, was part god and part man, but he later became a god of the lower world.

The first ten tablets are devoted mainly to the adventures of Gilgamesh and his close friend Enkidu. When Enkidu insulted a goddess and died, Gilgamesh was stricken with grief. He roamed the earth and crossed the waters of death in a boat, looking for immortality. Beyond the waters of death Gilgamesh encountered Utnapishtim, who related the story of the great flood. According to Utnapishtim the god of wisdom indicated to him that a flood was coming and that he should build a boat. The boat should be 120 cubits square, seven stories high, covered with bitumen, and loaded with food, gold, silver, his family, craftsmen, and animals. The storm lasted six days and nights. When the boat finally grounded on a mountain, a dove was sent out, then a swallow, and finally a raven. Then Utnapishtim offered sacrifices, around which the gods gathered like flies.[21]

A. Similarities to Genesis

Resemblances between this epic and the biblical flood account are numerous and striking: the deluge is divinely instigated; the hero receives divinely given information concerning the coming flood; the flood is associated with the sin of man (although the *Gilgameš Epic* leaves obscure the precise nature and extent of man's sin);[22] the hero and his family are delivered from the flood; they are delivered in a large boat; the physical causes and the duration of the flood are given; the delivered hero performs acts of worship which include sacrifice. The parallels between this epic and Genesis are much more numerous than those between *Enūma Eliš* and Genesis.[23]

B. Dissimilarities to Genesis

The divergencies between the *Gilgameš Epic* and Genesis, however, are also numerous, and at times they are fundamental.

---

21. For translations of the *Gilgameš Epic* see Speiser, "The Epic of Gilgamesh," in Pritchard, *ANET*, pp. 72–99; and Alexander Heidel, *The Gilgamesh Epic and Old Testament Parallels* (Chicago: University of Chicago Press, 1949), pp. 16–101.
22. Pritchard, *ANET*, p. 95 (lines 178–85).
23. For a thorough study of this point see Heidel, *The Gilgamesh Epic*, pp. 224–69.

For example, in the Bible there is one God and He is morally consistent; in the *Gilgameš Epic* there are many gods which, morally speaking, are scarcely distinguishable from sinful humanity. Divine judgment of human flesh, then, is far more justified in Genesis, where God is infinitely holy and above the weaknesses and frailties of human flesh.

The Genesis flood account is eminently more sober than any other ancient flood account. Such accounts did indeed exist in almost every major culture, and even though they are thoroughly corrupt, they point to a universal flood in antiquity. The biblical account, on the other hand, is divinely revealed, preserved from all contemporary superstitions. Once again we are forced to place the burden of proof on the naturalists who explain the Bible in purely evolutionary terms. Why are all accounts of the flood except the Bible's corrupted by superficial polytheism and inconsistencies? How can the unique monotheism and lofty character of the biblical account be explained apart from special revelation? The biblical narrative is sobering; it highlights holy demands and human responsibility, and reminds us that the judgments of God are sure.

III. The Archaeological Evidence

Since 1916 stories have circulated of sightings, or the discovery, of Noah's ark on Mt. Ararat. During World War I an airman named W. Roskovitsky reported observing on one of Mt. Ararat's slopes the remains of an ancient vessel. Shortly thereafter the Czar organized an expedition which claimed to have found remains of that ancient vessel. Since then renewed reports of such sightings have led to various expeditions to the traditional Mt. Ararat. Most of these, however, have not been conducted by trained scientists. The records of these expeditions read more like travelogues than scientific reports, and the accompanying photographs are usually devoted more to the expedition members, their equipment, and local natives than to scientific evidence.

These expeditions have created a great deal of excitement. Unfortunately, however, the wood recovered has not been unmistakably identified as the ark of Noah. It might also be pointed out that the Bible does not pinpoint the mountain on which the ark rested. It simply says that it was one of the mountains of Ararat; that is, the mountains of ancient Armenia in Turkey. The mountain currently identified as the one on which

132

the ark landed was once the location of the monastery of St. James. That monastery was situated at the base of the mountain until the earthquake of 1840 destroyed it with a mountain slide of rock, ice, and snow.[24] Near the monastery were the traditional sites of Noah's wife's grave and Noah's first vineyard, as well as the Garden of Eden. The traditions which mark this as the general vicinity in which the ark landed are unquestionably strong. It is also possible that the ark has been preserved. However, the attitude with which many believers approach this possibility is disconcerting. Some have stated candidly, "If we could just find the ark, we would end skepticism of the Bible forever." This is extremely naive. In the first place, visible evidences of any type are not really the answer to faith. Ancient Israelites saw an amazing series of miracles and visual demonstrations, and in spite of that, on numerous occasions they doubted God and apostatized. During His earthly ministry the Lord Jesus performed innumerable spectacular miracles for His countrymen, but they were not swept into belief by these miracles. It might also be pointed out that since the turn of the century literally hundreds of archaeological discoveries have directly verified Scripture, and still the world of scholarship doubts or denies the supernatural origin of Scripture. Therefore, we issue a caution with respect to the apologetic value of such discoveries. Even if the ark should be discovered, we should expect no worldwide change in attitude. The claims of Scripture and of Christ are accepted by faith and faith alone. Expeditions and research can and should continue. But until carefully evaluated evidence clearly indicates that the wood found on Mt. Ararat comes from that ancient vessel, the best attitude is one of caution and reserve.[25]

---

24. G. Ernest Wright, "The Ark Again?" pp. 1, 2.
25. To study this general topic further, see Violet M. Cummings, *Noah's Ark: Fact or Fable?*; and Montgomery, *The Quest for Noah's Ark.* The latter is more sober and scholarly.

10

The Earth's Population

Genesis 10, 11

Standing on Mars Hill in Athens, the apostle Paul declared that God had "made of one blood all nations of men for to dwell on all the face of the earth" (Acts 17:26). That is no superficial observation. One of its many anthropological and theological implications is that Genesis 10 and 11 are historically accurate. Many endure rather than enjoy reading these two chapters. Informed readers agree unanimously, however, that these chapters are strategic and historically significant. Their delineation of the family of nations illustrates the Old Testament's universal outlook. While subsequent chapters narrow the emphasis to Abraham and his offspring, the Book of Genesis teaches that divine mercy reaches beyond the bounds of the nation Israel, that God has made provision for the needs of men from all nations.

The majority of names in these chapters belonged to individuals, although the same names later identified nations—as did *Israel* and *Edom*, for example. "The natural sense of the chapter seems to make these the founders of their respective groups; but the interest lies in the group so founded and its relation to other peoples. This is borne out by the sprinkling of plural (e.g., Kittim, Dodanim, 4; cf. 13, 14), dual (Mizraim, 6) and

135

adjectival (16–18) forms, which also show that the compiler of the list did not automatically ascribe ancestors to the groups he recorded."[1] The names of cities (in vv. 10–12, for example) quite clearly indicate cities and not men, even though their names may have derived from men. These cities are spoken of as being "built" (v. 11) and as being part of a "kingdom" (v. 10).

Modern criticism generally dates this material in the seventh century B.C. and unanimously ascribes it to two principal sources—P and J. In chapter 10, verses 1a, 2–7, 20, 22, 23, 31, and 32 are from P; and verses 1b, 8–19, 21, and 24–30 are from J and are called the Yahwist table of nations.[2] Such analysis, however, is based upon faulty presuppositions. Earlier critical scholars had attempted to correlate Genesis 5 and 11 with the well-known Sumerian king list, and theorized that the materials for the former came from the latter. Subsequent studies suggested, however, that alleged parallels are too superficial, and the differences too significant, to support the theory.[3]

The descendants of Japheth and Ham are treated first in Genesis 10 and 11, saving Shem and his descendants for the remainder of the book. The two chapters, then, are arranged according to historical importance rather than chronology.

The Descendants of Noah's Sons (10:2–32)

Chapter 10 begins with the now familiar expression, "These are the generations [*'elleh tôlᵉdōt*]." This refrain is employed in sections of Genesis which are also related to genealogy (cf. 2:4; 5:1; 6:9; 11:10, 27; 25:12, 19; 36:1, 9; 37:2). The phrase seems to constitute a formal introduction to a passage, although some older writers regarded it instead as a conclusion.[4]

A. Japheth (10:2–5)

Noah's statement that "God shall enlarge Japheth" (9:27) indicated that Japheth's descendants would experience a

---

1. Derek Kidner, *Genesis,* p. 105.
2. Gerhard von Rad, *Genesis,* pp. 135ff.
3. Thomas C. Hartman, "Some Thoughts on the Sumerian King List and Genesis 5 and 11 B"; E. A. Speiser, "The Ethnic Divisions of Man"; A. H. Sayce, "The Tenth Chapter of Genesis"; D. J. Wiseman, "Genesis 10: Some Archaeological Considerations"; E. G. Kraeling, "Calneh, Genesis 10:10."
4. P. J. Wiseman, *New Discoveries in Babylonia About Genesis,* pp. 44–60.

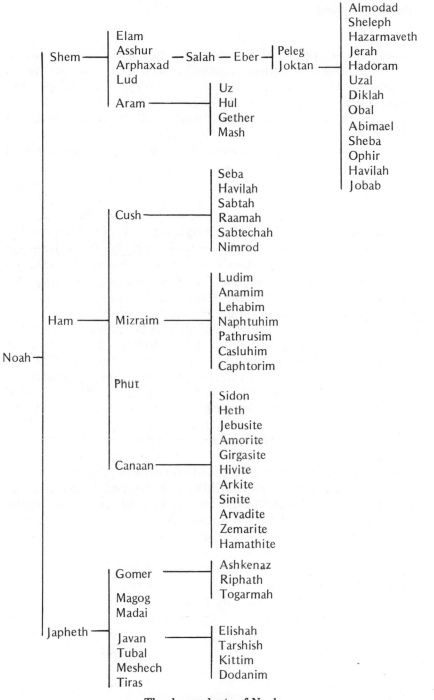

The descendants of Noah

remarkable prosperity and dispersion, and their names make it clear that they did indeed inhabit vast portions of the earth, migrating westward to the Aegean, northward into Europe, and eastward into the vast Asian continent.

Gomer (v. 2) is usually identified with the Cimmerians—in Assyrian inscriptions, Gamir or Gimirrai (cf. Ezek. 38:6). Gomer, therefore, would be the progenitor of the vast Indo-European family of nations. According to one commentator, "the Cimmerians migrated from Northern Europe and appeared in northern provinces of the Assyrian empire at the time of Sargon II, during the eighth century B.C. They invaded ancient Armenia, but were pushed westward by the Assyrians. An old Assyrian letter comments that none of their interpreters knew the language of the people of Gomer. The Cimmerians overthrew, in turn, the Phrygian and Lydian kingdoms of Asia Minor, but were gradually absorbed by the peoples of Anatolia."[5] The name Magog (v. 2) is more difficult to identify. According to Ezekiel, Magog, as well as Tubal and Meshech, originated in "the uttermost parts of the north" (38:2, 6; 39:1, 2). When a Babylonian king wrote to an Egyptian pharaoh in the fifteenth century, he referred to Magog as a barbaric tribe living in the north, presumably in the vicinity of the Black Sea. The name Madai is almost unanimously associated with the Medes who were located west of the Caspian Sea in the ninth century B.C. In the seventh century B.C. they made their mark on the ancient world under the leadership of King Cyaxares. Javan (v. 2) is to be identified with the Greeks or Ionians. The early Ionians first appeared in Hittite records as inhabitants of the western coastal regions of Asia Minor. Tubal and Meshech (v. 2) are well known from the prophecies of Ezekiel (cf. 27:13; 32:26; 38:2; 39:1), from which they appear to be best located in eastern Anatolia. Tubal should be identified with the Tibarenians of Herodotus and the Tabalaeans of Assyrian documents. Tubal is first identified as a country in the annals of Shalmaneser III in the ninth century B.C. The territory of Tubal was later captured by Tiglath-Pileser III, who made its king give him tribute: "I receive tribute from Kushtashpi of Commagene [Kummuhu], Rezon [Ra-hi-a-nu] of Damascus . . . Hiram [Hi-ru-um-mu] of Tyre . . . Uassurme of Tubal. . . ."[6] The descendants of Meshech first

---

5. Francis D. Nichol, ed., *The Seventh-Day Adventist Bible Commentary*, 1:269.
6. "Campaigns Against Syria and Palestine," translated by A. Leo Oppenheim in Pritchard, *ANET*, p. 283. Cf. p. 282 (lines 56–63).

appeared in the northern part of Mesopotamia during the reign of Tiglath-Pileser I about 1100 B.C.[7] Later they were referred to as the Muski in the inscriptions of Sargon II.[8] Tiras (v. 2) has been variously associated with the Etruscans of early Italy[9] and with an "Aegean counterpart of the Etruscans."[10]

The sons of Gomer were Ashkenaz, Riphath, and Togarmah (v. 3). Ashkenaz was most likely an ancestor of the Indo-European Ashkuza, who lived southeast of Lake Urmia in the time of Esarhaddon (seventh century B.C.),[11] although Speiser and Kidner associate them with the Scythians,[12] and Jewish tradition with the Germans or German Jews, for whom it is used to this day.[13] The name Riphath has not as yet appeared in ancient documents. His descendants were the Paphlagonians who lived by the Ragbas River, according to Josephus. Togarmah was probably the ancestor of a people mentioned in Hittite records from the fourteenth century B.C. Assyrian inscriptions refer to them as the Tilgarimmu of the Aurus Mountains. The name appears twice in Ezekiel (27:14; 38:6). The correct geographical location seems to be near Carchemish.[14]

The sons of Javan were Elishah, Tarshish, Kittim, and Dodanim (v. 4). Elishah probably refers to the inhabitants of Sicily and Sardinia (cf. Ezek. 27:7). Tarshish appears numerous times in the Old Testament and is almost always related to a land which was "afar off" (cf. Isa. 66:19 and Ps. 72:10). The Phoenicians imported silver, iron, tin, and lead from Tarshish (Ezek. 27:12). Jonah attempted to escape God's call for his life by taking a ship to Tarshish (Jonah 1:3). Solomon had a "fleet of Tarshish" (I Kings 10:22). Recent studies have indicated that the navy of Solomon was, in effect, a specialized "smeltery" or "refinery fleet" responsible for bringing smelted metal home from the colonial mines, an enterprise in which the Phoenicians probably were also very much engaged.[15] Sites proposed for Tarshish the city have ranged from the island of Rhodes to western Anatolia

---

7. Nichol, ed., *Bible Commentary*, 1:272.
8. "Inscriptions of a General Nature," in Pritchard, *ANET*, p. 285 (lines 72–76).
9. Kidner, *Genesis*, p. 106.
10. Speiser, *Genesis*, p. 66.
11. Nichol, ed., *Bible Commentary*, 1:272.
12. *Genesis*, p. 66; *Genesis*, p. 106.
13. H. C. Leupold, *Exposition of Genesis*, 1:361.
14. Speiser, *Genesis*, p. 66.
15. William F. Albright, "New Light on the Early History of Phoenician Colonization," p. 21.

and Sardinia; this biblical name might refer to more than one place. Kittim (v. 4) is usually identified with Kition, the capital of Cyprus (cf. Isa. 23:1, 12). The use of this name in Jeremiah 2:10 and Daniel 11:30 to refer to the Greeks in general apparently supports this identification. The name Dodanim (v. 4) presents special problems. The Hebrew text has "Dodanim" here but "Rodanim" in the parallel passage, I Chronicles 1:7 (where the translators of the Authorized Version unhappily translated it "Dodanim"), and the Septuagint reads "Rodioi" at Genesis 10:4. The letters *dālet* and *rēš* are easily confused. If "Dodanim" is correct, it refers to the northwestern coast of Asia Minor. If "Rodanim" is correct, it refers in Speiser's opinion to inhabitants of Rhodes.[16]

Verse 5 is quite important because it seems to imply that the events of 11:1–9 occurred before the "Gentiles" occupied the coastlands, an implication confirmed by the language of verses 25 and 32. Apparently the judgment at the Tower of Babel occurred during the life of Peleg.

[margin handwritten: during Peleg.]

B. Ham (10:6–20)

The Hamitic peoples played an important role in the history of Israel. In fact it is fair to say that the Hebrew people were more intimately associated with the descendants of Ham than with those of Japheth. Ham's descendants lived, by and large, south of Canaan. It would be incorrect, however, to simply identify Hamites with Africans (cf. for example vv. 8–12). The literary arrangement of verses 6–20 is to name four primary peoples (v. 6) and to trace the branches of three of them: Cush (vv. 7–12), Mizraim (vv. 13, 14), and Canaan (vv. 15–19). The other, Phut, may refer to either Libya (as the Septuagint translates Phut in verse 6) or Punt.

The sons of Cush are generally associated with two peoples, the Ethiopians to the south and the Kassites east of Assyria. Cush included not only Ethiopia but present-day Nubia and part of the Sudan. Some Cushites appear to have settled in the western part of Arabia bordering on the Red Sea (II Chron. 14:9; Isa. 45:14). The Egyptians descended from Ham's second son, Mizraim, which is what Egypt is called in the Old Testament. The Egyptians,

140

---

16. *Genesis*, p. 66.

The geographical distribution of Noah's descendants

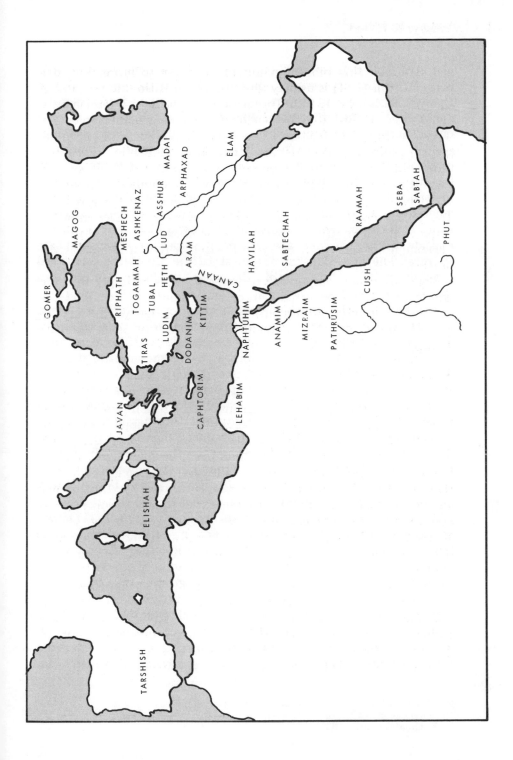

however, called their land either the "black land" or the "red land." The first expression depicts the fertility of the Nile Valley. In early Egyptian inscriptions the expression "two lands" is quite common. The fact that the Hebrew word for Egypt has a dual ending may reflect the Egyptian concept of two lands. It might seem strange that Canaan is listed as a descendant of Ham, especially since the people of Canaan, or the Canaanites, spoke Semitic languages. Hebrew is designated "the tongue of Canaan" in Isaiah 19:18, and Moabite, Aramaic, and Phoenician are other languages that are both Canaanite and Semitic. However, Canaan is listed as a descendant of Ham out of geographical, not linguistic, considerations. The language of a people does not always indicate its race. The great Muslim conquest of the Mediterranean world brought with it the Arabic language to both Semitic and non-Semitic peoples.

Cush's sons Seba and Havilah and Cush's grandson Dedan are all associated with Arabia.[17] One of the most famous descendants of Cush was Nimrod (v. 8). Arab traditions relating to Nimrod are obvious from such titles as Birs-Nimrod, the name for the ruins of Borsippa, and the well-known Nimrud of Calah. We know very little of this man, whose name is probably related to a verbal form meaning "to revolt," and who is described as a "mighty hunter before the Lord." His hunting may refer to outstanding prowess hunting animals in the field or to hunting men to enslave them. The expression "before the Lord," or "in the sight of the Lord," expresses neither approval nor disapproval; it expresses only that what Nimrod did was significant. Von Rad suggests that "'before the Lord' is here equivalent to 'on the earth' (cf. Jonah 3:3)."[18] Nimrod was also well known for his building projects (v. 11). The kingdom over which he ruled was located in southern Mesopotamia and included Babel, known to the Babylonians as *Bab-ilu* ("the gate of God"), and Erech, Uruk to the Babylonians. This area is located at modern Warka, and archaeological evidence indicates very early occupation. Erech, one of the earliest Sumerian city-states, is located about forty miles northwest of Ur, and it has yielded to excavators some very significant clay tablets. Akkad (v. 10) was probably located in the neighborhood of Babylon, but the ruins have not yet been identified with assurance. It was the seat

17. I Sam. 15:7 (Havilah) and Isa. 21:13 (Dedan).
18. *Genesis*, p. 142. Concerning Nimrod, see Speiser, "In Search of Nimrod," *Eretz-Israel* 5 (1958): 32–36.

of the early kings, Sargon I and Naram-sin. The site of Calneh (v. 10) has also not yet been identified with certainty. Some scholars associate it with Nippur or the present site of Nuffar. Its location "in the land of Shinar" (v. 10) would seem to put it somewhere near Babylon.

Verse 11 is obscure in the Authorized Version: "Out of that land went forth Asshur. . . ." The Hebrew text favors Nimrod as the subject and is better translated: "From that land he [Nimrod] went into Assyria" (RSV). Interestingly enough, Micah 5:6 refers to Assyria as "the land of Nimrod." It seems that Nimrod's activities at this point shifted from the south to the north. Nineveh, of course, is well known to us from biblical history and modern excavations. Perhaps the most startling discovery there has been the famous library of Ashurbanipal, containing thousands of baked clay tablets which have proved invaluable in reconstructing the history of the great Assyrian empire.

The remaining verses of this section, verses 12–20, concentrate on Egypt and its offshoots (vv. 13, 14), and on Canaan (vv. 15–19). The Caphtorim mentioned in verse 14 probably refers to the inhabitants of Crete, whose island later became the staging center of the Philistines (cf. Deut. 2:23; Amos 9:7; Jer. 47:4). This section of the chapter confirms that the earliest Canaanites were non-Semitic.

C. Shem (10:21–32)

Having dealt with the descendants of Japheth and Ham, the writer now shifts the focus to the descendants of Shem and keeps it on them through the remainder of the book. The importance of the Semitic line is delineated not only in chapter 10 (vv. 21ff.), but in chapter 11 (vv. 10ff.) as well. The descendant of Shem most important to the writer was Eber, the son of Arphaxad (v. 24) and the father of Peleg and Joktan (v. 25). The writer first focuses on Joktan (vv. 26ff.), the progenitor of many Arab races, reserving detailed treatment of Peleg and his descendants—the most important being Abraham—for chapter 11 (vv. 16ff.). The division of the earth referred to in verses 25 and 32 probably should be associated with the events of 11:1–9. It has been conjectured, however, that the verb *pālag*, translated "was divided" in verse 25, refers instead to irrigation canals.[19]

143

---

19. Kidner, *Genesis*, p. 109.

II. The Tower of Babel (11:1–9)

Perhaps as many as one thousand years elapsed between the great flood and Babel,[20] but one would think that mankind would never have forgotten the impressive lesson of the flood. However, the flood destroyed only sinful men, not sinful nature, a fact of which 9:20–29 is a grim reminder. When man gives it opportunity, his sinful nature drags him down in spite of the divine revelation and his spiritual knowledge. Chapter 11, like chapter 6, begins with a tragic rebellion against the authority and the commands of a sovereign God.

A. The Rebellion (11:1–4)

According to verse 1 all men spoke "one [*'ehāt*] language and one [*'ªhādîm*] speech." This could also be translated "one lip and one kind of words." All men spoke the same language and apparently even the same dialect.[21] The Revised Standard Version's translation, "one language and few words," seems unsuitable here. *'ªhādîm* can mean "few," but here it is parallel to the singular *'ehāt*. The traditional reading of the Authorized and Revised versions, then, is preferable.

That all men were of one language and dialect should not be surprising since they were fundamentally united in the sons of Noah. Research in the area of comparative grammar has demonstrated that known languages are related and could have descended from one language.[22] Of course it is unknown whether that language resembles any modern language, but until the nineteenth century the theory that the original language was Hebrew was practically unquestioned.[23] Some modern interpreters are still inclined toward an original Semitic language, if not Hebrew. "Personal names of the period preceding the confusion of tongues, as far as they can be interpreted, make sense only if considered to be originally Semitic. The record containing these names, the book of Genesis, is written in Hebrew, a Semitic tongue, by a Semitic author, and for Semitic readers. It is therefore possible, although unlikely, that Moses translated these

20. John C. Whitcomb and Henry M. Morris, *The Genesis Flood*, p. 486.
21. H. C. Leupold, *Exposition of Genesis*, 1:383.
22. Joseph P. Free, *Archaeology and Bible History*, pp. 46, 47.
23. Jerry A. Grieve, "The Origin of Languages," p. 15.

names from an original language unknown to his readers, into Hebrew names that would have had meaning for them."[24]

Verse 2 indicates that these early inhabitants traveled "*miqqedem*," translated "from the east" in the Authorized Version but better translated "eastward." Peoples in the region of Ararat (8:4) would have migrated to the Fertile Crescent, which would be southeast and east, as our text suggests.[25] Finding a fertile, open plain in southern Mesopotamia, they began to settle down. It was in this region that the early Sumerians left their mark both culturally and economically. The terms *Sumer* and *Sumerians* do not appear in the Bible, but through modern excavation they are well known to us as a highly sophisticated people. In the last part of the fourth millennium B.C., they developed a writing system which became the foundation of systems employed in Mesopotamia and elsewhere. Some of their great cities—such as Uruk, Aratta, and Kish—enjoyed well-organized governments. Each city had its own tutelary deity (Nanna of Ur, Enki of Eridu, Enlil of Nippur, etc.). Sumerian society was dominated by polytheism, and its pantheon was not unlike others in the ancient Near East. The origin of the Sumerians is still obscure and shrouded in mystery. In spite of extensive excavations in their major cities, the population of Sumer is still largely a matter of speculation. The Sumerians were an identifiable entity from approximately 3000 B.C. to 2000 B.C., when they were absorbed by other groups which occupied and controlled the area, and when the Sumerian language fell into disuse.[26]

As people gathered in that region—a very fertile one—they agreed among themselves to resist leaving it. Perhaps God had reiterated His command to "be fruitful and multiply and replenish the earth" (9:1), and they were resisting it.

The description in verse 3 of their building technique is informative, offering indirect support for our contention that Genesis was written by Moses. The inhabitants settled on using fire-hardened brick instead of stone. This was eminently appropriate since southern Mesopotamia, while rich in alluvial deposition, lacked significant quantities of stone of any kind. The

---

24. Nichol, ed., *Bible Commentary*, 1:283.
25. Cf. the usage of *miqqedem* in 2:8; 3:24; 12:8; 13:11.
26. Some thorough studies of the Sumerians are: Samuel N. Kramer, *History Begins at Sumer;* Kramer, *The Sumerians;* Sir Leonard Woolley, *The Sumerians;* H. Lenzen, *Die Sumerer;* Maurice Lambert, "La Période présargonique: Essai d'une histoire sumérienne"; Speiser, *Mesopotamian Origins.*

very earliest domestic structures were consistently made of mud-brick, often sun dried, but large public buildings or monuments were constructed from bricks which were baked to make them more durable. Moses, reared and trained in Egypt, must have seen the great, monumental, stone structures at Giza frequently. The widespread use of massive stones for construction in the Old Kingdom was well known to him. For this reason he here noted that these early builders in the Plain of Shinar employed mud instead of stone. He further observed that they used "slime . . . for mortar" (v. 3). The word translated "slime" is more accurately translated "asphalt" or "bitumen," substances which are very common in southern Mesopotamia.

The inhabitants of the Plain of Shinar concluded that they would prevent being "scattered abroad upon the face of the whole earth" (v. 4) by building a city and a tower. This, of course, is not the first hint of urbanization: Cain, having been cursed by God, removed himself to the land of Nod and built a "city" (cf. Gen. 4:16, 17). This is, however, the first mentioned—if not the first—urban project after the flood. The Lord did not react against the building of a city, but against the wicked motives for building it. Quite clearly these people were highhandedly rebelling against commandments of God. The nature and precise purpose of the "tower" (*migdāl*) mentioned in verse 4 has been the object of considerable speculation. Usually it is understood to be a very high landmark associated with the city and its worshipers. Several very large, staged temple-towers, or multi-storied ziggurats, have been discovered in Babylonia. One such ziggurat in Babylon was a marvel of colored, glazed tiles, standing over 297 feet high. Its name, *Etemenanki*, means "the building of the foundation-platform of heaven and earth." It was associated with the temple of Marduk, *Esagila*, "the building whose top is (in heaven)."[27] The Assyro-Babylonian word *ziqquratu* comes from the verbal root *zaqāru*, which means "to be high or raise up" and signifies the top of a mountain or a staged tower. Such towers in the flat plains of Mesopotamia served as a place for a god whose shrine belonged on a summit. The very first of these staged towers appeared in Uruk (Erech), located about thirty-five miles up the Euphrates Valley from Tell al 'Ubaid. More than two dozen such staged

146

---

27. D. J. Wiseman, "Babel," in J. D. Douglas, ed., *New Bible Dictionary*, p. 116.

The Great Ziggurat at Ur (Courtesy of Matson Photo Service)

towers are known today.[28] If the Tower of Babel was indeed the prototype of the later ziggurats, then it may well have represented highhanded rebellion against the true God. Its makers were resisting God's command to inhabit the whole earth, and they were attempting to protect themselves from, among other things, another divine judgment like the flood: "Such a citadel would protect them against attack, and enable them, they believed, to escape another flood, which God had promised should never be. The flood had covered the highest mountains of the antediluvian world, but had not reached 'unto the heaven.' If, therefore, a structure higher than the mountains could be erected, men reason, they would be safe whatever God might do."[29] Some scholars, however, feel that this *migdāl* was more of a military fortress than a temple-tower, and that it was part of the city's defensive system. It is well known that *migdāl* sometimes describes military structures (cf. Judg. 8:9; 9:46ff.; Isa. 2:15; II Chron. 14:6),[30] and such fortifications were said to be built "up in heaven" (Deut. 1:28; 9:21). While this interpretation is admissible on linguistic grounds, it seems to find no support from the context. Furthermore, it has not been determined that military defenses were this sophisticated in Mesopotamia by this time, although the amazing prepottery, Neolithic remains at Jericho provide some evidence of early, defensive-tower construction. The more likely interpretation, however, is that the Tower of Babel was religiously oriented and a prototype for the ziggurats. The mention of Babel's tower is in keeping with the prominence of these temple-towers in early Mesopotamian settlements. Furthermore, the clearly stated purpose of the tower was to make its makers men of renown ("let us make us a name") and to prevent their being "scattered abroad upon the face of the whole earth" (v. 4).

B. The Judgment (11:5–9)

During this rebellion the Lord "came down to see the city and the tower" (v. 5). "Jehovah's coming down is not the same here as in Exodus 19:20, 34:5, Numbers 11:25, 12:5, viz. the descent

28. Jack Finegan, *Light from the Ancient Past*, pp. 23, 24. Also see Andre Parrot, *Ziggurats et Tour de Babel* (Paris: Albin Michel, 1949), pp. 52–54; and Parrot, *Tower of Babel*.
29. Nichol, ed., *Bible Commentary*, 1:284.
30. See the Mesha Stone, line 22.

from heaven of some visible symbol of his presence, but is an anthropomorphic description of God's interposition in the actions of men, primarily 'judicial cognizance of the actual face,' and then, verse 7, a judicial infliction of punishment."[31] The Lord came down to see the city and tower "which the children of men builded [*bānû*]." Even though the verb *bānû* is perfect, commentators generally agree that the Lord came down before construction was completed. One reason for this consensus is that after the divine judgment upon them, the author says these men "left off to build the city" (v. 8). Man had arrogantly asserted: "*Let us* make brick. . . . *let us* build a city. . . . *let us* make us a name" (vv. 3, 4). Now the divine counsel responds: "*Let us* go down" (v. 7). The same plural idea is found in 1:26 and 3:22, so this should not be considered a direct reference to the holy trinity; it certainly allows for the trinity, however.

Opinions differ as to which came first, the scattering of men or the diversification of languages. The text says: " . . . let us go down, and there confound their language. . . . So the Lord scattered [*wayyāpes YHWH*] them abroad. . . ." Jerry A. Grieve suggests that "to bring about the diversity of language the Lord first caused a dispersion. The real miracle in the Tower of Babel, then, is not the confusion of tongues but the scattering of the people."[32] He offers three arguments: (1) The *wāw* prefix to *wayyāpes* is a *wāw* consecutive signifying logical result: " . . . so [in order to confound their language] the Lord scattered them abroad. . . ." The action in verse 8 proceeds directly and logically from verse 7. (2) Other references to this phenomenon mention only that the earth was divided (Gen. 10:5, 25, 32), which seems to indicate that the central idea of 11:1–9 is that great migrations occurred. (3) Linguistic science proves conclusively that different languages develop when a single community splits up and groups migrate to new territories. A more likely interpretation, however, is that the scattering of men abroad was the result of the confusion of tongues. What man refused to do voluntarily in obedience to God's command, man was forced to do. God's plan was not to destroy the human race, as it had been in the flood, but to scatter it. Verse 7 clearly states this purpose: the Lord went down to "confound their language *that they may*

---

31. C. F. Keil and Franz Delitzsch, *Biblical Commentary on the Old Testament*, 25 vols. (Edinburgh: T. and T. Clark, 1864–1901), 1:173.
32. "The Origin of Languages," p. 17.

not understand one another's speech." Once groups of people were isolated from each other by language, they would naturally scatter. Furthermore, verse 9 makes the sequence of events rather conclusive: " . . . the Lord did there confound the language of all the earth: and from thence did the Lord scatter them abroad upon the face of all the earth."

Exactly how God confused man's language has been the subject of considerable speculation. Some assert that the change was in the organs of speech, others that it "had a much deeper foundation in the human mind."[33] The text gives insufficient information to solve the problem with any degree of finality. The languages and dialects of the world now number approximately 3,000.

The name *Babel* appears to be linked with the Hebrew verb *bālal*, "to confuse." The ancient Babylonians, however, called the city *Bab-ilu*, meaning "gate of God." "It is, however, possible that this meaning was secondary, and that the name was originally from the Babylonian verb *babālu*, meaning 'to scatter,' or 'to disappear.' "[34]

Were the Babel-builders attempting to establish a centralized government and an unchangeable power structure? Would this not have been a good thing? Does not a plurality of nations and languages prevent worldwide advance—cultural, economic, and religious? The answer to the first question may well be yes, but the other two deserve an unqualified no. Man is fallen and the human heart corrupt. One world government probably would result ultimately not in human progress but in slavery. Alva J. McClain observes: "The judgment of God upon this first attempt at one world government was not only a clear warning against all such schemes but also an endorsement of what is called 'nationalism.' Although not the ideal form of human organization, nationalism has proven the safest for the preservation of personal liberty in a sinful world. In the world market of political ideas and forms, there will be competition and experiment just as long as there are many nations. And, in the end, such competition and experiment always work out for individual liberty and the development of distinctive cultural values which then may be mutually shared

33. Keil and Delitzsch, *Biblical Commentary*, 1:174.
34. Nichol, ed., *Bible Commentary*, 1:286. Also see René Labat, *Manuel d'Épigraphie Akkadienne* (Paris: Imprimerie Nationale de France, 1948), p. 299; Labat suggests the idea of "taking away."

between nations. In a sinful race left to its own devices, one monolithic world state might conceivably put an end to all further political experiment and result in an irreversible totalitarianism."[35]

One thing is clear from Genesis 11: God did not permit human rebellion to reach the level it had before the flood. In contrast to the disheartening confusion in this passage is the great blessing at Pentecost, recorded in Acts 2. The Holy Spirit's unique use of languages demonstrates that the gospel, far from being culturally or linguistically restricted, is for men of all nations. The greatest hope—an eschatological one—is expressed by the prophet Zephaniah: "Yea, at that time I will change the speech of the peoples to a pure speech, that all of them may call upon the name of the Lord and serve Him with one accord" (3:9 RSV).

III. The Ancestry of Abraham (11:10–32)

After introducing the table of nations, which showed the common descent of various tribes and races from Noah, the writer inserted the Tower of Babel incident to further explain the diversity of peoples and languages. In verse 10 the writer returns to the genealogy, introducing it with the typical formula, "These are the generations. . . ." (cf. 5:1; 6:9; 10:1; etc.). The focus is now on Shem, who had received from Noah a prophetic blessing with Messianic import (9:6). That Noah's prophecy conforms to the elective purposes of God for His people cannot be doubted when we trace the line of Shem through Terah and ultimately to Abraham. Shem was selected for special treatment solely because he was the progenitor of the Messianic line (cf. 5:32).

There are notable differences between the genealogical formulas in this chapter and those in chapter 5; for example, the age at death is omitted in chapter 11. Moses' chief interest is not the line of Shem in general but Terah, and as he does so often, Moses disposes of the less relevant matters in order to get to the essential. Ten generations are listed in this chapter, perhaps to make it parallel to chapter 5. It seems obvious that these genealogical lists were schematically arranged and contained considerable gaps.[36]

The name of Peleg's son Eber (*'ēḇer*) may have been the source of the word *Hebrew* (*'iḇrî*). *'Iḇrî* is first used in Genesis 14:13

151

---

35. *The Greatness of the Kingdom*, p. 48.
36. Kidner, *Genesis*, p. 111.

where it serves to identify Abraham. It is a noun form of the verb *'ābar*, which means "to pass over or through," so it might reflect the early travels of Abraham and his family (11:31). While in this respect *'ibrî* may be analogous to the term *Habiru*, which designated a people who moved about for various reasons (including military), the two words should not be equated. William F. Albright, however, sees *Habiru* as the source of *'ibrî; Habiru*, he writes, means "donkey-man, donkey driver, huckster, caravaneer."[37]

It is interesting to compare the ages of paternity in chapter 11 with those in chapter 5. Before the flood they ranged from 65 to 187 and averaged 117; after it they ranged (except in the cases of Shem, Terah, and Abraham) from 29 to 35. Terah was 70, and Abraham 100.

The genealogy of chapter 11 is not without its problems. According to verse 10 Seth was 100 years old "two years after the flood." But data appearing earlier in the book makes him 100 when the flood began (cf. 5:32 and 7:11). A variety of explanations has been offered, but the problem requires more investigation.[38]

A cursory reading of verse 27 might give the impression that Abraham, Nahor, and Haran were triplets, but this has been ably refuted by numerous writers.[39] Another matter of controversy, the location of "Ur of the Chaldees" (v. 28), will be discussed in chapter 11. The name *Abram* meant "father of elevation" or "exalted father," and signified the honor of being the progenitor of God's chosen people. Later his name was changed to *Abraham*, "father of a great number" (17:5).

Haran died, according to verse 28, "before his father Terah." This phrase is, literally, "in the face of his father Terah," and means "while his father Terah was still alive." This is the first mention of a son dying before his father.

While 11:24–32 tells relatively little about Terah, Joshua informs us that "your fathers dwelt on the other side of the flood in old time, even Terah, the father of Abraham, and the father of Nahor: and they served other gods" (24:2). This important statement reveals something about religion in Ur as well as the immediate background of Abraham. Abraham's wife, Sarah, was also his

37. *The Biblical Period from Abraham to Ezra*, p. 5.
38. See Leupold, *Exposition of Genesis*, 1:394; and Nichol, ed., *Bible Commentary*, 1:287.
39. Nichol, ed., *Bible Commentary*, 1:288.

half sister (20:12). Marriage to a half sister or another close relative would be forbidden in the Mosaic code (cf. Lev. 18:6, 9, 14) but it was apparently permitted during the patriarchal period. The mention of Sarah's barrenness seems incidental here, but it provides important background for subsequent events.

It might appear at first glance that at Ur the Lord revealed Himself to Terah rather than Abraham (v. 31), but a careful study of other passages (Acts 7:2, 3; 15:7; Neh. 9:7) quickly corrects this; God called Abraham, not Terah. The journey from Ur of the Chaldees would ultimately lead "into the land of Canaan," although Abraham could not have fully understood this at the time (cf. 12:1 and Heb. 11:8). Only two routes were really possible from Mesopotamia to Canaan: one crossed the great Arabian Desert, which would have been impossible for large flocks or herds; the other crossed the Fertile Crescent along the Euphrates, passed through a narrow desert of northern Syria, and followed the Orontes Valley south into Canaan. Apparently Abraham's family chose the latter. Why they stopped in Haran instead of continuing into Canaan is not explained, but their sojourn there was not, as we shall see later, disobedience to God.

Within Genesis 11, therefore, is a marked contrast: on the one hand human rebellion leading to the divine judgment of dispersion; on the other hand divine grace leading to the call of Abraham, a call which provided hope for the nations and salvation for the lost.

11

The Journeys of Abraham

Genesis 12–14

Some of the most suspense-filled narratives in Scripture are in this section of Genesis. At the heart of these stories is the divine promise of blessing upon Abraham and his descendants, and the pressures and complications which challenge its validity and appear to threaten its fulfillment. Romance, political intrigue, war, spiritual victory, and moral defeat all characterize these chapters. They are at once complex, requiring acute and sensitive analysis, and simple. Here are no great kings or empires, no massive temples being built or expanded. The life of Abraham is characterized more by tents and altars. The first eleven chapters of Genesis possess a universal and cosmic emphasis, but with the introduction of Abraham, Moses, under the inspiration of the Holy Spirit, begins to particularize redemptive history. God's covenant with Abraham, like a thin thread drawn taut, often appears about to be snapped by the impropriety of Abraham or the pressures of the people around him. It is at this very point of tension that we are able to view most clearly the spectacle of divine providence.

Biblical scholars have long been skeptical of the historicity of these chapters. "Until recently it was the fashion among biblical historians to treat the patriarchal sagas of Genesis as though they were artificial creations of Israelite scribes of the divided monarchy or tales by imaginative rhapsodists around Israelite campfires during the centuries following their occupation of the country."[1] Archaeological discoveries in Mesopotamia, Egypt, and Palestine since 1925 required a complete reevaluation. The Abrahamic narratives fit in so well with the culture and customs of the second millennium B.C. that they seem to demand an early date of composition. Scholars of an older generation were deeply influenced by Julius Wellhausen, who argued that most of the narratives were written rather late in Israel's history. But a shift has taken place. The approach now dominating Old Testament studies is "form criticism," the isolation of "units" of narration. Each unit has its own history. In the process of time various units were collected into larger bodies of material. While this method of biblical interpretation, which is reflected in the works of von Rad, is widely accepted, it is just as subjective as Wellhausen's. To assign historical value to one portion and deny it to another seems rather arbitrary and artificial. Of course, many discount the historicity of a large quantity of material on the basis of antisupernatural presuppositions. The accounts of Abraham and his descendants, which reflect the great acts of God, are best appreciated when considered historical and divinely inspired. Since there are no specific references to the patriarchs in contemporary documents, our only information about them comes from the Bible.

I. Abraham's Date

Dating Abraham is no small task because the chronological data available are scant. At present there are three principal proposals: the period between 2000 and 1700 B.C., proposed by a large group of scholars that includes Glueck,[2] Albright,[3] Roland de Vaux,[4] and G. Ernest Wright;[5] the seventeenth century B.C., by H. H. Rowley;[6] and the fourteenth century B.C., by Cyrus H. Gordon on the basis of genealogical lists.[7] The

---

1. William F. Albright, *The Biblical Period from Abraham to Ezra, p. 1.*
2. *Rivers in the Desert*, pp. 68–76.
3. *From Abraham to Ezra*, p. 3.
4. "Les patriarches hébreux et les découvertes modernes," *Revue Biblique* 53 (1946): 321ff.; 55 (1948): 321ff.
5. *Biblical Archaeology*, p. 50.
6. *From Joseph to Joshua*, pp. 113, 114.

Chronology of the ancient Near East

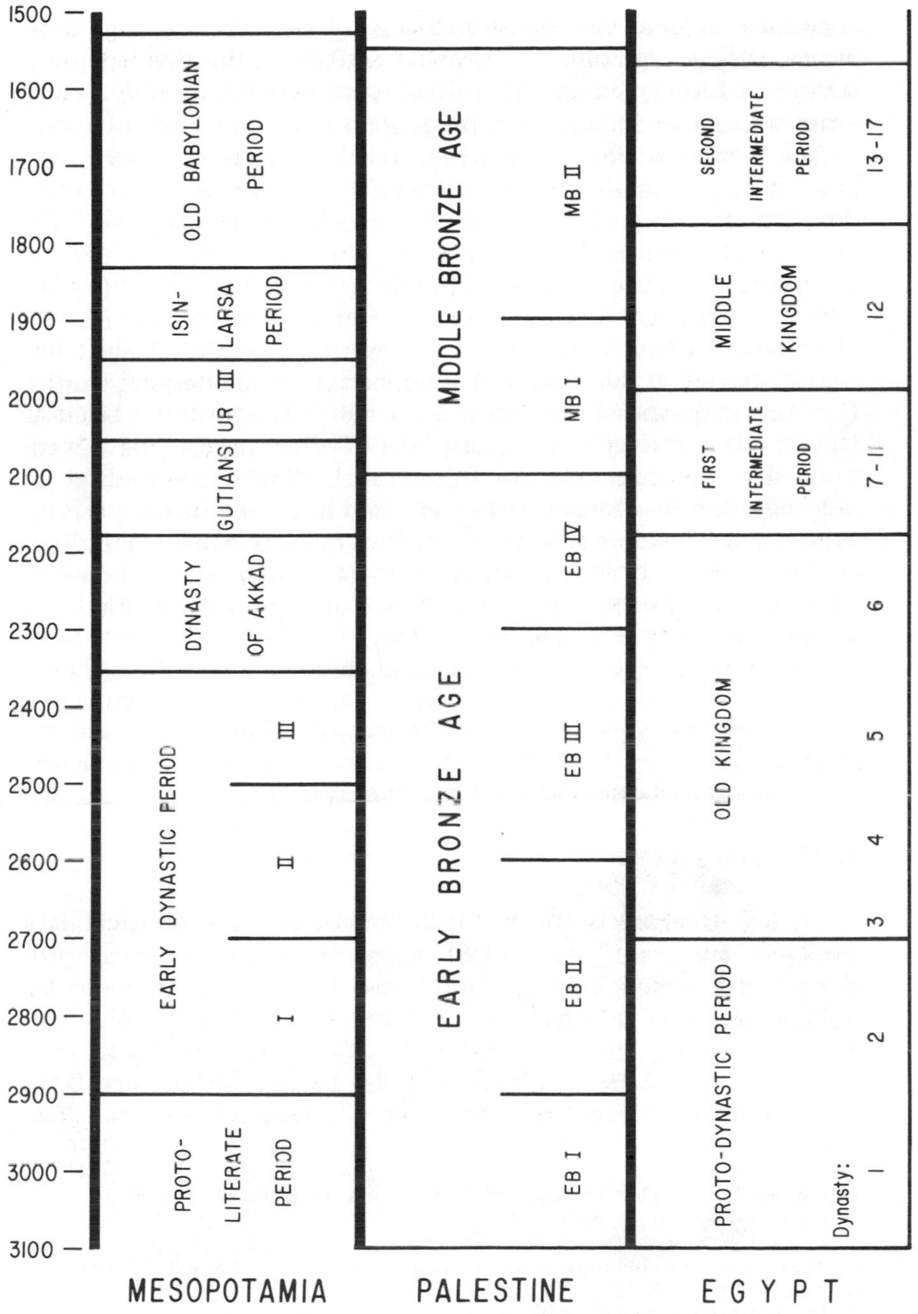
1500
1600
1700
1800
1900
2000
2100
2200
2300
2400
2500
2600
2700
2800
2900
3000
3100
OLD BABYLONIAN PERIOD
ISIN-LARSA PERIOD
UR III
GUTIANS
DYNASTY OF AKKAD
EARLY DYNASTIC PERIOD
III
II
I
PROTO-LITERATE PERIOD
MIDDLE BRONZE AGE
MB II
MB I
EARLY BRONZE AGE
EB IV
EB III
EB II
EB I
SECOND INTERMEDIATE PERIOD
13-17
MIDDLE KINGDOM
12
FIRST INTERMEDIATE PERIOD
7-11
OLD KINGDOM
6
5
4
3
PROTO-DYNASTIC PERIOD
2
Dynasty: 1
MESOPOTAMIA
PALESTINE
EGYPT

essential problems with the third proposal are its assumption that
the genealogies lack gaps and its conflict with year reckonings such
as those in I Kings 6:1 and Exodus 12:40. Gordon feels that genealogies were more important and accurate than such reckonings in
ancient Semitic societies.[8] However, the genealogies did have gaps.
The one in Exodus 6:16–20, for example, gives only the tribe,
clan, and family group to which Moses and Aaron belonged, not
their actual parents. Amram was not Moses' and Aaron's father;
the Amramites were already quite numerous at the exodus (Num.
3:27, 28), so Amram must have lived much before Moses' father.
The statement that "Jochebed . . . bare him [Amram] Aaron and
Moses" (Exod. 6:20) does not demonstrate immediate descent. [9]
The second proposal for Abraham's date likewise lacks biblical
support. It rests on the Septuagint's reading of Exodus 12:40
(" . . . the sojourning of the children of Israel, who dwelt in Egypt
and the land of Canaan, was four hundred and thirty years")
rather than the Hebrew text's (" . . . the sojourning of the children
of Israel, who dwelt in Egypt, was four hundred and thirty
years"). The latter reading which does not include the patriarchal
period in the 430 years seems preferable.

With all the evidence in view, it seems best to date Abraham and

---

7. *The Ancient Near East*, pp. 113ff.
8. Ibid., p. 116.
9. Note, for example, that children "born" to Jacob included great-grandsons
(Gen. 46:21, 22).

An inlaid game board and playing pieces, discovered in a twenty-fifth
century B.C. tomb at Ur (Courtesy of the British Museum)

his descendants between 2100 and 1800 B.C. The exodus from Egypt took place 480 years before the fourth year of Solomon (I Kings 6:1). Following Thiele's date of 931 B.C. for the end of Solomon's forty-year reign, the exodus occurred in 1445 B.C. Jacob's family arrived in Egypt 430 years before the exodus (Exod. 12:40), or in the year 1875 B.C. Jacob was 130 years old when he entered Egypt (Gen. 47:9) and therefore had been born in 2005 B.C. Isaac was sixty when Jacob was born (Gen. 25:26), and Abraham was 100 when Isaac was born (Gen. 21:5). Therefore, Abraham was born in 2165 B.C.

Perhaps the most impressive evidence for the earlier date of the patriarchal period is archaeological. The settlement patterns discovered by Glueck in Transjordan indicate that the events of Genesis 13 occurred somewhere between 2000 and 1900 B.C. Glueck discerned a drastic decrease in the density of occupation between the nineteenth and thirteenth centuries B.C., and he links this decrease with the destructive campaign mentioned in Genesis 14.[10] Furthermore, the names of the four eastern kings mentioned in Genesis 14 appear to fit the approximate period 2100 to 1700 B.C.[11] Kitchen points out that the system of power alliances (four kings against five) is typical in Mesopotamia only from 2000 to 1750 B.C.; different political patterns prevailed both before and after this.[12] Glueck's explorations in the Negev also point to this earlier date. The Negev was dotted with villages founded during the twenty-first century B.C. when Middle Bronze I began, and destroyed in the nineteenth century B.C. when that period ended. Abraham and his family moved quite freely through the Negev for extended periods of time, even with large flocks and a retinue of considerable size, and this would have been possible, it seems, only when the villages mentioned by Glueck existed. This fact is so significant that Glueck concludes: "Either the age of Abraham coincides with the Middle Bronze I period between the twenty-first and nineteenth centuries B.C. or the entire saga dealing with the patriarch must be dismissed, so far as its historical value is concerned, from scientific consideration."[13] Patriarchal customs, another important source for dating the era, generally reflect practices common in Mesopotamia from 2000 to 1500 B.C. Patri-

---

10. *Rivers in the Desert*, pp. 771–74.
11. Kenneth A. Kitchen, *Ancient Orient and Old Testament*, pp. 43, 44.
12. Ibid., p. 45.
13. *Rivers in the Desert*, p. 68.

archal customs find many parallels in written texts from Nuzi and Mari. [14]

II. Abraham's World

If Abraham was born in 2165 B.C., he lived during the latter phases of the great Sumerian culture of lower Mesopotamia. The Sumerians gave to Mesopotamia its earliest cities, government, law systems, and language. During the dynasty of Akkad (ca. 2360–2180 B.C.), Akkadian, a Semitic language, began to replace the earlier Sumerian tongue which had been spoken in southern Mesopotamia from the beginning of history. Approximately 2200 B.C. Mesopotamia was invaded by the Gutians from the mountains to the northeast. For a century the Gutians ruled the land, but they left no great cultural legacy. With the downfall of the Gutian dynasty came a renaissance of Sumerian rule under the Third Dynasty at Ur, and it lasted until about 1950 B.C. During this period Akkadian remained the spoken language of southern Mesopotamia, with Sumerian being used primarily by temple functionaries. The Semitic population of lower Mesopotamia now dominated the land.

Near the end of the third millennium B.C., the Fertile Crescent saw vast movements of people and sweeping destruction of settlements. Among those on the move were the Amorites, who were descendants of Canaan (Gen. 10:16). In the patriarchal period the Amorites inhabited the mountains (Deut. 1:19ff.) as well as the lowlands (Gen. 14:13). Biblical writers seemed to put them on the same level with the Canaanites (Exod. 3:18). During the period of the conquest, they apparently controlled five city-states—Jerusalem, Hebron, Jarmuth, Lachish, and Eglon (Josh. 10:5). There is widespread disagreement regarding the Amorites' place of origin. A. R. Millard suggests Syria, characterizing the Amorites as "a desert people unacquainted with civilized life, grain, houses, cities, government. Their headquarters were in the mountains of Basar, probably Jebel Bishri north of Palmyra. About 2000 B.C.

---

14. Further discussions of this material are in Kitchen, *Ancient Orient and Old Testament*, pp. 51, 52; Gordon, "Biblical Customs and the Nuzu Tablets," pp. 1–12; Loren R. Fisher, "Abraham and His Priest-King," pp. 264–70; Gordon, "The Patriarchal Narratives," pp. 56–59; C. Mullo Weir, "Nuzi," in D. Winton Thomas, ed., *Archaeology and Old Testament Study*, pp. 73–86; A. Malamat, "Mari," pp. 2–22.

The journeys of Abraham

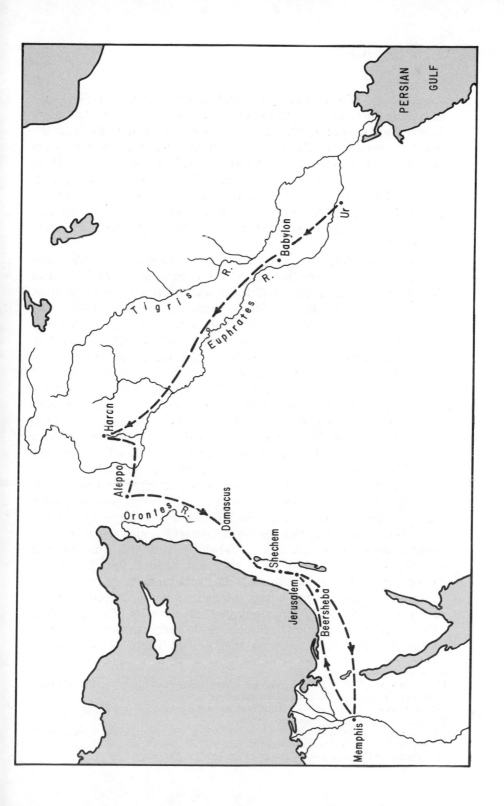

these people, who had been infiltrating for centuries, moved into Babylonia in force."[15] Others contend for the land of Arabia. [16] Alfred Haldar prefers the area between the Euphrates and the Mediterranean.[17] If the movement of the Amorites was as wide-spread and destructive as supposed, it made Abraham's migration from Mesopotamia to Palestine easier. If the general unrest from 2100 to 1800 B.C. in both Mesopotamia and Palestine was related to increased Amorite movement, this might explain the appearance of new burials in Palestine, as Kathleen Kenyon seems to suggest.[18]

Egypt, like Palestine, Syria, and Mesopotamia, was undergoing significant changes near the end of the third millennium B.C. After the Old Kingdom (2700–2200 B.C.) was a period of disintegration and chaos which lasted for a little more than 200 years (2200–1991 B.C.). This is commonly known as the First Inter-mediate Period and included the Seventh to Eleventh Dynasties in Egypt. The confusion and despair of the period is perhaps best reflected in the "Admonitions of Ipu-Wer": "A man regards his son as his enemy. . . . A man of character goes in mourning because of what has happened in the land. . . . Foreigners have become people everywhere. . . . The bowman is ready. Robbery is everywhere. There is no man of yesterday. . . . Why really, poor men have become the possessors of treasures. He who could not make himself a pair of sandals is (now) the possessor of riches. . . . Why really, the land spins around as a potter's wheel does. The robber is (now) the possessor of riches. . . ."[19] This was the period during which Abraham journeyed to Egypt. Some semblance of order was restored in the Eleventh Dynasty under the Intefs and Mentuhoteps, who ruled at Thebes, but it was the Twelfth Dynasty (ca. 1991–1786 B.C.) that stabilized Egypt. The native Thebans who constituted this dynasty ruled mainly from Memphis and the Fayyum. It was an age of enlightened and refined litera-ture and art. Not only kings enjoyed the benefits of immortality; others shared them as well. Special texts guaranteeing the blessing of the deceased are known as the "Coffin Texts." It was during

---

15. "Amorites," in J. D. Douglas, ed., *New Bible Dictionary*, p. 31. Also see Kathleen Kenyon, *Amorites and Canaanites.*
16. A. Poebel, "The Assyrian King List from Khorsabad," pp. 256ff.
17. *Who Were the Amorites?* pp. 6–28.
18. *Archaeology in the Holy Land*, pp. 135–61. This conclusion is challenged in Haldar, *Who Were the Amorites?* p. 14.
19. Translated by John A. Wilson in Pritchard, *ANET*, p. 441.

Canaanites as represented in Egyptian tomb paintings

the Middle Kingdom that Joseph and his brothers migrated to Egypt.

The situation in Palestine during the twenty-fourth to the twentieth centuries B.C. was not unlike that of Mesopotamia and Egypt. Early Bronze civilization suffered such violent destruction that "scarcely a vestige of it survived."[20] By the end of the twentieth century B.C., the situation in Palestine had stabilized. Archaeological data indicate that a new people were settling in unfortified villages located largely in the hill country but also in the Jordan Valley and southern Transjordan. Their pottery was crude; it was handmade except for the necks and rims of some large jars. Most Palestinologists attribute the new cultural elements to the Amorite settlements of the previous century. Occupation in Palestine during this period varied in type and extent. Probably the usual number of nomadic and seminomadic peoples were moving about in the fertile valleys and hillsides. Urban occupation ranged from 7 acres at Jericho to 13 at Megiddo and 182 at Hazor during its period of maximum expansion. It is difficult to arrive at any population statistics, but judging from the data now available, settlements were concentrated largely in the valleys and population was sparse in the hill country.

The lands through which Abraham moved, therefore, were populated by a variety of peoples whose movements had created considerable turmoil. These population movements may account for the lack of resistance and the minimal difficulty Abraham experienced in his wide-ranging travels. Of course one cannot forget that Abraham was called by God and protected by Him. This divine call and Abraham's journeys now demand our attention.

III. Abraham's Call to Canaan (12:1–9)

A. The Place of His Call (12:1–3)

Genesis 12:1 does not specify the city in which Abraham dwelled when God called him, but other passages (cf. Gen. 11:31 with Gen. 15:7; Josh. 24:2; Neh. 9:7; Acts 7:2) point to the city of Ur. In all probability Abraham grew up in this city just before

20. Wright, "The Archaeology of Palestine," in Wright, ed., *The Bible and the Ancient Near East*, p. 86. Also see Kenyon, *Archaeology in the Holy Land*, p. 134.

the rise of the Third Dynasty and the Sumerian renaissance. Ur was a center for the worship of the moon god Sin, and it is clear from Joshua 24:2 that Abraham and his father served some of these gods.

The location of Ur has long been debated. Moslems have traditionally identified it with Urfa, a city twenty miles northwest of Haran called Edessa by the Greeks. Gordon and others argue for a northern Ur. This is generally identified with Ura, a town northeast of Haran which was under the Hittites' control. Akkadian documents from Ugarit describe this as the home of merchants who traded with Ugarit. Gordon, accordingly, treats Abraham as a merchant-prince, a *tamkarum*, from the land of Hittites. He argues that (1) the term *Chaldees* can be applied to northern Mesopotamia as well as southern; (2) the image of the patriarchs as "city-merchants" fits the known facts from this time; and (3) a strong tradition connects Ur of the Chaldees with northern Mesopotamia.[21] The more likely and more generally accepted view is that Ur was located in southern Mesopotamia at Tell al-Muqayyar (Arabic for "mound of pitch"). This is located 160 miles from the present head of the Persian Gulf and 220 miles south-southeast of Baghdad. Originally it was on the east bank of the Euphrates, but today it is ten miles west of that river.

The ruins of this ancient city have been excavated several times, but the most significant excavation was conducted by Sir Leonard Woolley from 1922 to 1934. His efforts gave some insight into the splendor of Ur during the centuries just prior to Abraham's birth. Among the most interesting discoveries were the royal tombs of Ur, dating back to about 2500 B.C. The magnificent jewels, musical instruments, and statuettes found in them illustrate the fine craftsmanship of that period. The city was protected by a series of walls which were an average thirty feet high. The highest point of the city was the top of the Great Ziggurat, which rose from the plain along the Euphrates. The sacred area which surrounded this temple-tower covers a third of the northern half of the site and was by far the most important section of the city. Kings continually expanded, redesigned, and rebuilt it. The streets of Ur were unpaved, narrow, and winding, lined on both sides by

---

21. "Abraham and the Merchants of Ura," pp. 28–31. Cf. the response in H. W. F. Saggs, "Ur of the Chaldees: A Problem of Identification," pp. 200–209. Also see Albright, "Abraham and the Caravan Trade," pp. 44–54; and Joseph P. Free, "Abraham's Early Home," *Bible Today* 36 (1942).

house walls. Houses were usually constructed of burned mud brick, whitewashed or plastered on the outside; many were two stories high. The archaeological data give the impression that Abraham's Ur was a sophisticated, well-designed, wealthy city, one that provided the best available comforts. It is in this light that the nature and implications of Abraham's call to a land about which he knew nothing must be evaluated.

The title "Ur of the Chaldees" locates the city in the southern Mesopotamian land later called "Chaldaea." Many consider this term an "anachronism if a South Mesopotamian site is accepted, since the Chaldeans did not arrive in this area until the last of the second millennium B.C. or later."[22] Unger disagrees: "The qualifying phrase 'of the Chaldeans' is not an anachronism as many critics hold, but as in the case of numerous archaic place names, is a later scribal gloss to explain to a subsequent age, when Ur and its location had utterly perished, that the city was located in southern Babylonia. There after 1000 B.C. the race of the Chaldeans became dominant and eventually established the Neo-Babylonian or Chaldean empire, and it was, of course, quite natural for the Hebrew scribe to define the then incomprehensible foreign name by an appellation customary in his own day."[23] This explanation seems preferable since such glosses are not uncommon in the Book of Genesis (cf. 14:2, 3, 7, 8, 17).

B. The Nature of His Call (12:1–3)

The precise manner in which God contacted Abraham is not given; the text simply says, "And God said." It is quite probable that this call was accompanied by an appearance of the Lord (cf. Acts 7:2). God originally called Abraham in Ur, and God reiterated that call when Abraham was in Haran (Gen. 12:1–3). The Authorized Version reflects this in the pluperfect "had said." While the Hebrew text merely employs the imperfect with *wāw* consecutive, the pluperfect translation seems both grammatically permissible[24] and preferable. Some commentators have criticized Abraham for a delayed response, for insensitivity to God's mes-

---

22. Kyle M. Yates, "Ur," in Charles F. Pfeiffer, ed., *The Biblical World*, p. 602.

23. *Archaeology and the Old Testament* (Grand Rapids: Zondervan Publishing House, 1954), p. 108.

24. S. R. Driver, *Hebrew Tenses*, p. 82.

sage. This, however, seems both harsh and inaccurate. The delay could well have been a result of personal or family considerations, such as Terah's old age. It is not improbable that Abraham was awaiting the appropriate time to break with his family, and when that time came, God reiterated the call. Let it also be emphasized that God called, or elected, Abraham not because of any merit on his part. On the contrary, Abraham's background was polytheistic, and whatever he had from the hand of God was an expression of pure grace. What is said of Abraham can be said of everyone who comes to the Lord by faith. That which we deserve—judgment—He mercifully withholds, and that which we do not deserve—gracious blessing—He freely gives. This repeatedly caused the writers of Scripture to break out in doxologies to God.

To a man of lesser faith, God's requirement of Abraham (v. 1) would be staggering: leave your land, your kindred (cf. 43:7), and your father's house. In other words Abraham had to totally abandon all that was significant to him, a resident of Mesopotamia. His faith was not blind for he knew the power of God and possessed His promise to show him a new land. Of course God rarely demands personal sacrifice without the compensation of even greater blessings. Abraham's move from Mesopotamia and his father's house probably meant losing his inheritance, but how much greater were the things which God promised. He would, indeed, be leaving a land of large cities rich in material goods, but the Lord promised a new inheritance that would include another land (v. 1; cf. Gen. 13:15, 17). This promise was repeated to Isaac (Gen. 26:3) and Jacob (Gen. 28:13).[25] Even though Israel's possession of the land was threatened time and again, Israel never completely lost it. God's promise was sure and it was unconditional. Retaining the land did not depend on the might of Abraham or his descendants. Micah was able to say in days of despair and apostasy that the Lord would "perform the truth to Jacob, and the mercy to Abraham" which he had "sworn unto our fathers from the days of old" (7:18-20).

God's promised blessing included, in addition to his own land, a

---

25. It should be noted that the complete fulfillment of this promise awaits Israel's millennial restoration, for God "gave him none inheritance in it, no, not so much as to set his foot on; yet he promised that he would give it to him for a possession. . . ." (Acts 7:5; cf. Heb. 11:8-10). Cf. Howard W. Ferrin, "All Israel Shall Be Saved," pp. 235-47; John F. Walvoord, "The Fulfillment of the Abrahamic Covenant," pp. 27-36; and Alva J. McClain, *The Greatness of the Kingdom*, pp. 155, 212, 231.

future seed for Abraham (v. 2). This may have seemed incredible since Sarah was barren and Abraham was seventy-five years old (12:4; 15:2). While Abraham was commanded to leave his home and family in Mesopotamia, he had the promise that he would be the father of many people (cf. Gen. 13:16; 15:5; 17:4–7). The "seed of Abraham," compared with the dust of the earth and the stars of the heaven because of their number, goes beyond a mere natural progeny. The apostle Paul alludes to this in both Romans (2:29; 9:6, 7, 13) and Galatians (3:7).[26]

God also promised Abraham that He would "bless thee, and make thy name great; and thou shalt be a blessing" (Gen. 12:2). The essential word in this covenant is *blessing*, which occurs in this section no less than five times. Part of that blessing was to make Abraham's name great. The builders of Babel thought they could make themselves "a name" by defying God. But not one of their names survives today, while Abraham is remembered as a great man of faith, the father of the faithful, and a "friend of God." God's blessing was not limited to the Abrahamic nation of Israel; all nations of the earth would be blessed (v. 3). The universality of this covenant blessing is significant in the light of Paul's treatment of the Gentiles in Romans 9–11. The remarkable thing about Abraham was his deep, unwavering faith. He, and the other patriarchs, "died in faith, not having received the promises, but having seen them afar off, and were persuaded of them, and embraced them, and confessed that they were strangers and pilgrims on the earth" (Heb. 11:13). We are able to see things the patriarchs could not: the great growth of the nation Israel and the appearance of the Messiah, "the son of Abraham" (Matt. 1:1). While Abraham's life and dedication provide a pattern for faith, God's grace and mercy provide the encouragement of faith. With the apostle Paul we all declare, "O the depth of the riches both of the wisdom and knowledge of God! how unsearchable are his judgments, and his ways past finding out!" (Rom. 11:33).[27]

C. His Response to the Call (12:4–9)

In response to God's call and promises, seventy-five-year-old Abraham left the land of Mesopotamia (v. 4). Various motives

26. J. Dwight Pentecost, *Things to Come*, p. 88.
27. For additional study on Abraham's calls see Allan A. MacRae, "Abraham and the Stars"; and Peter L. Van Dyken, "Was God's Covenant with Abraham Ever Abolished?"

The world of the patriarchs

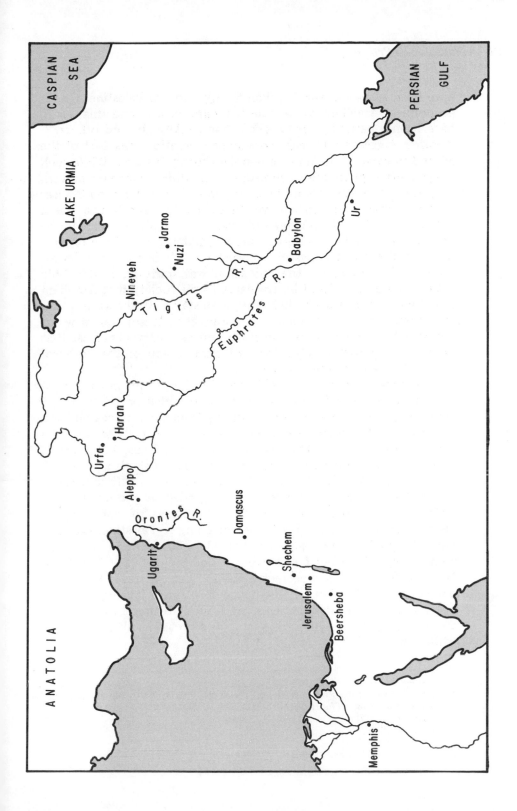

have been suggested for Abraham's migration to Palestine. One is economics; Abraham was a "donkey caravaneer," and this would have been a natural journey, according to Albright and others. [28] Another suggestion is that Abraham's migration was part of the general movement of Amorite peoples during this time. While such suggestions explain the circumstances in which Abraham moved, they do not explain his motives or goals. For that reason Speiser contends that Abraham's move, "reduced to basic terms, was a spiritual one."[29] He further observes, " . . . it would scarcely be normal for a native of Mesopotamia, whatever his ethnic origins, to look for greener pastures elsewhere."[30] Speiser concludes: "And if the reason for the migration was spiritual, as the Bible asserts, the cause should be traceable to the society that Abraham abandoned. Or to state it differently, we start with the assumption that Abraham found the spiritual solution of Mesopotamia wanting, and that the biblical process began as a protest against that failure."[31] Unfortunately, Speiser's explanation of the "biblical process" does not go far enough.

Of course it would not be impossible for Abraham to discern gross weaknesses and iniquities in Mesopotamian polytheism, but without special revelation and guidance from God, his search for a better alternative would have been futile and scarcely would have led him to Palestine. The apostle Paul reminds us that there is "none that understandeth, there is none that seeketh after God" (Rom. 3:11). Abraham's decision to forsake the wealth and security of Mesopotamia can hardly be regarded as purely natural. From a human point of view, the advantages of remaining in Mesopotamia far outweighed those of going to Palestine. Furthermore, it should be remembered that Abraham is cited not just for a single act of faith but for an attitude and life of faith (Heb. 11:9, 10). Charles R. Erdman correctly notes: "Yet the life of faith does not consist of one act of obedience in a single journey to some distant scene. It is an experience continually related to the unseen and the eternal. Its symbol is a tent, its secret is an altar. So it was with Abraham."[32]

---

28. *From Abraham to Ezra*, pp. 5–7; "From the Patriarchs to Moses: I. From Abraham to Joseph," *The Biblical Archaeologist* 36 (1973): 5–19.
29. *Genesis*, p. xlv.
30. Ibid., p. xlvii.
31. Ibid., p. xlvi.
32. *The Book of Genesis*, p. 52.

Women with copper water pots along the Euphrates River (Courtesy of Matson Photo Service)

Abraham did not move to a new land alone. Accompanying him were his wife, Sarah, his nephew Lot, and a considerable number of servants (Gen. 12:5). "Substance" in this verse probably refers to the large herds of cattle and flocks of sheep. Abraham crossed the Euphrates and went westward to Aleppo, then southward along the Orontes River through Lebanon, probably over the fertile land between the Lebanon and Anti-Lebanon mountains.

He finally stopped at Shechem, located in the "navel" of the land (Judg. 9:37) at the eastern end of the pass between Mt. Ebal and Mt. Gerizim, some forty miles north of Jerusalem. The ancient mound known today as Tell Balata was important not only to

171

Abraham but also to Jacob (cf. Gen. 33:18–20). In addition to the numerous biblical allusions to the site are a number of very significant allusions in extrabiblical sources. The name *Shechem* appears in an Egyptian "execration text" as a defeated enemy of a Twelfth-Dynasty pharaoh. Another inscription from about the same period relates the city's capture by Pharaoh Senusert III (Sesostris III). Since both of these inscriptions are Middle Bronze, they appear to verify the city's importance at that time and indicate its early opposition to Egyptian control.[33] Shechem also plays a prominent role in the Amarna period, when Lab'ayu established a confederation with the invading Habiru and incurred the wrath of other kings in the area, especially Abdu-Heba, King of Jerusalem.[34] Excavation of the site was begun by the Germans in 1903, with G. Walter and Ernst Sellin directing most of the work done before 1933. Better controlled excavations, directed by Wright, began in 1956. Subsequent campaigns were conducted in the summers of 1957, 1960, 1962, 1964, 1966, 1968, 1969, 1972, and 1973. The city was violently and completely destroyed on three occasions. It was destroyed when the Hyksos were expelled about 1550 B.C., but it was rebuilt again during the succeeding Late Bronze age. It was destroyed again in the eighth century B.C., probably as a result of the same Assyrian invasion which brought down Samaria in 722 B.C.; the city was rebuilt about 325 B.C. by the Samaritans. It was destroyed again near the end of the second century B.C., and the mound was never reoccupied.[35]

The "plain [*'ēlôn*] of Moreh" (v. 6) is more accurately rendered "tree of Moreh" or "oak of Moreh." This might be a grove of oaks, an interpretation supported by Moses' later reference to the same locality as the "plains [plural] of Moreh" (Deut. 11:30). Moses is careful to indicate that this land was occupied by hostile

---

33. Horace Hummel, "Shechem," in Pfeiffer, ed., *The Biblical World*, p. 518.
34. See "The Amarna Letters," in Pritchard, *ANET*, pp. 486–89.
35. For further study of this site see Wright, "Shechem," in Thomas, ed., *Archaeology and Old Testament Study*, pp. 355–70; and a series of articles by Wright in *The Biblical Archaeologist*, vols. 20, 26, and 32. Preliminary reports on the campaigns of 1956, 1957, 1960, and 1962 may be found in *Bulletin of the American Schools of Oriental Research*, vols. 144, 148, 161, and 169, respectively. Also see Wright, "The Samaritans at Shechem," pp. 357–66; Siegfried H. Horn, "Scarabs from Shechem," *Journal of Near Eastern Studies* 21 (1962): 1–14; James F. Ross and Lawrence C. Toombs, "Three Campaigns at Biblical Shechem," *Archaeology* 14 (1961): 171–79; Wright, *Shechem;* and Horn, "Shechem in the Light of Archaeological Evidence," pp. 9–19.

Canaanites (v. 6). This was the context of the Lord's appearance to Abraham and of His reiteration of the promise (v. 7). Abraham responded by building an altar to the Lord, a visible evidence of the strength of his faith.

From here he journeyed to Bethel, twenty miles farther south, pitched his tent on a hilltop between Bethel and Ai, again built an altar to the Lord, and called upon His name (v. 8). The nature of Abraham's existence in the land is very nicely reflected in the two verbs *pitched* and *built*. He pitched a tent, a temporary structure, for his own comfort; he built an altar, a permanent structure, for worshiping God. Abraham left behind him in Canaan no sign of his wealth or prestige, only the altars he had constructed to worship his God.

Ancient Bethel has been identified with the ruins on the north side of the Arab village Beitin, where Albright made soundings in 1927. James L. Kelso joined Albright in 1934, July through September, for full-scale excavations. This site is thought to have been first occupied early in the Middle Bronze age (ca. 2200 B.C.). At the beginning of the Late Bronze age (1550 B.C.), a strong wall was built and the city became quite prosperous, presumably because of Egyptian contacts. The site underwent a major destruction in the latter part of the thirteenth century B.C. It was destroyed again in the sixth century B.C. by fire, after which it was settled by some returning exiles (Neh. 9:31). The real center of worship for these exiles, of course, was Jerusalem (Zech. 7:2). Bethel was quite evidently an important place for the patriarchs, especially Abraham. This is where he went after his visit to Egypt (13:3).[36]

The other site near which Abraham had located is *hā'ay* ("Ai"), a mound located one mile east of Beitin and known today as Et-tell.[37] *Ai* always has the article in Hebrew, and it means "the ruin," which may well have been an acquired name rather than its original Canaanite one.[38] Brief excavations were conducted there in 1928 by John Garstang, then director of Palestine's Department of

---

36. Additional information on Bethel is in James L. Kelso, "Excavations at Bethel," pp. 36–43; and "The Third Campaign at Bethel," pp. 3–8.
37. This identification has been challenged, however, in David Livingstone, "Location of Biblical Bethel and Ai Reconsidered," pp. 20ff. The traditional identification is defended in W. Winter, "Biblical and Archaeological Data on Ai Reappraised"; and Anson F. Rainey, "Bethel is Still Beitin," pp. 175–88.
38. E. F. Campbell and Bruce T. Dahlberg, "Archaeological News from Jordan," *The Biblical Archaeologist* 28 (1965): 27.

Antiquities. From 1933 to 1935 the Rothschild expedition worked at the site under the direction of Mme. J. Marquet-Krause and S. Yeivin. They unearthed evidence, including great walls and houses constructed of stones, that the city had flourished during the third millennium B.C. Sometime before 2200 B.C. the city was destroyed, and it was not reoccupied until approximately 1100 B.C., a fact which makes it difficult to identify the site with the Ai of the conquest period. Hoping to clarify the problem, Joseph A. Callaway began excavations at the site in 1964. His conclusions regarding the occupational gap were essentially the same as those of his predecessors, however, so the problem still exists.

From Bethel and Ai Abraham journeyed south to the Negev. The Negev of our passage is generally regarded to be the area west and southwest of the Dead Sea. This area is now quite dry and barren, but Glueck's archaeological surveys there demonstrated that the

The northern Negev (Courtesy of Levant Photo Service)

area between Palestine and Egypt was once dotted with many villages. He maintains that this narrative "is the background of the Negev as a land where Abraham and his people could and did sojourn and find means of livelihood for fairly long periods of time, where domesticated beasts could find forage and both men and animals obtain water."[39] According to Glueck's surveys these villages were founded around the beginning of Middle Bronze I in the twenty-first century B.C., and were destroyed about the nineteenth century B.C. This archaeological evidence caused Glueck to conclude: "The flesh and blood personage of Abraham—if indeed he did live, which we have no reason to doubt—could not have existed later than the nineteenth century B.C., at the end of Middle Bronze I, for otherwise there would have been no historical framework into which his life could have been set."[40] Not only were there permanent settlements in the Negev, but apparently peace generally prevailed there.[41] Why Abraham journeyed southward into the Negev is not explained in the text; possibly the famine of verse 10 had already begun.

IV. Abraham's Sojourn in Egypt (12:10–13:4)

Famines were not uncommon in Canaan. During the patriarchal period, there were three major ones (cf. 12:10; 26:1; 41:56). Canaan's agriculture, unlike Egypt's, was dependent upon rain, and at times the November and December rains either failed or were insufficient.[42] Famine resulted in Abraham's migrating to Egypt (v. 10), something which many consider a moral failure on his part. The text says Abraham "went down to Egypt," and they consider the verb "went down" evidence for their interpretation. Many interpret the same verb similarly in Jonah 1:3, 5. But such terms as this describe topography and nothing else. When Abraham traveled from the central hill country through the Negev, he had to go down. So did Jonah when he went from the north hill country near Samaria to Joppa. John writes that the Lord Jesus "went up" to Jerusalem (John 5:11): Are we to assume that Jesus was returning to a higher spiritual position after a period of

---

39. *Rivers in the Desert*, pp. 67, 68; "The Age of Abraham in the Negev," pp. 2—9.
40. *Rivers in the Desert*, p. 68.
41. Ibid., p. 69.
42. Also cf. Ruth 1:1; I Kings 17:1; Hag. 1:10, 11.

failure? Indeed not! If Abraham's trip to Egypt was in some sense a lapse of faith, this is not proven by the verb "went down." [43] Faced with famine, Abraham's decision to go to Egypt was perfectly natural since food was always abundant there. Kidner observes: "It is unrealistic to regard Egypt as necessarily forbidden territory to God's people at this stage, for it was soon to be expressly allotted to them as a refuge and their presence there would not invalidate their claim to Canaan. Abraham had to feel his way forward (vv. 8, 9) without a special revelation at every step, guided like us largely by circumstances (cf. Ruth 1:1; Matt. 12:14, 15). In a famine it might well seem of providence that Egypt was nearby, watered by the flooding of the Nile."[44] One must admit that Abraham seems to have made his decision without consulting God; this was unfortunate because the Lord is perfectly capable and willing to take care of His own during such disasters (cf. Ps. 105:14, 15).

Palestinian Semites coming to Egypt to acquire food were well received only by those native Egyptians who profited from the transactions. The resentment of other Egyptians is clearly expressed in the "Admonitions of Ipu-Wer": "Behold, he who had no grain is (now) the owner of granaries. He who had to get a loan for himself (now) issues it. . . . So lower Egypt weeps. The storehouse of the king is a (mere) come-and-get-it for everybody, and the entire palace is without its taxes."[45] After more lamenting, Ipu-Wer suggests that Asiatics migrating to Egypt for food and water be barred: "There will be built the Wall of the Ruler—life, prosperity, health!—and the Asiatics will not be permitted to come down into Egypt that they might beg for water in the customary manner, in order to let their beasts drink. And justice will come into its place, while wrongdoing is driven out."[46]

As they approached Egypt, Abraham had his wife, Sarah, agree to identify herself as his sister (v. 13): Abraham knew that she was "a fair woman to look upon" and that the king would desire her, and Abraham feared for his life.[47] This seems to be the interpreta-

---

43. Applying moral qualities to the topographical designations of Gen. 19:30 and I Kings 22:20 should clearly demonstrate the folly of such a practice.
44. Derek Kidner, *Genesis*, pp. 115, 116.
45. Pritchard, *ANET*, p. 443.
46. Ibid., p. 446.
47. The beauty of Sarah is a problem because she was 65 years old. It must be remembered, however, that patriarchal life spans were twice what ours are. Abraham died at 175, Sarah at 127. At 65, therefore, Sarah might have had the beauty and vigor of a modern woman of 30.

tion suggested by Moses. However, Speiser notes that in Hurrian society "the bonds of marriage were strongest and most solemn when the wife had simultaneously the judicial status of a sister, regardless of actual blood ties."[48] While there may have been legal advantages to such an adoption in Hurrian society, it is not clear that there were any in either Canaan or Egypt. The only advantage mentioned in the biblical text was the saving of Abraham's life. Speiser assumes that the author of the material was unfamiliar with the traditions of Abraham's day, and that he injected into the narrative embellishments and anachronisms.[49] Until it can be firmly established that Hurrian customs were known and recognized in Egyptian society, we must suspend judgment on Speiser's interpretation.

Of course Sarah was Abraham's half sister (Gen. 20:12), but using half of the truth to disguise the other half must be regarded a lie. Abraham tacitly admitted this when he offered no defense for his act (vv. 18–20). With the true identity of Sarah concealed from him, the king treated Abraham extremely well for her sake, giving him sheep, oxen, servants, and camels (v. 16). In time, however, God "plagued Pharaoh and his house with great plagues" (v. 17). The nature of these plagues is not given but they must have been severe. Apparently the king discovered the full truth about Sarah, and he called for Abraham. As incredible as it sounds, the "father of the faithful" was rebuked by the pagan king. The fact that this incident is included in the text at all illustrates the impartiality of Moses' historiography and proves the uniqueness of Scripture. It is extremely doubtful that an uninspired Hebrew historian would have so emphasized the weaknesses and failures of Abraham. Of course lies for the sake of expediency were not uncommon. They were told by Isaac (Gen. 26:6–10), Rachel (Gen. 31:33–35), the midwives in Egypt (Exod. 1:15–22), Michal (I Sam. 19:14) and David (I Sam. 21:1–5, 8, 9). Some have attempted to justify such lies as means to a good end. The moral nature of a lie, then, should be determined by the situation and not by an "arbitrary, absolute" standard. Such a proposition, however, finds no support in Scripture. It never views a lie in a favorable light. God honors truth. It is presumptuous for a man ever to assume that circumstances might turn out badly if he does not lie. His faith in the providential care of God is weak. Passages such as

177

48. *Genesis*, p. 92.
49. Ibid., p. 93.

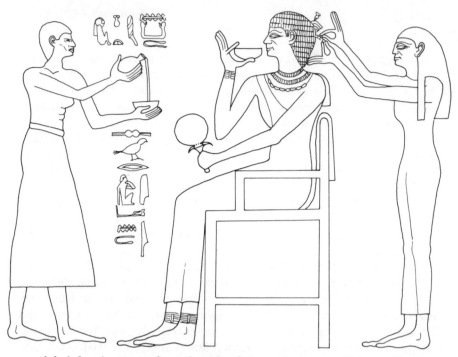

A hairdressing scene from the side of the sarcophagus of Princess Kawit (Eleventh Dynasty). The servant at the left is pouring milk from a flask.

the one at hand admonish us never to succumb to such a temptation. The integrity and honesty of a child of God are among his most potent weapons in spreading the gospel.

We have no specific information on the length of Abraham's sojourn in Egypt, but it probably was not an extended stay. Lot, Sarah, and Abraham's servants went with him back to the Negev (Gen. 13:1). Abraham "was very rich in cattle, in silver, and in gold" (v. 2). He did not stay in the Negev but journeyed on to Bethel, where he had once built an altar and worshiped his God (12:7, 8). This may have been a time of reflection and meditation for Abraham. The very fact that he survived a potentially disastrous situation in Egypt must have been cause for special praise to his God.

V. Abraham's Relationship to Lot (13:5–14:24)

A. Separating from Lot (13:5–18)

178

Lot, like Abraham, possessed flocks, herds, and tents (v. 5). The limited areas available for grazing created a problem, and ultimately it led to strife between the herdsmen of each man (vv. 6,

7). Abraham, Lot's senior, very generously gave Lot first choice of the land available, and Abraham would take what was left (v. 9). This act gives us insight into Abraham's sensitive nature. Lot selected the "plain of Jordan," which apparently was well irrigated and filled with vegetation,[50] while Abraham selected the "land of Canaan." The Jordan Valley, possibly a center for moon worship, was characterized by an unbridled wickedness that centered in the city of Sodom. All indications are that Lot tolerated this decadence but not without vexed conscience (II Peter 2:7, 8). Little did he know that the physical beauty of the area was small compensation for the destruction and calamity yet to come.

When Lot separated from Abraham, God came to Abraham and reaffirmed His covenant promise (vv. 14–17). That, and the emphasis on the immutability of the promise (v. 15), must have greatly consoled Abraham. He then moved northward to Mamre, which was in the vicinity of Hebron, and once again built an altar to the Lord (v. 18). The city of Hebron lies twenty-two miles south of Jerusalem on the road to Beersheba. The antiquity of the site is implied by the fact that it was built seven years before Zoan (Tanis) in Egypt (Num. 13:22).

B. Rescuing Lot (14:1–16)

Many interpreters have dismissed chapter 14 as a historical impossibility and, therefore, as apocryphal. Recent archaeological discoveries and linguistic studies, however, demand the opposite conclusion. Albright notes that "Genesis 14 contains so many archaisms in language, in personal and place names, etc., that it has been long impossible for a serious scholar to deny that its source material must go back to early times. My own attitude toward the historicity of the chapter has oscillated over the decades, but has tended to grow more conservative as new material turns up to elucidate this or that obscurity."[51] Of particular interest is Glueck's identification of some of the cities in Transjordan which, according to the text, were defeated by the kings from the east. This is significant: "Archaeological discovery has thus buttressed the accuracy of the Biblical account of the existence and destruction of this long line of Middle Bronze I cities by the Kings of the

50. Such irrigation systems were in use long before Lot's time. Kenyon, *Archaeology in the Holy Land*, pp. 45, 46.
51. *Archaeology, Historical Analogy and Early Biblical Tradition*, p. 26.

179

East. Particularly remarkable and worthy of special emphasis is the fact that all of them were destroyed at the end of that period in the nineteenth century B.C., with only a few of them having ever been reoccupied."[52]

Some scholars have attempted to trace the material in this chapter to a poetic original, or to an Akkadian document written in cuneiform. J. A. Emerton finds the arguments for both unconvincing and considers them false clues to the chapter's correct interpretation.[53]

One of the four kings who invaded Sodom and its environs was Amraphel. Commentators once identified him with Hammurabi, but this seems untenable on two grounds: (1) Hammurabi did not reign until the mid-eighteenth century B.C. at the earliest, and this is too late for the Abrahamic period; and (2) a philological identification between *Amraphel* and *Hammurabi* has its difficulties. The names do, however, fit the general pattern of names established by recent discoveries in Babylon and nearby city-states.[54]

The invasion was successful, and for twelve years these kings dominated that territory (v. 4). Then a revolt brought the kings back to the Jordan Valley, and they soundly defeated the rebel kings, taking much booty and some captives—including Lot (vv. 5–12). One of Lot's countrymen escaped and brought word of the tragedy to Abraham (v. 13). (Abraham is referred to in verse 13 as "the Hebrew," a common thing for outsiders to call Israelites [cf. 34:14], and for Israelites to call themselves around foreigners [40:15; 43:32]). Abraham responded by arming "his trained servants, born in his own house, three hundred and eighteen. . . ." Some have attempted to find mystical significance in the number 318, but they have been unsuccessful.[55] That Abraham selected servants "born in his own house" does have significance. Such servants are normally given more freedom and responsibility than those captured during warfare. To free Lot, Abraham had to travel far north to the city of Dan, a long, difficult journey. (The name *Dan*

---

52. *Rivers in the Desert,* p. 74. Also see Glueck, "Abraham in the Negev," pp. 6–9.
53. "Some False Clues in the Study of Genesis XIV," pp. 24–47.
54. Free, *Archaeology and Bible History,* p. 57.
55. This is discussed in John J. Davis, *Biblical Numerology,* pp. 142, 143. From a reference in an Egyptian inscription to a Mitannian princess and a retinue of 317 girls, Gordon concludes that "318 looks like a conventional number for a large group." "The Patriarchal Narratives," p. 57. His conclusions seems a bit premature.

is here substituted for *Laish*, the original name [cf. Josh. 19:47]; the very fact place names have been editorially updated [cf. v. 2] is strong evidence for this chapter's antiquity.) Abraham was completely successful in freeing Lot and his servants (v. 16). This episode again shows the unique character of Abraham. He could have let Lot remain in captivity as vengeance for the difficulties Lot had caused him. But whatever weaknesses Abraham had, vindictiveness was not one of them.

C. Meeting Melchizedek (14:17—24)

When Abraham returned from his venture, he was met by the kings of the Jordan Valley. One of them, Melchizedek, king of Salem and "priest of the most high God," brought Abraham bread and wine. This priest-king blessed Abraham and received tithes from him, and was therefore superior to him. This remarkable individual appears abruptly and is described only briefly. He is mentioned elsewhere in Scripture only in Psalm 110:4 and Hebrews 7:1ff. His identity has been the subject of considerable debate. There have been four basic proposals: (1) he was a theophany of the preincarnate Christ; (2) he was a historical, human person who typified Christ; (3) he was a Canaanite priest; and (4) he was Shem.[56] The fourth proposal is the least likely; the second is the most likely.[57] The titles for God in verses 18 and 19 demonstrate that Melchizedek worshiped no Canaanite god. "Most high God [*'ēl 'elyôn*]" emphasizes God's strength and sovereignty, distinguishing Him from the gods of Canaan who were subject to the same weaknesses as their worshipers. "Possessor of heaven and earth" is similar to titles used in Daniel 4.

After the king of Sodom, the first one to meet Abraham (v. 17), gave precedence to Melchizedek, he requested that Abraham keep the goods he had recovered but return the king's subjects. Abraham refused to keep anything, not wanting to obligate himself in any way to this wicked king (v. 23). Perhaps Abraham was better able to refuse the king's gifts after his experience in Egypt. His

---

56. Howard B. Rand, *Primogenesis*, p. 65. Rand also suggests that the bread and wine brought by Melchizedek were for "the celebration of what was afterward known as the Lord's Supper." Ibid., p. 66.
57. This problem is discussed more completely in Homer A. Kent, Jr., *The Epistle to the Hebrews* (Grand Rapids: Baker Book House, 1972), pp. 123–35; Fisher, "Abraham and His Priest-King," pp. 264–70; John G. Gammie, "Loci of the Melchizedek Tradition of Genesis 14:18–20," pp. 385–96.

refusal showed that his motivation in warfare was loftier than that of the ungodly. The believer can learn an important lesson from this narrative: the gifts of the ungodly are often attached to deadly strings. May God grant each of us the power to keep our eyes on the Author and Finisher of our faith and to look constantly for "a better country, that is, an heavenly" (Heb. 11:16).

12

Covenant Renewal

Genesis 15–17

Believers have often found themselves in the gulf between divine promise and personal experience: God's promise is clear but circumstances do not seem to be leading to its fulfillment. The failure in these situations is not God's but man's. What is true of believers today was true of Abraham. God had given him a great promise, but events raised such deep questions in his heart that he began to fear (15:1). Traveling through a strange land was not easy. A famine had driven him to Egypt, and he had left in humiliation. Back in Canaan he had mediated a serious dispute between his men and Lot's. The invasion of the kings from the east and Lot's capture had also complicated things. Surely Abraham, like many of us, was perplexed about how circumstances could possibly fulfill God's promises to him. In chapters 15–17 God resolved that dilemma. Chapter 15 is especially important, for the apostle Paul built his case for justification by faith on it (cf. Rom. 4 and Gal. 3).

This section of Genesis greatly frustrates those scholars who are given to source analysis. Skinner remarked many years ago that chapter 15 "shows unmistakable signs of composition, but the analysis is beset with peculiar, and perhaps insurmountable, difficulties."[1] Von Rad observed more recently but similarly: "The source analysis of the text of this chapter is very difficult. . . . We have given the text in its present form (a satisfactory source analysis seems absolutely impossible); but the variations in the narratives before and after the chief joint [between verses 6 and 7] will occupy us in the theology of our interpretation."[2] The language and flow of the text are such that there seems to be no difficulty with assuming it to be a single literary unit. Its vocabulary and style are in harmony with the rest of the book and, therefore, should be considered Mosaic in origin.

I. The Covenant Reaffirmed (15:1–21)

A. A Promised Heir (15:1–6)

After Abraham's difficulties with Lot, the Lord appeared to Abraham "in a vision [*maḥᵃzeh*]" (15:1). This was the fifth revelation of God to the patriarch.[3] *Maḥᵃzeh* appears elsewhere only in Numbers 24:4, 16, and in Ezekiel 13:7, and it always seems to refer to a divinely initiated vision. In any event, this was the means by which God communicated with Abraham, assuring him in his adversity that God was his "shield and exceedingly great reward." This phrase indicates that God would both protect him and fulfill all the covenant promises to him. Abraham's response indicated the depth of his concern about his lack of a son and heir. He addressed God as "Lord Jehovah" (ASV). Abraham was the first to combine '*ᵃḏōnāy* and *YHWH*, and this gives us some insight into Abraham's theology. He called God "Lord" because He was his master; he called God "Jehovah" because He had given him the covenant promises. Abraham clearly had no doubts about God's omnipotence.

Abraham asked God if "the heir of my house is Eliezer of Damascus?" (v. 2). This is a difficult clause in the Hebrew text, although verse 3 does explain it.[4] Abraham was suggesting that

1. *A Critical and Exegetical Commentary on Genesis*, p. 276.
2. *Genesis*, pp. 177, 178.
3. H. C. Leupold, *Exposition of Genesis*, 1:471.
4. For further study of the problem and suggested solutions see E. A. Speiser, *Genesis*, pp. 111, 112; H. L. Ginsberg, "Abram's 'Damascene' Steward," pp. 31, 32; Otto Eissfeldt, "The Alphabetical Cuneiform Texts from Ras Shamra Published in 'Le Palais Royal d'Ugarit,'" p. 48; and C. F. Keil and Franz Delitzsch, *Biblical Commentary on the Old Testament*, 25 vols. (Edinburgh: T. and T. Clark, 1864–1901), 1:211.

Eliezer, "one born in his house [*ben bêṯî*]" become his heir. *Ben bêṯî* means literally "son of my house" (cf. in 14:14 *yᵉlî ḏê ḇêṯô*, "home born"). Childlessness, of course, was always considered by oriental women the greatest tragedy. But Abraham was concerned primarily about a male heir to inherit his present possessions and, even more significantly, the future blessings promised by God. Influenced by human values, Abraham concluded that he and Sarah were beyond the point of childbearing and therefore should "adopt" a son for an heir. Perhaps there is a touch of impatience here, but Abraham's solution of adopting an heir was a well-known practice in Mesopotamia. Wealthy but childless couples adopted one of their slaves to inherit their property and also to care for them in old age. A number of such "adoption tablets" have been found at Nuzi, which is identified with the mound Yorghan Tepe located about ten miles southwest of modern Kirkuk in Iraq. Excavations were begun there in 1925 by the American Schools of Oriental Research in Baghdad; in charge was Edward Chiera. Harvard University and the University Museum of Pennsylvania further excavated the site from 1927 through 1931. The Hurrian culture which dominated the site has left us with literary materials invaluable for illuminating patriarchal customs. There were two types of adoption in ancient Nuzi. The first, "sale-adoption" or "fictive adoption," was no more than a formal exchange of property. The second, "real adoption," was a childless couple adopting a servant—or any other young man, for that matter—who would receive their inheritance. One "adoption tablet" reads: "The tablet of adoption belonging to [Zike], the son of Akkuya: he gave his son Shennima in adoption to Shuriha-ilu, and Shuriha-ilu, with reference to Shennima, (from) all the lands . . . (and) his earnings of every sort gave to Shennima one (portion) of his property. If Shuriha-ilu should have a son of his own, as the principal (son) he shall take a double share; Shennima shall then be next in order (and) take his proper share. As long as Shuriha-ilu is alive, Shennima shall revere him. When Shuriha-ilu [dies], Shennima shall become the heir."[5] While this practice may have been commonly accepted, God did not choose to use it to fulfill

---

5. "Mesopotamian Legal Documents," translated by Theophile J. Meek, in Pritchard, *ANET*, p. 220. On this custom also see S. Kardimon, "Adoption as a Remedy for Infertility in the Period of the Patriarchs," pp. 123—36; Cyrus H. Gordon, "Biblical Customs and the Nuzu Tablets," pp. 1—12; Gordon, "The Patriarchal Narratives," pp. 56—59; and Clifford A. Wilson, "The Problems of Childlessness in Near Eastern Law," pp. 106—14.

His promises to Abraham: "This shall not be thine heir" (v. 4). Abraham's heir would be his own child, not an adopted servant.

To strengthen the faith of Abraham and enlarge his vision, God encouraged him to look at the vast expanses of the heavens and "count the stars." This is not a bad idea for any believer who is suffering frustration and hardship. Numerous trips to Palestine have demonstrated to this writer its value. The Palestinian sky is unclouded by pollutants, and the evening stars are magnificent. Sitting in an open space on the Judean hills, one feels he can almost touch the myriad stars before him. Probably just such an experience caused David to declare, "The heavens declare the glory of God" (Ps. 19:1). God promised Abraham a seed as innumerable as the stars (cf. 22:17; 26:4; Exod. 32:13).[6] This helped Abraham reaffirm his faith. He may still have questioned how God would fulfill His promise, but he "believed in the Lord" (v. 6). This reveals much about the nature of true faith. It does not ignore natural processes, but it does recognize that God is superior to them all and can alter them to suit His purposes. Abraham believed, and God justified him, or declared him righteous. We probably should not consider this the first exercise of saving faith; that probably occurred when God first called Abraham in Ur (cf. Heb. 11:8–10). The fact that he was justified fourteen years before he was circumcised is the basis for Paul's argument that circumcision is a sign of faith, not a basis for justification (Rom. 4:9–12).

B. A Promised Land (15:7–21)

With the matter of an heir settled, God proceeded to reaffirm His promise of an inheritance, reminding Abraham that He had "brought him out of Ur to make this land his inheritance. Again, unsure of how this would be accomplished, Abraham asked, "Whereby shall I know that I shall inherit it?" This request for a sign has often been understood as further evidence of extremely weak faith, but this is both a harsh and unnecessary conclusion. Requests for signs were not unusual in Old Testament times. They were not so much to discover God's will as to confirm it. Such signs were requested by Gideon (Judg. 6:17, 36–40) and Hezekiah (II Kings 20:8; contrast this with Ahaz' attitude in Isa. 7:12). Far

6. On this phrase see Allan A. MacRae, "Abraham and the Stars," pp. 97–100.

from being a symptom of unbelief or doubt, it expressed heartfelt longing to see God fulfill His covenant promises. To visibly confirm His covenant, God condescended to the customary practice of walking between the divided parts of animals (thus the expression "to cut a covenant" for "to make a covenant" [v. 18]). The two parties to a covenant would pass between the pieces of butchered animals to confirm their agreement (cf. Jer. 34:18, 19).[7] In the instance at hand, however, only God, in the form of "a smoking furnace and a burning lamp," walked; Abraham did not because God's promises to him were unconditional. He was responsible only to set the scene and guard it from violation (v. 11). The symbols of God's presence (v. 17) were eminently appropriate, reflecting the awesome power and absolute holiness of God. Note, for example, the symbols of His presence witnessed by Israel at Sinai (Exod. 19:1–19) and by Isaiah (Isa. 6:3–5).

"When the sun was going down" (v. 12), Abraham fell into a "deep sleep" and was struck with the horror of the darkness. The same Hebrew expression translated here "deep sleep" is employed in 2:21 to describe Adam's divinely induced unconscious state during the creation of Eve. It is not clear whether Abraham's deep sleep was also divinely induced, but it may well have been (cf. I Sam. 26:12). The nature of the great darkness which overwhelmed him is not described, but in all likelihood it was designed to impress upon Abraham the great difficulties his posterity would experience in Egypt (v. 13). God told him that his seed would sojourn in a foreign land for about 400 years (in all likelihood this is 430 rounded off [cf. Exod. 12:40]). Then they would be freed and would "come out with great substance" (v. 14), a prophecy which was literally fulfilled (cf. Exod. 12:34–36). God promised Abraham a long life (v. 15), and explained that not until his seed was in the fourth generation would it enter Canaan and conquer its inhabitants, "for the iniquity of the Amorites is not yet full" (v. 16). This helps put the conquest into perspective. The campaigns under Joshua were not purely militaristic or nationalistic; they were also judicial, as verse 16 clearly states.[8]

The boundaries of the promised land are given in Scripture for the first time in verses 18–21. While these boundaries were

---

7. In Mari the expression "to slay an ass" was idiomatic for "to enter into a compact." Apparently asses were cut in pieces for purposes of making covenants. See George E. Mendenhall, "Puppy and Lettuce in Northwest-Semitic Covenant Making," pp. 26–30.
8. John J. Davis, *Conquest and Crisis*, pp. 48–50.

approached in David's reign, they will not be reached until the Lord returns and establishes His kingdom. One of the borders is the "river of Egypt"—that is, the Nile. Elsewhere this border is a wadi, or brook (*naḥal*), the modern Wadi el-Arish (cf. Num. 34:5; Josh. 15:4, 47). The northern boundary is the Euphrates. The Kenites and Kenizzites of verse 19 were tribal groups which Judah eventually absorbed.

II. The Birth of Ishmael (16:1–16)

10 yrs. in Canaan

Ten years had elapsed since God's original promise of an heir (16:3), and Abraham and Sarah became even more concerned. Once again they resorted to a contemporary custom to resolve the dilemma. The childless Sarah gave her Egyptian slave, Hagar, to Abraham as a concubine, a practice widely sanctioned in the ancient Near East (see also Gen. 30:3). Hagar is introduced in the text without lengthy explanation. Her name was Hebrew, not Egyptian; perhaps she was given this name, which means "flight," after joining Abraham and Sarah on their flight from Egypt. The Code of Hammurabi allowed a priestess of the *naditum* rank, who was free to marry but not have children, to give to her husband a female slave by whom he could have children: "When a seignior married a hierodule and she gave a female slave to her husband and she has then borne children, if later that female slave has claimed equality with her mistress because she bore children, her mistress may not sell her; she may mark her with the slave-mark and count her among the slaves."[9] While this provision illustrates the general practice, it is less pertinent than a custom at Nuzi. One text reads: "If Gilimninu fails to bear children, Gilimninu shall get for Shennima a woman from the Lullu country (i.e., a slave girl) as concubine. In that case, Gilimninu herself shall have authority over the offspring. . . ."[10] Of course, establishing the existence of the custom does not justify it.

From the union of Hagar and Abraham a son was conceived. The dispute which then erupted between Sarah and Hagar (which reminds us of that between Hannah and Peninnah in I Samuel 1:2–18) evidently was common; the Code of Hammurabi even made provision for a settlement between the wife and her slave

188

9. Translated by Theophile J. Meek, in Pritchard, *ANET*, p. 172 (paragraph 149). Also cf. paragraphs 144, 145, 170, and 171.
10. Translated by Speiser in *Genesis*, p. 120.

girl. As far as Sarah was concerned, the continuing presence of Hagar and Ishmael in her household threatened her position and authority. Not wanting to become embroiled in the dispute, which was legally Sarah's to settle, Abraham suggested that she do to Hagar "as it pleaseth thee." So Sarah made life difficult for Hagar, perhaps by returning her to slave status (which the Code of Hammurabi permitted the wife to do) and making unrealistic demands upon her.[11] In any event, Hagar was forced to flee, and she got as far as the wilderness on the way to Shur (v. 7), near the Egyptian border (20:1; 25:13).

It is not surprising that Hagar fled toward her native homeland. Before she reached it, however, she met "the angel of the Lord." This is usually understood as a preincarnate appearance of the second person of the trinity, and the angel's character, deeds, and power confirm this interpretation. After a brief inquiry and response, the angel recommended that Hagar return and submit to her mistress (v. 9), and promised that the seed of Hagar would be multiplied exceedingly (v. 10). Then the Lord named her unborn son *Ishmael*, which meant "God hears" and was intended to remind Hagar of God's special intervention in her behalf. Ishmael was the first unborn child named by God, but not the last (cf. Gen. 17:19; Luke 1:13; 13:31). Many Arabs claim Ishmael as their father and, therefore, Palestine as their land. The prophetic description of Ishmael as "a wild ass of a man" (RSV) is rather intriguing. The animal referred to is the wild and untameable onager, which roams the desert at will. This figure of speech depicts very accurately the freedom-loving Bedouin moving across vast stretches of land. When Hagar finally gave birth to Ishmael (v. 15), Abraham was eighty-six years old. Eleven years had passed since God first promised an heir, and His promise was still unfulfilled.

III. The Covenant Again Reaffirmed (17:1–27)

A. The Maker of the Covenant: Almighty God (17:1–3)

After Ishmael's birth God was silent for thirteen more years (17:1). This long silence could well have been a test of Abraham's faith, or it could have been "a remedial penalty for Abram's

189

---

11. Some have defended Sarah's actions on the basis of the "Law Code of Lipit-Ishtar" (ca. 1850 B.C.), paragraphs 24–27. In Pritchard, *ANET*, p. 160.

impatience in not waiting for God to work things out in His own good time and way."[12] When God appeared to Abraham (exactly how He appeared we are not told), He identified Himself as "the Almighty God" ('*ēl šadday*). Commentators do not agree on the significance of this divine name. It appears forty-eight times in the Hebrew Bible, nine times in the Pentateuch and thirty-one in Job. The prevailing view, that it comes from the Akkadian *šadû* ("mountain"), was proposed by Friedrich Delitzsch in his *Prolegomena* (1886) and developed and popularized by Albright in an important article which appeared in 1935.[13] A second view has it mean "God ['*ēl*] who [*ša-*] is sufficient [*day*]."[14] A third traces *šadday* to the Hebrew *šad* ("breast").[15] The fourth and most appropriate traces *šadday* to the root *šādad*, "to be strong or powerful."[16] The strongest support for this contention is furnished by the contexts of the term in its forty-eight occurrences. The majority seem to emphasize some aspect of God's power and might. Of the six times the word is used in Genesis, it is almost always connected with some divine blessing; the fulfillment of these blessings seems contingent on the power and omnipotence of God. In Ruth 1:20, 21 and Job,[17] it clearly emphasizes the Lord's might and power: in Job 37:23 Shaddai is characterized as "excellent in power." Its use in Psalms 68:14 and 91:1 is also related to this general idea. In the majority of cases it is translated in the Septuagint "the Almighty." For God to so identify Himself at this point in Abraham's life was both appropriate and significant. It was also a fitting introduction to God's reaffirmation of His covenant.

After identifying Himself, God specifically instructed Abraham to be "perfect" (*tāmîm*). *Tāmîm* here means "upright, blameless, or mature"; in Genesis 6:9 Moses used it to describe Noah. While

---

12. Francis D. Nichol, ed., *The Seventh-Day Adventist Bible Commentary* 1:320.

13. "The Names *Shaddai* and *Abram*," pp. 180–93. Also see Albright, *From the Stone Age to Christianity* (Baltimore: The Johns Hopkins Press, 1940), p. 185.

14. Derek Kidner, *Genesis*, p. 128.

15. Andrew Jukes, *The Names of God*, p. 66.

16. Gustav F. Oehler, *Theology of the Old Testament* (New York: Funk and Wagnalls, 1883; reprinted by Zondervan Publishing House, n.d.), p. 90; Keil and Delitzsch, *Biblical Commentary*, 1:223; and C. J. Ellicott, *Ellicott's Commentary on the Whole Bible*, ed. R. Payne Smith (Grand Rapids: Zondervan Publishing House, 1954), p. 70.

17. Job 5:17; 6:4, 14; 8:2; 15:25; 21:20; 22:25; 23:16; 27:2; 34:12.

God reaffirmed His covenant again (v. 2), a humbled Abraham fell on his face (v. 3).

B. The Beneficiary of the Covenant: Abraham (17:4, 5)

The literary formula "as for me" according to Kidner reflects God's part in the covenant-making procedure.[18] God's blessing and promise are unconditional, depending not on the genius or capabilities of Abraham, but on the faithfulness of God. This was so important that God changed the patriarch's name from *Abram*, "exalted father," to *Abraham*, "father of the multitude." *Abraham* has generally been associated with two roots: *'ab* and *raham* (Arabic *ruham*, "multitude"). The word *rûham*, meaning "great number" does not occur in ancient Hebrew literature now available, but it may have existed in ancient Hebrew nonetheless.[19] The last phrase of verse 5 seems to associate Abraham's new name with the special covenant promise of a numerous progeny.

C. The Sign of the Covenant: Circumcision (17:6–14)

In verses 6–14 God reiterated the covenant He had established with Abraham fourteen years earlier (Gen. 15), repeating and emphasizing certain aspects of it. This is no common covenant; it is "everlasting" (v. 7), and the land which it promises will be an "everlasting possession" (v. 8). This has much theological significance. Verses 9–14 stipulate Abraham's part in the covenant-making process: he was to circumcise eight days after birth every male child born in his house, whether to him or to his servants (vv. 10–12). To refuse was to break the covenant (v. 14).

It has been alleged that this passage, Exodus 4:24ff., and Joshua 5:2ff. offer conflicting accounts of the origin of circumcision. However, the last two passages clearly do not discuss its origin. As a ritual it was, first of all, a spiritual sign, and then of course a national sign. All members of the covenant community were expected to demonstrate their faith by this sign. But the rite outlived the memory of its significance, which is why the apostle

191

---

18. *Genesis*, p. 129.
19. Nichol, ed., *Bible Commentary*, 1:321, 322; Albright, "The Names *Shaddai* and *Abram*," pp. 193–204.

Paul pointed out that circumcision apart from obedience is uncircumcision (Rom. 2:25–29).

Circumcision was not unique to the Hebrews. It was practiced by Egyptians, Edomites, Ammonites, Moabites, and some other nomadic peoples (cf. Jer. 9:25). The Philistines, of course, did not practice it and were commonly designated "the uncircumcised" (cf. II Sam. 1:20). Nor was this custom in vogue in Mesopotamia.

D. The Promise of the Covenant: Isaac (17:15–27)

God changed Sarah's name as well as Abraham's (v. 15), but this change was less significant: her old name, *Sarai*, meant "my princess," and her new name, *Sarah*, meant "a princess." Why her name was changed the text does not say; maybe it was simply to mark the occasion as important.[20] The Lord promised to bless Sarah with a son, whose offspring would make her the mother of nations and kings (v. 16). Abraham's response has perplexed commentators: he laughed and said, "shall a child be born unto him that is an hundred years old? and shall Sarah, that is ninety years old, bear?" (v. 17). Was his laughter an expression of joy or doubt? Calvin thought the former: "Hence also we infer that he laughed, not because he either despised, or regarded as fabulous, or rejected, the promise of God; but, as is commonly wont to happen in things which are least expected, partly exulting with joy, and partly being carried beyond himself in admiration, he breaks forth into laughter."[21] However, Abraham's attempt to steer God toward a more realistic path (v. 18) and God's response to that (vv. 19–21) are more consistent with a laughter of incredulity or skepticism than of rejoicing. This was one of many great struggles of faith experienced by godly men. It was momentary and spontaneous. Abraham's earlier suggestion that Eliezer be his heir had been rejected (15:2–4), so he offered another suggestion: Ishmael. However suitable it may have seemed to Abraham, it was completely unsuitable to God. The recipient of His covenant blessings, God said unequivocally, would be a son named Isaac born to Sarah (v. 19). The idea of a 100-year-old man fathering a son should not have sounded strange to Abraham; when he was

20. On this change see von Rad, *Genesis*, p. 197; and Speiser, *Genesis*, p. 125.
21. *Genesis*, trans. John King (Grand Rapids: Wm. B. Eerdmans Co., 1948), pp. 459, 460.

born his father had been 130, and Abraham himself would father sons by a second wife when he was more than 137 years old—his age when Sarah died (Gen. 25:1–6).

God then repeated to Abraham what He had already told Hagar (Gen. 16:10–13): Ishmael would be the father of a great nation (17:20). If the Arabs are in fact the descendants of Ishmael, we can fully appreciate this divine promise, for the Arabs have become both numerous and great. The West owes much, for example, to Arab medical technology. However, the promise of national greatness must be distinguished from that of the covenant. Verse 21 does just that: "But my covenant will I establish with Isaac." This in no way implies racial inferiority; it indicates only that God's elective purposes will be fulfilled through the descendants of Isaac. This statement, along with the previous one, definitely tested Abraham's faith and commitment. Moses records no response from him; when the Lord finished speaking, He left (v. 22). The end result of this encounter with God was the strengthening of Abraham's faith. He, his servants, and his thirteen-year-old son Ishmael were circumcised (vv. 24–27).

Abraham had his spiritual lapses, but they were always brief and they were always followed by victories which vindicated his inclusion in Hebrews 11. He did not understand the natural processes by which all of God's promises would be fulfilled, but he was "fully assured that what he had promised he was able to perform" (Rom. 4:21).

It is strange indeed that believers throughout the ages have been so slow to meet God's minimal requirements when the blessings have been so great. In fact it is incredible that we stumble over the smallest obstacles when God has provided more than enough strength to overcome them. Abraham's experiences should teach us that natural law is no barrier to the purposes and plans for God. A miracle cannot be scientifically analyzed or explained. For this reason God asked Abraham, as He asks us, simply to believe, and He rewards faith with great blessing.

13

The Destruction of Sodom

Genesis 18, 19

As we approached the crest of the hill in the 110-degree heat, we saw the most welcome sight of the afternoon, the little black tent of our Bedouin friend, Muhammad Radin. That he would warmly welcome us was beyond question; more than once we had been the benefactors of the warm hospitality of the Ta'amri Bedouin who roam these hills. After the usual introductions and greetings we were invited into the large section of the tent where other men were seated on a large, ornate rug. We joined them and enjoyed hot tea prepared in typical Bedouin fashion. On the other side of a partition the ladies talked excitedly as they prepared a meal. The whole scene was reminiscent of Abraham's intimate fellowship with his three visitors, as recorded in Genesis 18.

The eighteenth chapter of Genesis contrasts with the nineteenth, the former depicting Abraham's tender, sensitive fellowship with his guests; the latter, God's awesome judgment and violent destruction of wicked Sodom. Perhaps this contrast can give us new glimpses into God's character and activities. On one hand He fellowships with us as He did with Abraham, but on the other our infinitely holy God is moved by, and concerned about, the wickedness of this world. When Abraham captured that heart-

195

beat of his divine visitor, he interceded with God. Could it be that our generation's seeming inability to intercede effectively is due to a lack of personal, continuous fellowship with the Savior?

I. Abraham's Fellowship with God (18:1–22)

Our introduction to the scene is brief but effective. "The Lord [*YHWH*] appeared" to Abraham by the oaks of Mamre when the patriarch was resting quietly in front of his tent on a typically hot day for that region. His visitor was called *YHWH*, although in the rest of the narrative Abraham calls him *'ᵃdōnāy*. The exact location of the oaks of Mamre is unknown today, but they were in the vicinity of Hebron (cf. 13:18). The oak trees grew freely and made the area attractive enough for Abraham to spend considerable time there. And as we observed earlier, Abraham's sojourn in Palestine was characterized not by palaces and temples but by tents and altars.

A. His Guests (18:2)

When Abraham saw three men approaching his tent, he ran to meet them and bowed himself to the ground. One of the three was the Lord Himself, and the other two were angels (cf. Gen. 19:1, 15; Heb. 13:2) who looked like men (Gen. 19:10, 12, 16). Some commentators argue that the three men were the three persons of the trinity, but their argument is unconvincing. Some question whether Abraham immediately recognized who his three visitors were. The Masoretes who pointed the Hebrew text seem to have had little doubt that Abraham promptly recognized one of his visitors as the Lord; they pointed *'ᵃdōnāy* ("my Lord" in v. 3) like a plural noun, a common designation for deity. But Speiser disagrees,[1] and both the context and Hebrews 13:2 ("some have entertained angels unawares") seem to bear him out. Perhaps Abraham's experience was similar to that of Samson's father, Manoah, who conversed with the Angel of the Lord for some time before realizing it was the Lord Himself (cf. Judg. 13:15–23). Abraham's bowing to his visitors (v. 2), then, was nothing more than his expression of humility to all his visitors.

196

---

1. *Genesis*, p. 129.

B. His Hospitality (18:3–8)

After exchanging appropriate greetings, Abraham addressed one of the visitors as "my Lord" ($^{a}\underline{d}\bar{o}n\bar{a}y$), a respectful form of greeting. The expression "if now I have found favor" was often used when talking to someone of higher rank or when honoring someone; Abraham's use of it furnishes no evidence that he recognized one of his visitors to be a theophany.[2] Abraham's concern that his visitors not pass him by is typical of oriental hospitality. After their feet were washed and a place arranged for their rest (v. 4), Abraham arranged a meal for his guests. With considerable haste he put a number of people to work on the project. Grinding and baking were women's tasks, but butchering was done by the men. Abraham selected a calf from his herd and then prepared drinks and trimmings for the meal. His visitors accepted his hospitality to prove to him that this was no mere dream or vision.[3]

C. His Wife's Denial (18:9–19)

The visitors' question, "Where is Sarah?" was out of keeping with oriental custom, since strangers would neither know nor use a wife's given name. The fact that they knew Sarah's name indicated that they were not mere men and that the purpose of their visit had to do with her. She was "in the tent" but in another section of the tent and out of view; oriental women were commonly near where men and guests were seated but not visible. Even today Bedouin women will sit close to the partition and listen to the conversation between the men in the other section, and Sarah was evidently "listening" in the same way (v. 10 RSV).

The visitor's promise to "certainly return unto thee according to the time of life" (v. 10) can mean that he would return in one year (cf. Rom. 9:9 and the Septuagint or that he would return in nine months, the normal period of pregnancy. In either case Sarah would have given birth by then. Verse 11 is parenthetical, providing a reason for the response of Sarah noted in the next verse: ". . . Sarah laughed within herself." Her laugh was clearly derisive, suggesting

---

2. This same expression was also used by Laban (30:27), Jacob (32:5; 33:8, 10, 15; 47:29), Shechem (34:11), and the Egyptians (47:25).
3. Josephus (*Antiquities,* 1:11:2) and others say that the guests only appeared to eat.

that Abraham either had not told her of the promise (17:6, 19) or failed to convince her that it could be kept. The visitor's ability to discern Sarah's inner laughter when he could not even see her proved conclusively that he was the Lord Himself (vv. 12, 13). His response to Sarah—"Is anything too hard for the Lord?"—proves that Sarah's laughter expressed unbelief. The visitor's question was similar to the angel's statement to Mary: "For with God nothing is impossible" (Luke 1:37). When Sarah realized that she may have offended her guest, she denied that she had laughed (v. 15). The fact that she would even attempt to deny the act indicates that her laugh and remark of verse 12 were scarcely audible, if not inaudible. The visitor's surprising detection of her attitude had forced her into "a moment of confusion from which she sought escape by the route of falsehood."[4] Sarah's denial was quickly rebuffed and the conversation ended. The visitor left, Abraham with them, and headed for Sodom (v. 16). Abraham was the friend of God (II Chron. 20:7; Isa. 41:8), and this is evident in the intimate revelation recorded in verses 17ff. Since he sustained such a close relationship to his Lord, God thought it appropriate to reveal to him the impending judgment. The Lord's confidence in Abraham is further delineated in verse 19. What a tribute it is to be evaluated by the Lord Himself as faithful, obedient, and consistent.

D. His Intercession for Sodom (18:20–33)

The great "cry of Sodom and Gomorrah" could refer to the outcry against it (as the RSV interprets it) or simply to the evil which was so apparent in the cities. The same expression occurs in 19:13. Verse 21 implies not that God was uninformed about what was going on in the city, but that He would handle the situation justly. He already knew the city was wicked (13:13), but He wanted to demonstrate that His decision to destroy it was fully justified and not arbitrary. Then two of the travelers continued toward Sodom while the Lord Himself remained with Abraham (v. 22). When "Abraham drew near [*nāgaš*]," he did more than draw close physically. *Nāgaš* is often used in the Old Testament of the mind and heart reaching out toward God in worship and confession (cf. Exod. 30:20; Isa. 29:13; Jer. 30:21). Hebrews 4:16 and

198

---

4. Francis D. Nichol, ed., *The Seventh-Day Adventist Bible Commentary*, 1:328.

James 4:8 express the same idea. Abraham's inquiry, "Wilt thou also destroy the righteous with the wicked?" is a supreme example of his sensitive concern for those about him. We observed this same characteristic during his dispute with Lot (chapter 13).

The nature and context of Abraham's intercessory prayer are eminently instructive for believers today. Far too often we pray as if we must overcome God's reluctance rather than seize upon His willingness. The fact that God was the one to bring up the situation in Sodom is revealing. It may further be observed that intercessory prayer is only effective when one realizes how awesome the judgment of God is. It is extremely difficult, if not impossible, to pray effectively for lost souls if one is not convinced that lostness will ultimately result in literal, eternal punishment.

Abraham was concerned about the "righteous" of Sodom and Gomorrah. Indeed he had an underlying concern for Lot, but his sense of justice did not stop with his nephew. One should not get the impression that Abraham was merely haggling with God; his questions were exploratory and perceptive. He knew well that God would judge the city in righteousness and justice, but he was not familiar with the situation in Sodom. His supposition of fifty righteous men in the city (v. 24) might have been based on Lot's potential influence. Lot's decision to live in Sodom, a city known for its wickedness (13:13), had been a gross impropriety, but II Peter 2:7 makes it clear that Lot was a righteous man. He was a believer, and Abraham had great concern for him. Abraham continued to intercede, reducing the number of righteous men as low as ten (v. 32). Abraham wanted to know if God would spare the city for a mere handful of righteous men, and the answer was a resounding yes. It should always be remembered that God's attitude is, "As I live . . . I have no pleasure in the death of the wicked; but that the wicked turn from his way and live" (Ezek. 33:11). With his question answered, Abraham ended his prayer and the two separated (v. 33).[5]

It may be well to reflect upon these verses. Why did God reveal to Abraham His decision to destroy the cities of the plain? Several observations can be made: (1) The Lord wanted to call to Abraham's attention the nature and extent of human depravity. (2) He

---

5. Further discussion of Abraham's intercession is in L. Paul Moore, Jr., "Prayer in the Pentateuch," pp. 329–34; and Reginald E. O. White, *They Teach Us To Pray*, pp. 13–23.

wanted to impress upon Abraham that His absolute holiness required Him to judge such unbridled wickedness. (3) He wanted Abraham to understand fully that His judgment was perfectly just; thus the Lord went to "see" (v. 21) the wickedness of the Sodomites, to see if "they have done altogether according to the cry of it." (4) He wanted Abraham to learn that He responded to intercession of others. The psalmist expressed the same truth: "Therefore he said that he would destroy them, had not Moses his chosen stood before him in the breach, to turn away his wrath, lest he should destroy them" (106:23).

As we shall see, the intercession of Abraham was not fruitless: Lot and his immediate family were delivered by sovereign grace. And many others have followed Abraham's example: Moses and Samuel both stood in the gap before God to turn away His wrath (Jer. 15:1; Ezek. 22:30). Perhaps the lack of spiritual power and effective witness in the church today is caused primarily by the lack of sufficient intercessory prayer.

II. Sodom's Judgment by God (19:1–38)

A. Sodom's Wickedness (19:1–14)

The two angels who had visited Abraham reached Sodom that evening. The article with the word *angels* is evidence that these were the same two angels who had visited Abraham that afternoon (18:22). The journey from Hebron to Sodom would have covered at least twenty-five miles of rugged, mountainous terrain. "Lot sat in the gate of Sodom," which may indicate that he occupied an office such as judge. Verse 9 may hint at this, and his relationship to Abraham who had earlier saved the city from slavery would have helped him gain such a dignified position. In any event, Lot's move from a tent pitched near Sodom (13:12, 13) to a permanent residence in the city showed his willingness to coexist with unbridled wickedness. The gate of an ancient city was a center of public activity. The markets were there (II Kings 7:1; Neh. 13:19) and court was held there (Deut. 21:19; 22:15; 25:7; Josh. 20:4; Ruth 4:1). David often appeared at the gate to greet the people (cf., e.g., II Sam. 19:8). In typical oriental fashion Lot greeted the two visitors and politely invited them to his house for the evening. The two angels, however, declined the invitation, perhaps to test Lot's sincerity (v. 2). But Lot pressed his invitation until they accepted it, and then cared for them accordingly (v. 3).

The evening had not been far spent before the men of the city came to Lot's house and demanded that the visitors be given to them, "that we may know them." Verses 4 and 5 vividly describe the incredible depravity of the Sodomites. Casting aside the good traditions of oriental hospitality, they wanted only to gratify their unnatural lusts. The verb *know* designates sexual activity many times in the Old Testament (cf. Gen. 4:1; 19:8; Judg. 19:25), and this is clearly what it designates here. Some recent writers have attempted to argue otherwise, but without success.[6] Such immoral offenses would later result in capital punishment and would be grouped with incest and bestiality (Lev. 18:22, 29; 20:13). It is also forthrightly condemned in the New Testament (Rom. 1:26, 27; I Cor. 6:9; I Tim. 1:10).

Hoping to persuade them to forget such a demand, Lot came out of the house, locked the door behind him (v. 6), and pleaded with the men, but his pleas evidently fell on deaf ears and hardened hearts. Not wanting to violate his responsibility to protect his guests, he offered to the men instead his two virgin daughters (v. 8). Such an offer is almost incredible, but Lot considered his obligation to his guests greater than his obligation to his children. His sense of the demands of hospitality explains his act, but of course does not justify it. When a man took in a stranger, he was bound to protect him, even at the expense of the host's life. Lot's decision to offer his daughters was neither superficial nor uncalculated. He probably saw it as the lesser of two evils. But his evil countrymen completely rejected his proposal (v. 9).

Once the situation was far beyond Lot's control, the two angelic visitors stepped in and supernaturally blinded the men of Sodom (v. 11). *Sanwērîm* ("blindness"), which appears only here and in II Kings 6:18, is probably a partial blindness and a mental bewilderment.[7] Keil and Delitzsch suggest that the term signifies "mental blindness, in which the eye sees but does not see the right object."[8] Speiser, on the other hand, considers the term a loan word based on the Akkadian *šunwurum*, "an adjectival form with

---

6. D. Sherwin Bailey, *Homosexuality and the Western Christian Tradition* (London: Longmans, 1955), pp. 3, 4. This view is definitively disproven in Derek Kidner, *Genesis*, pp. 136, 137.
7. Nichol, ed., *Bible Commentary*, 1:334.
8. *Biblical Commentary on the Old Testament*, 25 vols. (Edinburgh: T. and T. Clark, 1864–1901), 1:233.

superlative or 'elative' force: 'having extraordinary brightness.' "[9] The idea of mental confusion resulting from distorted vision seems to be best; verse 11 tells us that "they wearied themselves to find the door," while completely blind men would probably never have tried. If Lot had not realized before this miracle that his two visitors were no mere men, he certainly realized it then.

The angelic visitors quickly told Lot the purpose of their visit and charged him to gather his immediate family and rescue them from impending judgment. Sodom would be destroyed because "the cry of them has become great before the face of the Lord" (v. 13; cf. Jonah 1:2). His sons and daughters are not mentioned again in the text, but we should not assume that Lot contacted only his "sons in law"—young men who were betrothed to Lot's two unmarried daughters. Lot's sons-in-law completely rejected his warning (v. 14). They responded as do many who, upon hearing of God's final judgment, mock and deride the very possibility of such an event.

B. Lot's Deliverance (19:15–22)

The next morning, the angels encouraged Lot to take his wife and two daughters, and leave the city quickly. But his deep attachment to the wealth which he had accumulated in the city made it impossible for him to leave with dispatch. It was a lingering Lot that the two men grasped and mercifully led out of the city (v. 16). Lot's affection for the things of this world is all too typical of our generation's materialism. One is reminded of the very tragic discoveries in Pompeii and Herculaneum of people sprawling on the streets with jewelry and other precious objects in their hands. Apparently when Mt. Vesuvius erupted and destroyed these cities, the inhabitants' affection for their riches proved inordinate.

So important was a rapid escape that Lot and his family were commanded not even to look back. When they learned their destination—the mountains—Lot said "Oh, not so, my Lord." This is an amazing response, indeed. His reason for preferring the small neighboring city of Bela (14:2), afterward called Zoar, to the mountains was a mere excuse. In fact he ultimately forsook Zoar (v. 30) for the mountains, indicating that he considered Zoar to be

---

9. *Genesis*, p. 139.

subject to like destruction. Albright and Glueck have located Zoar in the Ghor es-Safi, the fertile valley at the present mouth of the Seil (stream) el-Qurahi. "The Ghor es-Safi was cultivated to a greater extent in Byzantine and Mediaeval times than now and 'supported flourishing sugar and indigo plantations.' Graves have been found in it which can be dated by the pottery to about 2000 B.C., in the period in which the Cities of the Plain seemed to have flourished. Hence near the Byzantine Zoar in this fertile district the Zoar of the Old Testament may be found, but, Glueck adds, 'it is probably so covered with accretions of later ages that it will be found, if at all, only by accident.' "[10]

C. Sodom's Destruction (19:23–29)

The next morning the Lord destroyed Sodom and Gomorrah, as well as other towns in the plain, with "brimstone and fire" (v. 24). Precisely what "brimstone and fire" signify has been the subject of considerable study and speculation. Massive volcanic eruptions have generally been ruled out by geological research in the area. The most prominent explanation, suggested by J. Penrose Harland, is that a massive earthquake resulted in enormous explosions: "A great earthquake, perhaps accompanied by lightning, brought utter ruin and a terrible conflagration to Sodom and the other communities in the vicinity. The destructive fire may have been caused by the ignition of gases and of seepages of asphalt emanating from the region, through lightning or the scattering of fires from hearths." [11] Of course, while God may have used such natural means, His timing of the event was strictly supernatural.

The location of Sodom and Gomorrah is equally uncertain even though it has been studied in detail. Albright locates it on the lowest course of the Seil en-Numeirah, which flows into the Dead Sea today at approximately the center of the east side of the embayment. Gomorrah would then be further north on the Seil 'Esal.[12] Most scholars who have studied the matter locate these cities in an area south of the Lisan Peninsula that is now the Dead

10. J. Penrose Harland, "Sodom and Gomorrah," p. 58.
11. Ibid., p. 67.
12. Ibid., p. 58. Also see William F. Albright, "The Jordan Valley in the Bronze Age," *Annual of the American Schools of Oriental Research* 6 (1924–25): 13–74; and Albright, "The Archaeological Results of an Expedition to Moab and the Dead Sea," pp. 2–12.

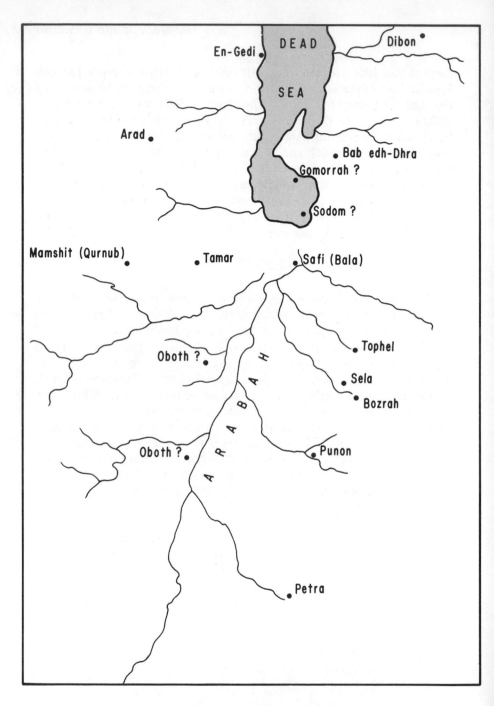

The Dead Sea and the Arabah

Sea.[13] Substantial evidence for this location has come from the excavations at Bab edh-Dhra', five hundred feet from the eastern shore of the Dead Sea. Numerous burials with pottery evidence point to general use between 2300 and 1900 B.C.[14] The lack of a permanent settlement in the immediate vicinity might indicate that the cities have disappeared beneath the waters of the Dead Sea.

The very fact that God destroyed the cities is clear evidence that not even ten of their inhabitants were righteous (cf. 18:32). Only four were led out of the cities, and Lot's wife, unable to detach herself from Sodom's material goods, looked back and "became a pillar of salt" (v. 26). Whether she was covered by "molten materials of the explosion" raining down on her,[15] or she was chemically changed to salt is difficult to determine with certainty. Nor is there any way of knowing how long that pillar remained visible. On the southwestern shore of the Dead Sea are many salt-rock formations, and some of them resemble a human figure. Visitors are tempted to identify one or another of these "pillars" with Lot's wife, but this is, of course, a useless exercise. So vivid and tragic was this event that it is often rehearsed in the New Testament to warn others against turning back (cf. Luke 17:31–33; Heb. 10:38, 39).

The morning after the great disaster Abraham returned to the place where he had "stood before the Lord" (v. 27; cf. 18:22), probably in the hills to the east of Hebron. Here he could view the smoldering ruins of Sodom and Gomorrah. He may have been disappointed that the cities had been destroyed, but he was certainly comforted by the knowledge that his intercessory prayer

---

13. For further study on the subject see Elmer B. Smick, *Archaeology of the Jordan Valley*, pp. 47–51; Frederick G. Clapp, "The Site of Sodom and Gomorrah," *American Journal of Archaeology* 40 (1936): 323–44; M. A. Lamberty, "Fluctuations in the Level of the Dead Sea," *Geographical Review* 52 (1962): 602, 603; Nelson Glueck, "Explorations in Eastern Palestine, II"; and Glueck, "An Aerial Reconnaissance in Southern Transjordan," pp. 19–26.
14. Albright, "The Archaeological Results of an Expedition to Moab and the Dead Sea," pp. 5–7; Paul W. Lapp, "The Cemetery at Bâb edh-Dhrâ'," pp. 104–11; Lapp, "Bâb edh-Dhrâ' Tomb A 76 and Early Bronze I in Palestine," pp. 2–19; G. Ernest Wright, "The Chronology of Palestinian Pottery in Middle Bronze I," pp. 27–34; and James L. Kelso and J. P. Horley, "Early Bronze Pottery from Bâb ed-Drâ' in Moab," pp. 3–13.
15. Kidner, *Genesis*, p. 135.

had been answered (v. 29). "God remembered Abraham" in the time of divine judgment just as He had remembered Noah (8:1).

D. Lot's Shame (19:30–38)

Lot was able to take his daughters out of Sodom, but he was not able to take the philosophy of Sodom out of his daughters. They made him drunk in order to cohabit with him. The close relationship here between wine and sexual immorality is no accident (cf. Gen. 9:21, 22; Hab. 2:15). Von Rad describes the event aptly: "There, in the insensibility of his intoxication he becomes a tool, without any will of his own, of his two unmarried

Jebel Usdum ("Hill of Sodom") along the western shore of the Dead Sea (Courtesy of Matson Photo Service)

and childless daughters. Through incestuous intercourse with their own father they raise up descendants for the family which is threatened with extinction. The tribes born of them are the tribal ancestors of the later Ammonites and Moabites."[16] Lot's daughters were unashamed. The names they gave their sons immortalized their paternity. *Moab* (v. 37) is a variant of the Hebrew *mē'āb*, "from the father," as indicated in the Septuagint. *Ben-ammî* (v. 38) literally means "son of my people" and indicates that his father and mother were of the same family stock. The Moabites originally inhabited the territory between the Arnon and the Zered east of the Dead Sea, while the Ammonites roamed widely in the eastern part of the region between the Jabbok and the Arnon.

The story of Lot and his family should provide a sobering reminder that all of our decisions are significant, even that of where we will live. Our moral environment significantly influences our lives. For this and many other reasons the New Testament constantly implores the believer to fellowship with those of like precious faith.

---

16. *Genesis*, p. 218.

14

Life and Death

Genesis 20–23

To a man of weak faith, God's failure after so long to fulfill His promises would have been sufficient reason to abandon His covenant. Abraham still lacked an heir, and he exercised very little control over the land. But his faith, in spite of his deficiencies of character, was genuine and unconditional. This does not imply that Abraham was not desperately struggling to realize the promises made to him. At times he did express impatience and anxiety, but never to the point of abandoning his commitment to God. Chapters 20–23 reflect something of Abraham's life in Canaan, his struggles and his blessings from the Lord.

I. Abraham's Deception of Abimelech (20:1–18)

No reason is given in the text for Abraham's departure from the grove at Mamre near Hebron. His flocks may have exhausted the grazing areas there, or political changes may have interrupted the peace. He journeyed southwest to the Negev, a trip of more than sixty miles. There he "sojourned" (*nāsa'*), and "dwelled" (*yāšab*), words which indicate that his residence there was rather permanent. The precise location of Gerar, where Abraham settled, has

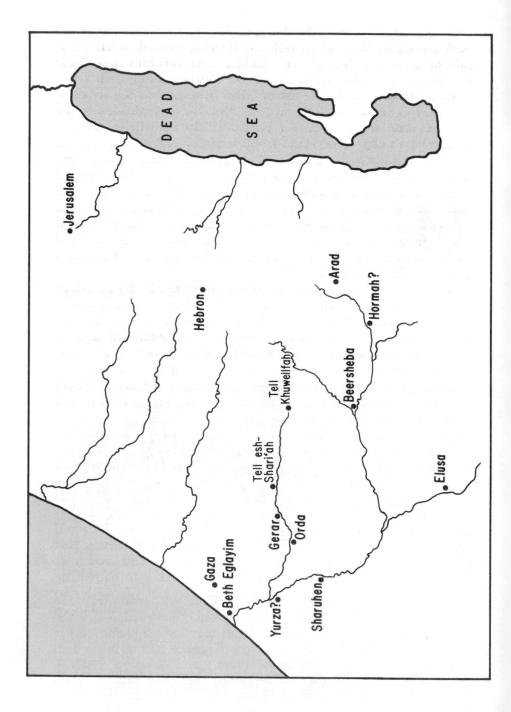

been the object of considerable speculation. The most important evidence seems to point to Tell Abu Hureira, located on the north side of Wadi esh-Shari'ah. The biblical text indicates that Gerar was near a big wadi in whose bed the patriarchs dug their wells. Gerar's omission from the list of cities belonging to the tribes of Simeon and Judah (Josh. 15:19; I Chron. 4) may indicate that the area was still largely under the control of the Philistines, as it was in Abraham's day. Gerar is not mentioned in Egyptian sources, but important information about it is preserved in Roman and Byzantine sources.[1] The famous Medeba map locates Gerar north of Orda and west of Beersheba. The identification of Gerar with Tell Abu Hureira was once rejected by many scholars, but recent archaeological surveys seem to support it.[2] The territory of Gerar was strategically located between settled land to the east and grazing land to the west, so it is understandable that the Philistines gained control of it rather early.

Abraham had deep suspicions about Abimelech, king of Gerar. *Abimelech* was a dynastic title: the king of Gerar in Isaac's time is called Abimelech (26:8), as is King Achish of Gath in David's day (I Sam. 21:10; cf. the title of Ps. 34). Evidently the king of Gerar, like the king of Egypt, took significant numbers of unmarried women into his harem. One would think that after his humiliation in Egypt twenty-five years earlier, Abraham would have abandoned the use of deception. It is equally incredible that he thought Abimelech might be attracted to Sarah who was now ninety years old, and one might be inclined to fault Abraham with poor judgment or shallow jealousy. But Abimelech did take Sarah (20:2), indicating that she was indeed blessed with unusual beauty.[3] As had the king of Egypt, Abimelech discovered the deception quickly, not by any genius of his own but by special revelation (v. 3). In the same dream God informed Abimelech that He had kept him from sinning with Sarah (vv. 4–6). To avoid judgment, however, the king was to return Sarah to Abraham, "for he is a prophet [*nābi'*], and he shall pray for thee, and thou shalt live. . . ." (v. 7). Abraham is identified as a prophet to emphasize the official nature of his intercessory prayer, not his ability to foretell events. In a real sense he is God's chosen spokesman on

---

1. Yohanan Aharoni, "The Land of Gerar," p. 28.
2. Ibid., p. 31.
3. More than one woman has wished that the text revealed Sarah's secret. In society today the struggle to maintain beauty begins quite early—say, forty?

211

Gerar and neighboring sites

this occasion. *Nāḇî'*, used here for the first time in Scripture, is derived from the verbal root *nāḇā'*, which means "to proclaim, call out, declare." It also means "to speak as an intermediary." The English word *prophet* comes from the Greek *prophētēs*, a combination of the preposition *pro* ("for, on behalf of") and the verb *phēmi* ("to speak"). Abraham's intercession saved Abimelech's life (vv. 3, 7) and ended the barrenness which God had imposed on his household (vv. 17, 18).

Abimelech's rebuke of Abraham is reminiscent of Pharaoh's (cf. 12:17–20). Abraham's naivete in thinking that God would allow him to get away with the deception this time is startling. Nor could Abimelech understand why Abraham would do such a thing (v. 10). The excuses Abraham offered were inadequate and indicate weak faith on this occasion. He suggested, first of all, that since the fear of God was not in Gerar, he had been sure that he would be slain for the sake of his wife (v. 11). He noted further that Sarah was his sister; both had the same father, although not the same mother (v. 12). Finally, he and Sarah had told the same lie for twenty-five years (v. 13). Abimelech's kindness after Abraham confessed was not unlike Pharaoh's. Abimelech gave Abraham sheep, oxen, and servants, and granted him freedom to settle anywhere in his territory (vv. 14–16).

In spite of Abraham's failures he still was a man of prayer, an effective intercessor. Chapter 20 is an eloquent commentary on the patience of God with His servants. Even though Abraham had perpetuated a half-lie for twenty-five years, God was tolerant, forgiving, and willing to answer Abraham's request. God did not ignore the sin of Abraham, however. Quite the contrary, God exposed his deception both times, thereby warning him of the serious consequences of his sin.

II. Isaac's Birth (21:1–21)

A. A Promise Fulfilled (21:1–8)

When "the Lord visited [*pāqaḏ*] Sarah" in 21:1, the great suspense that had begun in chapter 12 ended. *Pāqaḏ* has two uses in the Old Testament: the Lord's coming to judge (Isa. 24:21; Jer. 9:25; Hos. 12:3) and His coming to bless someone (Gen. 50:24; Ruth 1:6; etc.). The child was born "at the set time of which God had spoken to him" (v. 2), and Abraham gave his son the divinely appointed name, *Isaac*, which literally means "laughter" (cf.

212

17:19). The name undoubtedly reflects the laughter of both Abraham and Sarah when God promised them a son. In accordance with the covenant agreement, Isaac was circumcised on the eighth day (v. 4). His birth when Abraham was one hundred and Sarah ninety (v. 5) was an evidence of God's particular blessing and grace. Whether Isaac was born at Gerar or Beersheba is not clear.

B. Conflict and Separation (21:9—21)

While the birth of Isaac was a happy event for Abraham and Sarah, it was also distressing, as we see in the remaining part of chapter 21. Erdman explains why: "The prospects and expectations of Ishmael are suddenly shattered. He had grown to youthful vigor, confident that he was to inherit the great wealth and power of his father. Now the true heir appears. Ishmael is moved to mad hatred. Proud and impetuous, he does not conceal his chagrin. On the occasion of a great feast given in honor of Isaac he is guilty of insolence, of mockery and insult."[4] Sarah saw Ishmael "mocking" ($m^e\d{s}ah\bar{e}q$). This participle comes from the same root as *Isaac*, and that root means "to laugh." The intensive form of the participle here indicates that this was not simple laughter but "ridicule." The word is so used in Genesis 19:14; 39:14—17. Since Ishmael was fourteen years older than Isaac and therefore the eldest son of Abraham, it was natural for him to consider himself the heir.

The events that followed brought great distress and heartbreak to Abraham, who had deep affection for Ishmael. The situation had deteriorated so badly between Sarah and both Hagar and Ishmael that the only solution seemed to be complete separation. The suggestion of Sarah is viewed in Galatians 4:30 as inspired. Giving Hagar enough food and water for the journey was not easy for Abraham (v. 14); it would not take long for the meager provisions which she and Ishmael could carry to be exhausted. Once they were, Ishmael became so weak that Hagar had to "drag" him to the shade of a shrub (v. 15). The word *cast* (AV) seems inappropriate since Ishmael was approximately seventeen years old. Hagar was familiar enough with the relentless oppression of the Negev to realize that death was imminent unless God intervened. So she and the young lad prayed, and God responded (vv.

213

---

4. *The Book of Genesis*, p. 74.

16, 17), assuring them that Ishmael would be made a great nation
(v. 18). This response might seem inappropriate, but it guaranteed
the lad's survival. God then directed Hagar to a nearby well (v.
19). Ishmael was reared in the wilderness near Egypt, became an
archer, and eventually married a woman from Egypt, his mother's
original homeland (vv. 20, 21).

III. Abraham's Covenant with Abimelech (21:22–34)

At some point Abraham migrated from Gerar southeast to
Beersheba. The journey would not have been a long one, although
it would have covered some rugged territory. One gets the impression that Abimelech exercised significant control over a vast area
southeast of Gerar, and he and Abraham covenanted at Beersheba
to coexist in the area peacefully (v. 32). Tel Beer-sheba, located on
the outskirts of modern Beersheba, was excavated in 1969 and
1973 by the Tel Aviv University Institute of Archaeology. Of
course in Abraham's day Beersheba may have been nothing more
than a small settlement or oasis, as excavations seem to indicate.
"Our excavation showed that the city was founded only in the
Iron Age; and one of our great surprises was an unusually strong
fortification of that period, creating an imposing mound. . . ."[5]
Where in this area was Abraham's residence, or as Yohanan
Aharoni puts it, " . . . where was the sanctified well of the patriarchal traditions near which Abraham planted his tamarisk tree
(Gen. 21:33)? Comparing it with the Kenite high place at Arad,
surrounded by the civilian settlement, Abraham's high place might
be on the prominent hill surrounded by river beds near which the
wells were located."[6] A covenant between Abraham and
Abimelech was necessary apparently because each wanted control
of the valuable water sources in Wadi esh-Shari'ah (vv. 25, 26).
Abimelech's willingness to make a settlement with Abraham indicates the latter's considerable strength and influence in the area.
Neither wanted an armed conflict, so the covenant was easily
made. It was concluded with an exchange of appropriate gifts (vv.
28–30). Abraham celebrated by planting "a grove" and worshiping
God. This is the "tamarisk tree" the location of which Aharoni
discussed above.

The mention of Philistines in verse 34 has long been considered

214

---

5. Aharoni, "Excavations at Tel Beer-Sheba," p. 111.
6. Ibid., p. 115.

Left, an ancient well near Beersheba, showing rope marks along the sides; *below*, Beersheba viewed from the south (Courtesy of Matson Photo Service)

anachronistic by scholars. They are mentioned again in Genesis 26:1, 8, 14, 15, 18. Many maintain that the Philistines first appeared in Canaan only after they had attacked Egypt and been repulsed by Rameses III in 1190 B.C. Among the "sea peoples" who mounted the attack was a group listed as *prst* in Egyptian monuments. This group has generally been identified with the Philistines of later biblical narratives. However, it is not impossible that there had been migrations of peoples from the Aegean world. "There is evidence of a major expansion of Aegean trade in the Middle Minoan II period (c. 1900–1700 B.C.); and objects of Aegean manufacture or influence have been found from this period at Ras Shamra in Syria, Hazor, and perhaps Megiddo in Palestine, and Tod, Harageh, Lahun, and Abydos in Egypt."[7] It is therefore possible that the Philistines of the patriarchal period were peaceful tradesmen who had settled along the southwest coast of Palestine. In all likelihood they quickly assimilated Canaanite culture, as perhaps is evidenced by the King of Gerar's dynastic title, Abimelech, a Semitic name. Some years ago Sir Flinders Petrie suggested the rationale for this early migration: to export grain back to the rocky, non-self-supporting homeland.[8]

IV. Abraham's Obedience to God (22:1–24)

A. God's Command (22:1, 2)

The Lord's startling command to Abraham, "take now thy son . . . and offer him there for a burnt offering. . . ." has challenged the genius of more than one commentator. There are at least three ways of looking at it.

A large group of scholars contend that human sacrifice was a common custom in Abraham's day, and this passage must be seen in that context. Advocates of this position usually adopt a more or less evolutionary approach to Israel's religion. Human sacrifice was

---

7. T. C. Mitchell, "Philistines," in J. D. Douglas, ed., *New Bible Dictionary*, p. 990.
8. *Palestine and Israel*, p. 62. Other studies of the Philistines are Edward E. Hindson, *The Philistines and the Old Testament*; G. Bonfante, "Who Were the Philistines?" pp. 251–62; Kenneth A. Kitchen, *Ancient Orient and Old Testament*, pp. 80, 81; E. F. Campbell, "In Search of the Philistines," pp. 30, 32; T. Dothan, "Archaeological Reflections on the Philistine Problem," *Antiquity and Survival* 2 (1957): 151–64; Cyrus H. Gordon, "The Role of the Philistines," pp. 22–26; E. Grant, "The Philistines," *Journal of Biblical Literature* 55 (1936): 175–94.

unquestionably practiced in Old Testament times. A Babylonian cylinder seal, for example, unmistakably portrays the execution of a human sacrifice,[9] and the translation of an Akkadian poem describes the sacrifice of a first-born son.[10] However, the unguarded generalizations of a generation ago require reevaluation in the light of recent evidence. Albright observes, "The extent to which human sacrifice was practiced among the Canaanites has not been clarified by the discoveries at Ugarit, which nowhere appeared to mention it at all."[11] There is little question that Abraham would have been acquainted with it in Mesopotamia, but he may never have practiced it.

Another reaction to this passage is that God never expected Abraham literally to sacrifice Isaac but only to dedicate him completely. Marcus Dods writes: "God meant Abraham to make the sacrifice in spirit, not in the outward act; He meant to write deeply on the Jewish mind that fundamental lesson regarding sacrifice, that it is in the spirit and will that all true sacrifice is made. . . . The sacrifice God seeks is devotion of the living soul, not the consumption of a dead body."[12] The danger in this view, however, is that "carried to its logical conclusion, [it] would eliminate the necessity of the sacrificial death of Christ."[13] Furthermore, Abraham responded to God's command by gathering wood (22:3), taking a knife and fire (v. 6), and building an altar (v. 9), all of which indicate that Abraham fully intended to physically sacrifice Isaac. The language of the passage is very similar to that of Jephthah's vow in Judges 11:30–40.[14]

The third and best approach to the passage is that God commanded an actual human sacrifice and Abraham intended to obey Him fully. Such a conclusion may seem harsh, but it is in keeping with the language of the text and in harmony with the outcome. God later prohibited human sacrifice in the Mosaic law,[15] and while He commanded Abraham to practice it, He then prevented

---

9. R. A. S. Macalister, "Human Sacrifice: Semitic," in James Hastings, ed., *Encyclopedia of Religion and Ethics*, 13 vols. (New York: Charles Scribner and Co., 1913–27), 6:863.
10. A. H. Sayce, *Patriarchal Palestine*, p. 183.
11. William F. Albright, *Archaeology and the Religion of Israel* (Baltimore: The Johns Hopkins Press, 1942), p. 93.
12. *The Book of Genesis* (New York: Funk and Wagnalls, 1900), p. 200.
13. David R. Dilling, "The Atonement and Human Sacrifice," p. 25.
14. Jephthah's vow and its interpretation are discussed in John J. Davis, *Conquest and Crisis*, pp. 124–28.
15. Cf. Lev. 18:21; 20:1–5; Deut. 12:31; 18:10.

217

him from practicing it. This largely relieves the moral tension. The only sacrifice of a human being which God has required and accepted was that of His own Son, who was a propitiation for our sins. And it should be remembered that Jesus Christ was no mere man; as the God-Man He provided a substitutionary atonement which is eternally unique.[16]

Abraham's faith was tried by God and no one else (v. 1). God did not tempt him to evil, but challenged his faith. James states, "Let no man say when he is tempted, I am tempted of God: for God cannot be tempted with evil, neither tempteth he any man: but every man is tempted, when he is drawn away from his own lusts and enticed" (1:13, 14). God's command to Abraham is characteristic of the emotionally-charged narrative: "Take now thy son, thine only son Isaac" (v. 2). In this ascending climax the description becomes more particular and the challenge more intense. This was the supreme test of Abraham's faith since the promises of God involved Isaac and his descendants. God's command clashed with His promise of blessing through Abraham's posterity. Abraham did not, however, attempt to resolve the conflict, but moved ahead on faith, realizing that an infinitely perfect God does not make mistakes.

B. Abraham's Response (22:3—14)

Abraham's unqualified obedience was evident when he rose up the next morning and made the necessary preparations for the sacrifice (v. 3). It was a long journey to Mt. Moriah where the fateful event was to take place, giving Abraham three days to change his mind and return (v. 4). The two young men who accompanied Abraham and Isaac (vv. 3, 5) are identified in Jewish tradition as Ishmael and Eliezer, but this is pure speculation. Abraham said to the two, "I and the lad will go yonder and worship and we will return unto you" (v. 5). His confidence that his son would return with him from the place of sacrifice is ascribed by the New Testament to an explicit belief in resurrection (Heb. 11:17—19). The record of the intimate conversation between Abraham and Isaac on their journey to the mount (vv. 7, 8) might give us a glimpse into the heart of God as the Father witnessed His Son bearing the cross to Calvary. Isaac's penetrating

218

---

16. This problem is further discussed in Dilling, "The Atonement and Human Sacrifice," pp. 28—39.

questions are without parallel in the Old Testament, and Abraham's responses demonstrated his unadulterated faith in God. The sudden appearance of the Angel of the Lord, who provided the substitute for Isaac, brought the intrigue to an end (vv. 11–13). Abraham's faithfulness did not take God by surprise. He knew His servant well, but the trial of faith was necessary to mature and develop Abraham's spiritual character. The patriarch triumphantly named the site *YHWH yir'eh*, "Yahweh will see to it," or "Yahweh will provide" (v. 14). This mountain would see even more important events than this: Solomon would build his temple on it (II Chron. 3:1), and the cross of Christ would be positioned in the vicinity.[17]

C. The Covenant Reaffirmed (22:15–24)

Abraham's obedience resulted in renewed assurance that God would fulfill His covenant. Not only did God reaffirm His covenant but He reemphasized its universal aspect with two similes in verse 17. God promised that Abraham's seed would "possess the gate of his enemies" (v. 17), which anticipates the successful conquest of the land under Joshua and may have eschatological overtones as well. After the events at Moriah, Abraham and his young men returned to his semipermanent residence at Beersheba (v. 19). The chapter concludes with a brief table of the descendants of Nahor, Abraham's brother. The most important persons mentioned are Bethuel and his daughter Rebekah, who figure prominently in later accounts (cf. 24:15, 24, 47, 50; 25:20; 28:2, 5).

V. Sarah's Death and Burial (23:1–20)

Sarah died, according to 23:1, at the age of 127. She is the only woman whose age at death is recorded in Scripture, and this indicates her importance. She died in Kiriath-arba ("city of four quarters"), an early name for Hebron (cf. 35:27; Josh. 14:15; Judg. 1:10). Why Abraham had left Beersheba and settled in Hebron we are not told.

To secure a place to bury Sarah, Abraham negotiated with natives of the area (v. 3), men identified as "the sons of Heth" (*bᵉnê hēt*); that is, the Hittites. The mention of Hittites (cf. Num.

219

---

17. For additional study of this chapter see Jesse L. Boyd, Jr., "The Sacrifice of Isaac," pp. 112–21.

Two views of Hebron (bottom photo courtesy of Levant Photo Service)

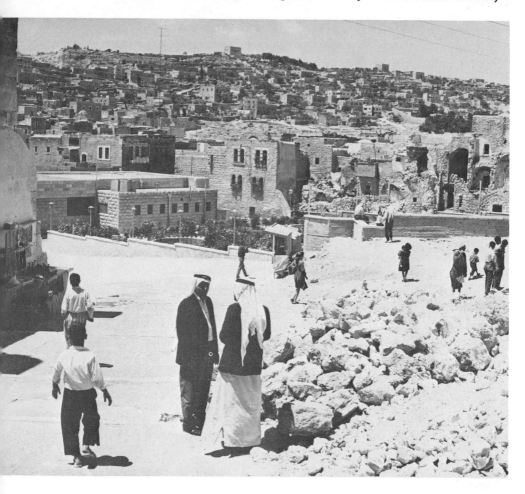

13:29) has long been a problem to commentators because there is no other evidence that Hittites of ancient Anatolia were ever interested in territories as far south as Hebron. Their armies reached Damascus but apparently never Palestine.[18] Their culture definitely had an influence in Palestine, however. Excavations at Megiddo uncovered a small bronze figure of a Syro-Hittite god of war, armed with a sword and shield and wearing the characteristic conical headdress. It is generally dated to the Late Bronze II period.[19] At Bethshan numerous Syro-Hittite seals, a curved scimitar, and a pronged Hittite battle-ax were found.[20] Also discovered was a jar handle stamped with Hittite hieroglyphs representing a solar disk, a mountain, and the familiar conical hat.[21] Of course most of these artifacts are postpatriarchal. O.R. Gurney offers two possible solutions to the problem. The first, originally suggested by E. Forrer, is that during the reign of Mursilis II, a Hittite migration reached Egyptian territory and could also have populated the Palestinian hills. Gurney is quick to point out, however, that "immigration of Anatolian Hittites to Palestine cannot have been a frequent occurrence."[22] The second solution is that *Hittite* might be a purely linguistic designation; that is, the people in the Judean hills who were called Hittites merely spoke the Hittite language or some form of it.[23] Additional archaeological evidence is essential to any final conclusions on the matter. That Hittites could have migrated and settled in the central Judean hill country, however, is consistent with known settlement patterns.

The negotiations between Abraham and the Hittites have always greatly interested Bible scholars, but only recently, as archaeology has illuminated Hittite law, the interpretation of the passage has undergone drastic change. No longer is it understood as typical oriental haggling for a parcel of land.

Abraham was a "stranger and sojourner," not legally part of the community of Hittites, and therefore had to negotiate for the land in a special manner. He asked the Hittites, according to the Authorized Version, to "give [*nātan*] me a possession of a buryingplace,"

18. O. R. Gurney, *The Hittites*, p. 59.
19. James B. Pritchard, ed., *The Ancient Near East in Pictures*, p. 169 (no. 496).
20. Ibid., p. 54 (no. 178).
21. John Garstang, *The Hittite Empire*, p. 333.
22. *The Hittite Empire*, pp. 61, 62.
23. Ibid. p. 62.

but *nātan* here means "sell"; the same root in verse 13 means "pay." Abraham was asking to buy the cave of Machpelah for an equitable price. Why Ephron refused to sell him only the cave (v. 11) relates to Hittite law. That law, as Manfred R. Lehmann has established, required the owner of a complete unit of land to perform the king's *ilku*, or feudal services.[24] Paragraphs 46 and 47 of the Hittite code say: "If in a village anyone holds fields under socage as inheritance—if the fields have all been given to him, he shall render the services; if the fields have been given to him only to a small part, he shall not render the services, they shall render them from his father's house. . . . If anyone buys all the fields of a craftsman, they shall ask the king, and he shall render those services which the king orders. If there remain fields in the hands of the man from whom he buys, he shall not render the services. If the field (and) fallow are vacant or the people of the village give it to him, he shall render the services."[25] Thus Ephron the wealthy prince was reluctant to sell Abraham only the cave because he did not wish to remain responsible for the feudal services that the owner of the field must render. So Abraham purchased the field along with the cave (v. 17). The Hittites were not the only ones who attached *ilku* services to the land; the Code of Hammurabi did something similar.[26] The prominent mention of trees in the final agreement (v. 17) was also characteristic of Hittite business documents.[27]

The obvious parallels between this transaction and those preserved in Hittite documents have at least two possible implications. First, they might indicate that the Hittites dwelling in the southern hill country of Palestine were indeed generically related to those in ancient Anatolia. Second, they seem to preclude a late date for the composition of Genesis. "We have thus found that Genesis 23 is permeated with intimate knowledge of intricate subtilties of Hittite laws and customs, correctly corresponding to the time of Abraham and fitting in the Hittite features of the Biblical account. With the final destruction of the Hittite capital of Hattusas about 1200 B.C.E., these laws must have fallen into utter oblivion. This study again confirms the authenticity of the

---

24. "Abraham's Purchase of Machpelah and Hittite Law," pp. 15–18.
25. "The Hittite Laws," translated by Albrecht Goetze, in Pritchard, *ANET,* p. 191.
26. In Pritchard, *ANET,* pp. 167, 168 (paragraphs 27–41). Also see G. M. Tucker, "The Legal Background of Genesis 23," pp. 77–84.
27. Lehmann, "Abraham's Purchase," pp. 17, 18.

'background material' of the Old Testament, which makes it such an invaluable source for the study of all aspects of social, economic, and legal aspects of the periods of history it depicts."[28]

The cave of Machpelah (v. 9) became the burial place of, in addition to Sarah, Abraham, Isaac, Rebekah, Leah, and Jacob (cf. 25:9; 49:31; 50:13). Rachel was the only significant exception (cf. 35:19). The cave of Machpelah has been identified with two caves, one above the other and both beneath a modern mosque near Hebron. Because scholars have not been permitted to study the caves, however, verification of the site has been nearly impossible. A few visitors have been given access to the upper cave, but none the lower cave. The four hundred shekels Abraham was forced to pay for the land were far more than it was worth. The price has been estimated in American currency at $116, which may seem modest enough to us but in the ancient Near East was clearly exorbitant.[29] The average cost of a field was four shekels an acre, and the most fertile gardens went for forty shekels an acre.[30]

The very fact that Abraham buried Sarah in the land of Canaan is proof of his unwavering faith. Knowing that his descendants would have to endure four hundred years of bitter bondage in a foreign country (15:13), he looked beyond that to the ultimate fulfillment of God's promise. The true saint has no buried hopes, only anticipation of a glorious future. Abraham is remembered for his far-reaching faith which caused him to look for a city "whose builder and maker is God."

---

28. Ibid., p. 18.
29. For the weight and value of the shekel which underlies the $116 price, see Francis D. Nichol, ed., *The Seventh-Day Adventist Bible Commentary*, 1:341, 356.
30. Ibid., p. 356.

15

The Last Days of Abraham

Genesis 24–27

Romance, intrigue, conflict, and hatred are all part of the narratives which lie before us. The description of Abraham's last days follows the same simple historical format as the first part of the story. He is still a sensitive man, not overwhelmed by his own interests and very committed to the good of others. The selection of a bride for Isaac was no burdensome chore but a welcomed opportunity to insure a godly progeny. This section provides us with greater detail about the life of Isaac, putting his fortunes and failures in historical and spiritual perspective. The emotion-charged story of Jacob's theft of the patriarchal blessing is one of the most captivating in all of the Book of Genesis; there are not many actors on the scene, but the drama is intense. The death of Abraham is a strategic transition in the historical narrative. The question immediately arises, what will become of Abraham's descendants and how will their unique covenant relationship with the Lord fare? The chosen line is at this point but a thin thread threatened by innumerable forces from both within and without. The perpetuation of the promised seed in spite of these threats furnishes one of the greatest exhibitions of divine providence ever recorded.

225

A relief map of Palestine (Courtesy of Matson Photo Service)

I. The Marriage of Isaac (24:1–67)

A. Abraham's Instructions (24:1–9)

According to an old maxim it takes two to make a marriage—a single daughter and an anxious mother! In chapter 24 there are an unmarried son and a father, now "stricken in age" (v. 1), who appears to have been anxious to at least some degree. Abraham was about 140 years old at this time: he was 100 when Isaac was born (17:17) and Isaac was 40 when he married Rebekah (25:20).

Abraham was deeply concerned that Isaac's wife believe in the Lord and that her culture and Isaac's be compatible. A Canaanite daughter-in-law was thoroughly unacceptable. He summoned his eldest servant and instructed him to seek a wife for Isaac, specifying where to look for her and how to select her. The "eldest servant of his house" (v. 2) is not named but commentators almost unanimously identify him with Eliezer, whom Abraham had previously proposed to be the heir to his property (15:2). He carried out his mission with such good judgment and firmness that he must be considered one of the outstanding characters in Scripture.

One might conclude not only from this narrative but from those that follow that Isaac was somewhat passive and unimportant. Such a conclusion is not without some foundation. "The figure of even a great man may be dwarfed by comparison with that of a distinguished father or of a famous son. Thus the character of Isaac is overshadowed by the majesty of Abraham and the dramatic interest of Jacob. There was a third factor which diminished the importance of Isaac; he was the husband of a clever and masterful wife. No matter how exciting the scene in which he may appear, he is always assigned to a minor part. At least, by contrast with these other actors, his role in life was prosaic, uneventful, obscure."[1] This does not mean that Isaac lacked character or an unquestioning faith in God. His voluntary cooperation with Abraham in Genesis 22 indicated that his faith and obedience were as deep as Abraham's.

Abraham instructed his servant to select a woman for Isaac from among Abraham's kindred in Nahor (v. 4). The servant, afraid that no woman would be willing to travel that far to meet Isaac, asked permission to take Isaac to Nahor if the woman

227

---

1. Charles R. Erdman, *The Book of Genesis*, p. 86.

refused to come to Palestine. Abraham's negative response was quick and decisive: he was under oath to remain in the promised land and did not desire Isaac to return to Mesopotamia (vv. 5–8). The agreement was settled by the servant putting his hand under Abraham's thigh (vv. 2–9). The only other instance of such a ceremony is in 47:29. The thigh, or "loins," were regarded as the source of posterity (cf. Gen. 35:11; 46:26; Exod. 1:5). The agreement, then, extended beyond Abraham to his posterity.

B. His Servant's Journey (24:10–67)

Details concerning the 450-mile journey do not appear in the biblical text. The terrain probably was well enough known to render such a description unnecessary. The servant probably crossed the Jordan River and took the King's Highway north to Damascus. From there he traveled northwest, then north through the Beqa Valley, following the Orontes River. Upon reaching Aleppo he went to the Euphrates, then north to the city of Nahor, which probably was not far from Haran (v. 10).

The mention of camels in verse 10 (as well as elsewhere in patriarchal narratives)[2] has long been a problem to commentators because there is little evidence of widespread domestication of this animal prior to the end of the thirteenth century B.C. There are, however, some extrabiblical indications that camels were domesticated, at least to a limited degree, in the patriarchal period. For example, camel bones have been found in the ruins of a house in Mari which dates from about 2400 B.C.[3] And a camel is listed among domesticated animals in an eighteenth century B.C. tablet found in Alalakh.[4] Other significant evidences are distributed widely enough in the Fertile Crescent to indicate at least a limited domestication, and this may be all that the patriarchal narratives require.[5]

2. Gen. 12:16; 24:10, 11, 14, 20, 22, 64; 30:43; 31:17, 34; 32:8, 16; 37:25.
3. André Parrot, *Abraham et son Temps* (Neuchâtel, Switzerland: Delachaux and Niestlé, 1962), p. 89.
4. Albrecht Goetze, "Remarks on the Ration Lists from Alalakh VII," p. 37.
5. See Joseph P. Free, "Abraham's Camels," pp. 187–93; Kenneth A. Kitchen, "Camel," in J. D. Douglas, ed., *New Bible Dictionary*, pp. 181–83; W. G. Lambert, "The Domesticated Camel in the Second Millennium—Evidence from Alalakh and Ugarit," pp. 42, 43; B. S. J. Isserlin, "On Some Possible Early Occurrences of the Camel in Palestine," pp. 50–53. For William F. Albright's objections to the early domestication of the camel, see the review of *Hebrew Union College Annual*, vol. 16, in *Journal of Biblical Literature* 64

Above, the Beqa Valley; *below*, a relief of Baal-Hadad from the ruins of Baalbek, located in the Beqa Valley

The servant's journey, as it turned out, was an immediate success. This was not because of his natural genius but because of his persistent prayer and his sensitivity to God's Spirit. Upon arriving at the well near Nahor that evening, he immediately prayed for divine blessing (vv. 11, 12). His selection of a well as a meeting place was, of course, only natural. Wells were frequently used as meeting places by townsfolk, shepherds, and travelers.[6] No sooner had he completed his prayer than Rebekah appeared (v. 15). The promptness of God's response to his request was not at all unusual (cf. Dan. 9:23; Isa. 65:24). Recall how soon Peter's spectacular release from prison followed the prayers of the church (Acts 12:5–19), so soon that the praying saints were totally unprepared for Peter's arrival in their midst (vv. 15, 16).

Rebekah's appearance at the well was not unusual for a woman of her day. She is described as "very fair to look upon, a virgin" (v. 16). Apparently the servant had been some distance away from the well while praying, for he had to run to meet her (v. 17). Her willingness to help impressed him, and in gratitude he gave her a gold ring and two bracelets (v. 22). He inquired who her father was and requested lodging for himself (v. 23). Her response to his inquiry and request (vv. 24, 25) caused him to bow down and worship the Lord; his prayer had indeed been answered. The believer's greatest thrill is to see God answer prayer, but he must keep in mind that the answer to his prayer might require effort on his part, as it did on the servant's. Many are perfectly willing to pray for the poor and hungry but consistently refuse to open their refrigerators to make the answer to their prayers possible.

The servant was warmly received by Rebekah's brother, Laban, and then described his mission. Laban must have been impressed with the godly sensitivity of the servant, for he immediately observed that the whole matter originated from the Lord (vv. 50, 51). This response brought great joy to the servant, and for the second time he worshiped his Lord, recognizing His hand in the whole matter (v. 52).

The ultimate decision to go to Palestine and marry Isaac was Rebekah's (vv. 57, 58). This was no arbitrarily contracted marriage, arranged without due regard for the emotions and wishes of the couple. Rebekah decided to go, and Isaac soon developed a

230

(1945): 287, 288; "Cuneiform Material for Egyptian Prosopography," p. 25 (n. 14); and "Abram the Hebrew: A New Archaeological Interpretation," p. 38 (n. 9).
6. Cf. the experiences of Jacob (Gen. 29:15) and Moses (Exod. 2:15).

genuine love for her (v. 67). The qualities which the servant observed in Rebekah require a special study in themselves.[7]

II. The Death of Abraham (25:1–11)

Abraham enjoyed physical and mental strength until the day he died. After Sarah died and Isaac married, Abraham may have been extremely lonely, and this might explain why he married Keturah. It is not impossible, however, that he took Keturah even before Sarah died.[8] A number of the names in verses 2–4 have been identified with various Arab tribes.[9]

Abraham died at age 175 (thirty-eight years after Sarah's death) and "was gathered to his people" (v. 8). Commentators have handled this expression in various ways: as a mere euphemism for death;[10] as a reference to a multiple burial, a common practice among both Canaanites and Israelites;[11] and, the majority view, as a reference to immortality.[12] He was buried in the cave of Machpelah, which he had earlier purchased from the Hittites (vv. 9, 10; cf. Gen. 23), by his two sons, Isaac and Ishmael, which may indicate that some reconciliation had taken place between them. The sons of Keturah are not mentioned, either because their role in the funeral was insignificant or because they were so widely scattered that attendance at the funeral ceremony was impossible.

III. The Descendants of Abraham's Sons (25:12–34)

A. Ishmael (25:12–18)

The mention of Ishmael at the funeral of Abraham gave the writer occasion to point out that God's promises to this man (cf. 16:10ff. and 17:20) had been fulfilled. The names of the twelve princes descending from Ishmael are applied not only to tribal divisions but also to geographical localities (cf. v. 16). Some of

---

7. One such study is Wolfgang M. W. Roth, "The Wooing of Rebekah," pp. 177–87.
8. C. F. Keil and Franz Delitzsch, *Biblical Commentary on the Old Testament*, 25 vols. (Edinburgh: T. and T. Clark, 1864–1901), 1:261.
9. Ibid., 2:202; and Francis D. Nichol, ed., *The Seventh-Day Adventist Bible Commentary*, 1:367.
10. Nichol, ed., *Bible Commentary*, 1:314, 315.
11. Eric M. Meyers, "Secondary Burials in Palestine," p. 17.
12. See Derek Kidner, *Genesis*, p. 150; Keil and Delitzsch, *Biblical Commentary*, 1:263; G. Henton Davies, *Genesis*, p. 207.

these well-known names appear elsewhere in Scripture, and many are common in northern Arabia.[13] Since Ishmael was the elder son, his descendants were appropriately mentioned first. The narrator's primary interest, however, was quite clearly Isaac and his family.

B. Isaac (25:19–34)

1. His sons' births (25:19–26). Like Sarah, Rebekah was barren, and only divine intervention could change that. Isaac prayed for her (v. 21), and Rebekah conceived. However, she became apprehensive and perplexed as "the children struggled together within her" (v. 22), and she prayed to the Lord about it. He revealed to her that in her womb were two sons, and they would be the progenitors of two nations. The struggle within the womb was typical of the great struggle between the two peoples in years to follow. Quite surprisingly God further stated that "the elder shall serve the younger" (v. 23). This was contrary to ancient Near Eastern custom, but the elective purposes of God transcend custom.[14] Esau became the progenitor of the Edomites, Jacob of the Israelites. They were brothers, but they became bitter enemies. Not only their futures were different, but their physical and mental characteristics were also. Esau was a rugged outdoorsman, physically and emotionally restless; Jacob was a "plain [*tām*] man" (v. 27) who dwelt in tents. *Tām* means "amiable, pious, and cultured."[15]

2. The birthright (25:27–34). The eldest son enjoyed particular privileges in the ancient patriarchal household. During his father's lifetime he took precedence over his brothers (Gen. 43:33); after his father died, he received a double share of the inheritance (Deut. 21:17) and became head and priest (cf. Exod. 22:29; Num. 8:14–17; Deut. 21:17) of the family. He could lose the rights of primogeniture, however, if he committed a grave offense:[16] "The status of the first-born was thus bound up with responsibilities and obligations on the one hand, and rights, privileges and prerogatives on the other, including a double portion of the patrimony. All

---

13. These names are discussed in more detail in Nichol, ed., *Bible Commentary*, 1:368; E. A. Speiser, *Genesis*, p. 188; and Davies, *Genesis*, pp. 207, 208.
14. Note Hosea's comment on Jacob in Hos. 12:3.
15. Nichol, ed., *Bible Commentary*, 1:369.
16. As did Reuben, for example, for committing incest (Gen. 35:22; cf. 49:3, 4 and I Chron. 5:1).

these were formalized by the father's testamentary blessing."[17] A knowledge of Genesis 25 is, of course, essential to an understanding of the great tension and intrigue which develops in chapter 27.

The story about Esau and Jacob furnishes some interesting glimpses into Isaac's character and interests in his latter years. He had a decided preference for Esau. This may have been because Esau was the first-born, but other factors also entered in: Esau was a rugged individualist and he regularly supplied his father with venison, which he loved. The conflict and tragedy which follow in the family provide a practical warning to parents who give one child preferential treatment over another.

On one occasion Esau returned from the fields desperately hungry. Jacob was willing to feed him—probably lentils—only if Esau would "sell" his birthright. "Sell" might better be translated "barter" in verse 31, although "sold" seems appropriate in verse 33. It might be noted that red lentils are still a favorite food in Palestine. They are generally prepared with onions, garlic, rice, and olive oil, and are served with lamb or other meat. Jacob probably would never have made such a demand had Esau cared at all for the privileges of his birthright. Exchanging the birthright for something else was legitimate in the ancient Near East. One Nuzi tablet records the transfer of inheritance rights to an adopted brother, and another the sale of a birthright: "On the day they divide the grove . . . Tupkitilla shall give it to Kurpazah as his inheritance share. And Kurpazah has taken three sheep to Tupkitilla in exchange for his inheritance share."[18] Esau impetuously forfeited important rights, responsibilities, and honors which were his by birth. He "despised his birthright"; he considered the responsibilities and honors unimportant, or he was totally uninterested in them. The agreement was solidified by a formal oath (v. 33).

IV. The Conduct of Isaac (26:1—35)

A. Deception and Discovery (26:1—16)

Famine struck the land, as it had during Abraham's early days in Canaan (cf. 12:10). Gerar was not as affected by the drought as the

---

17. Nahum M. Sarna, *Understanding Genesis*, p. 185. Also see Roland de Vaux, *Ancient Israel*, pp. 41, 42, 53; and I. Mendelsohn, "On the Preferential Status of the Eldest Son," pp. 38—40.
18. Cyrus H. Gordon, "Biblical Customs and the Nuzu Tablets," p. 5.

less fertile regions of the Negev, so Isaac and his family went there in search of food. The king of that region was Abimelech. He may have been the same king with whom Abraham had had dealings, but since ninety-seven years had passed since Abraham's first treaty with Abimelech (21:8, 22; 25:26; 26:34), the Abimelech of this chapter probably was not the one in 21:22. As has been previously observed, *Abimelech* is in all likelihood a dynastic title. The Lord appeared to Isaac, perhaps in a theophany, and instructed him not to continue on into Egypt (v. 2), a prohibition which had not been given to Abraham. The Lord promised that if Isaac would remain in Canaan, He would continue to bless Isaac's family and fulfill His covenant promises.

While in Gerar Isaac fell prey to the same lie that Abraham had used for at least twenty-five years. Fearing that Abimelech would kill him in order to take his attractive wife, he declared Rebekah his sister (v. 7). This, of course, is the third such episode, and some have argued that all three are based on a single historical event. However, the differences in detail and orientation between the three accounts are sufficient to conclude that they represent three separate events. Isaac's lie and his preferential treatment of Esau are blotches on his life. Again we are reminded that only a divinely inspired text would have preserved in such detail these weaknesses. The text does not say that Abraham had warned Isaac about lying, but it seems rather likely that he had. Unfortunately, as so often happens, Isaac refused the counsel of his father and had to endure a bitter and humiliating experience. After being sternly rebuked by the King, Isaac continued to live in the area. His agricultural efforts were very successful (v. 12), and he acquired large flocks and herds, and many servants (v. 14). Isaac's prosperity made the Philistines so jealous that Abimelech asked him to leave the area (vv. 15, 16). Abimelech's statement that Isaac was "much mightier than we" probably confirms that the Philistines of the patriarchal period were limited in number and power. They were peaceful Minoan settlers and not the later warriors of Egyptian records.

B. Conflict and Covenant (26:17–35)

Hoping to avoid open conflict with the Philistines without leaving the valley of Gerar, Isaac abandoned the wells which the Philistines had filled up (cf. vv. 15, 17) and moved to the east of the city. There he reopened the wells which his father had dug (v. 18). But just as soon as the wells were working again, the Philistines claimed them and reopened the conflict (vv. 19–21). So Isaac moved further eastward and dug another well, and this one the

234

Philistines left alone. He named the well *Rehoboth*, meaning "wide spaces." This spring has been identified with the present er-Ruchebeh, twenty miles southwest of Beersheba in the Wadi Ruchebeh. It is interesting that the name of this wadi has remained the same since the days of Isaac. Without explanation or reason Isaac continued further eastward and north to Beersheba (v. 23). There the Lord "appeared" unto him and reiterated the covenant He had made with Abraham. Isaac responded by building an altar and worshiping God (v. 25). The altars which the patriarchs built are significant signposts throughout Genesis (cf. 12:7; 13:17, 18; 35:7) of their thanksgiving for God's revelations and providential care.

Abimelech, who had admitted that Isaac was "mightier than we" (v. 16), became deeply concerned about the recent events, fearing reprisal from Isaac. So he and Phicol, the chief captain of his army, made the first move to establish a formal and lasting peace agreement (v. 26). (The name *Phicol* [cf. 21:22], like *Abimelech*, may have been either an official title or a recurring family name.)[19] The appearance of Abimelech and Phicol somewhat surprised Isaac. Their candid admission that the Lord was with Isaac is further evidence that the king generally feared Isaac's power. Presumably the covenant between Isaac and Abimelech was a reaffirmation of the one between Abraham and Abimelech (cf. 21:22–34).

Chapter 26 concludes with a brief note about the marriage of Esau to foreign women. At forty years of age he married two women. Both were Hittites, and this openly defied the principles which Abraham had so judiciously followed earlier (Gen. 25). The names of these Hittite women are Semitic, which probably indicates that their families had dwelt in the land of Canaan for a considerable period of time and that they had adopted the language of the Canaanites. Esau's marriages, as might be expected, caused Isaac and Rebekah great grief, and they highlight the folly and superficiality of Isaac's preferential treatment of him.

V. The Blessing of Isaac (27:1–46)

A. Rebekah's Scheme (27:1–33)

The great tension which had developed between Isaac and Jacob, as well as between Isaac and Rebekah, culminates in Gen-

---

19. For an example of this from a later period see Frank M. Cross, Jr., "The Discovery of the Samaria Papyri," p. 121.

esis 27, a chapter saturated with intrigue, suspense, and agony. Isaac was approximately 137 years old, and since Ishmael had died fourteen years before at the age of 137 (25:17), Isaac may have felt that his days were numbered. So the nearly blind patriarch summoned Esau and promised him the final oral blessing in exchange for some venison (vv. 1–4). Isaac's continued preference for Esau is a sad commentary on his spiritual discernment this late in life. He seems to have completely ignored Esau's barter of the birthright and his grievous marriages (26:35). Isaac's natural desires were evidently more important to him than spiritual and moral values. This dependence on his senses turned out to be his undoing.

Upon hearing of the impending blessing, Rebekah devised a plan by which Isaac would bless Jacob instead of Esau, thus preserving for Jacob the birthright he had acquired. Isaac would have to be deceived. While Esau was hunting venison, Jacob secured goats and Rebekah prepared the meat in such a way that Isaac apparently could not distinguish it from venison (vv. 8–10). Why was Rebekah so sure that he could not? Might she have worked the same deception before? In any event, Jacob was not so confident. He was principally concerned about the physical difference between himself and Esau: " . . . Esau . . . is a hairy man, and I am a smooth man: my father peradventure will feel me, and I shall seem to him as a deceiver" (vv. 11, 12). If the plan did not work, Jacob was sure that he would be cursed. Rebekah assuaged his fears by dressing him in Esau's clothes, putting on his hands and neck "the skins of the kids of the goats" to simulate Esau's hairy skin, and promised to take upon herself any curse that might result (v. 13). Jacob followed his mother's plan, but he was not without some tense moments.

Isaac quickly recognized that the voice he heard was not Esau's. He also wondered how the venison could have been secured so quickly. The plan required Jacob to lie: he identified himself as Esau (v. 19), then asserted that he had been able to return so quickly because God had brought the animal to him (v. 20). Isaac's dependence upon his five senses resulted in his deception, and this provides a rather subtle warning to all who would depend solely on empirical evidence for truth! Satan has for millennia provided impressive substitutes for the real thing, and unfortunately many do not discover the deception until tragedy has occurred. Rebekah's plan succeeded and Isaac blessed Jacob (vv. 27–29).

236

A hunter with his game, part of an eighth-century B.C. Assyrian relief

It should be remembered that God appointed that "the elder would serve the younger" (25:23; cf. Rom. 9:12). What appears on the surface to be a series of accidents, failures, and deceptions turns out in the long run to be God's providential working, which includes human frailty as well as strength. As Joseph observed when greeting his brothers after a long separation, even man's evil acts are, in effect, part of the plan of God (Gen. 45:3–9; 50:20). What man intends for evil God utilizes for good. This is a great mystery, and should cause each of us to stand before the Creator in complete humility.

B. Esau's Reaction (27:34–46)

The pitiful remorse and tears of the heartbroken Esau present one of the tenderest and most revealing scenes in Scripture. To put it into proper perspective, we must consider the divine commentary recorded in Hebrews 12:16, 17. This passage makes it clear that when Esau sold his birthright, he formally denied himself the blessing of the first-born. Apparently neither he nor Isaac took that event very seriously. His cry, on the surface at least, was that of an innocent man who had twice been cheated (v. 36), but such was not the case. He pled for a blessing from his father and was granted one (vv. 39, 40). Isaac's promise in verse 39 has been interpreted in two ways, differing on the force of the preposition *min:* "thy dwelling shall be *in* the fatness of the earth"; and "thy dwelling shall be *away from* the fatness of the earth."[20] The first interpretation, which is implied in the Authorized Version, would make this essentially the same as the blessing on Jacob in verse 28. The second, however, makes this more of a curse: the Edomites would inhabit a region less fertile than Canaan.[21]

As a result of the deception, Esau deeply hated Jacob and fully intended to slay him after Isaac died (v. 41), not realizing that Isaac would live another forty-three years (35:28). Rebekah heard about Esau's intentions and suggested to Jacob that he flee to Haran and reside with her brother Laban "a few days" (vv. 43, 44); she apparently agreed that the death of Isaac was not far away. She feared the loss of both sons through the process of blood revenge; if Esau killed Jacob, then the nearest elder relative

---

20. Keil and Delitzsch, *Biblical Commentary*, 1:278; Kidner, *Genesis*, p. 156.
21. Nichol, ed., *Bible Commentary*, 1:378, 379.

A cuneiform tablet from Nuzi with a list of personal names, dating from the fifteenth century B.C. (Courtesy of the Oriental Institute, University of Chicago)

would kill Esau and she would be "deprived also of you both in one day" (v. 45).

Rebekah's explanation to Isaac of why Jacob should depart was quite different from the truth. She said she was sending Jacob to Haran because she had wearied of Esau's Hittite wives and wanted Jacob to marry a woman from her family. Her explanation pleased Isaac for obvious reasons. Rebekah's deceit had worked, but it meant that she would never see Jacob again.

C. The Oral Testament's Importance

It might seem strange to members of Western society that such importance was placed on an oral blessing or testament. However, recent discoveries have verified that an oral benediction was legally as valid as a written "last will and testament." A Nuzi court record tells about Tarmiya, whose two older brothers contested his inheritance of a slave girl. Tarmiya argued that his father's oral testament legally entitled him to her: "My father, Huya, was sick and lay on a couch; then my father seized my hand and spoke thus to me, 'My other sons, being older, have acquired a wife; so I give

239

herewith Sululi-Ishtar as your wife."[22]   After witnesses were examined, the judges decided in Tarmiya's favor. It is significant that Isaac introduced his oral testament by saying, "I am old, I know not the day of my death" (27:2); a similar statement in a Nuzi text introduces the final disposition of property.[23]

The amazing correspondence between the judicial process recorded in Genesis and the one in Nuzi texts substantiates the historical accuracy of the Old Testament. It also indicates that the patriarchs were influenced by Mesopotamian practices. Of course the patriarchs were distinguished by their monotheism, which is without parallel in either Mesopotamian or Egyptian literature. In spite of repeated efforts to produce some, there is no sound evidence of any ethical monotheism outside of Israel. If the theological concepts of Israel were "discovered" or "developed" rather than revealed by God, why did no other nations produce a similar theology? The uniqueness of the faith of the patriarchs sets them apart from their polytheistic background and again reminds us of the amazing mercy and grace of a loving God.

---

22. "Mesopotamian Legal Documents," translated by Theophile J. Meek, in Pritchard, *ANET*, p. 220.
23. Speiser, " 'I Know Not the Day of My Death,' " pp. 252–56.

16

The Adventures of Jacob

Genesis 28–36

The record of Jacob's life in chapters 28–36 is a compilation of episodes which fluctuate between mature spirituality and a brash disinterest in that which is right. We see Jacob on one hand as a man of faith and prayer, and on the other as a man of slick maneuvers and cunning ways. He was by nature strong-willed, ambitious, self-reliant, shrewd, and at times unethical. While Jacob was a man of domestic capability and fidelity, Esau was a brave, generous, heroic, and rugged hunter who broke away from the quiet pastoral life of his father to enjoy a reckless, self-indulgent career of pleasure. The most important way in which Jacob differed from Esau, however, was that Jacob was heir to God's promise and a man of faith, although his faith was at times rather weak and imperfect.

Jacob's separation from his parents was difficult for him. He feared the reprisal of Esau who hated him uncontrollably for stealing the birthright. As it turned out, however, Jacob's survival and journey to Mesopotamia were no mere accident of patriarchal history. As He would Joseph in Egypt, God blessed Jacob in Mesopotamia, and Jacob became the progenitor of the great nation of Israel.

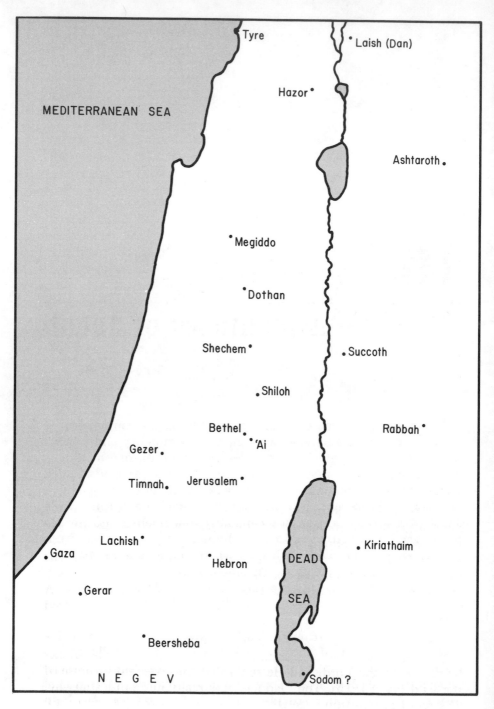

The land of Palestine

I. The Journey to Haran (28:1–22)

A. Isaac's Command (28:1–9)

Agreeing with Rebekah about whom Jacob should marry (27:46), Isaac advised Jacob not to marry a daughter of Canaan. Because of this—and, if Isaac had learned of Esau's plot to kill Jacob, because of that, too—Isaac commanded Jacob to go to Paddan-Aram, the home of Laban, Rebekah's brother. *Paddan-Aram* means "the plain of Aram," and it was located near Haran in northwest Mesopotamia. While blessing Jacob, Isaac referred to God as El Shaddai ("God Almighty" in 28:3). Since this divine title was earlier associated with the covenant of Abraham (17:1), Isaac was reminding Jacob that he would receive the land promised to Abraham (v. 4). Isaac followed the advice of his father and lived with Laban among the Arameans ("Syrian" in v. 5) for twenty years. We should note in passing that the order of Jacob's and Esau's names in verse 5 was no slip of Moses' pen; Jacob's name is first because God had elected him and Isaac had given him his blessing. Esau then attempted to please his father by fetching a wife from the family of his grandfather Abraham (v. 9). Esau went "unto Ishmael," which must mean "the family of Ishmael" since Ishmael had died fourteen years earlier, and married Mahalath, Ishmael's daughter.

B. Jacob's Dream (28:10–22)

Jacob began his journey, one that would cover more than four hundred miles—an indication of the importance of his mission. He stopped for an evening's rest on the west side of the Jordan in the vicinity of Luz, about fifty miles north of Beersheba (v. 19). His use of stones for pillows seems strange, but in ancient times a pillow was more of a headrest than what we consider a pillow. A number of headrests made of wood or stone have been discovered in Egypt. While sleeping on the ground, lonely and weary, Jacob dreamed about a ladder extending from earth to heaven, with angels "ascending and descending on it" (v. 12). At the top of the ladder stood the Lord, and He reiterated the covenant promise of the land (vv. 13–15). The "ladder" was really more of a stairway. The word in question is related to the *mound* thrown up against a walled city (II Sam. 20:15). A stairway better fits the picture of

243

messengers ascending and descending than does a ladder.[1] The suggestion, however, that "the stairway that Jacob saw concerning heaven and earth recalls at once the picture of the ziggurat with its external ramp linking each stage of the tower to the other,"[2] may be overstating the case.

The stairway symbolized the genuine and uninterrupted fellowship between God in heaven and His people on earth. The angelic messengers reflect God's constant care of His own. Whatever loneliness and despair Jacob may have felt, his dream certainly lifted and encouraged him. He was convinced that it was no ordinary dream but a revelation, for "the Lord is in this place" (v. 16). To commemorate the event he made a pillar of one of the stones he had used for headrests and anointed it with oil (v. 18). This pillar is not to be confused with those later erected for the worship of Baal (Deut. 12:23).[3] "Normally, a stone was holy and an object of worship because it was thought to be the abode of a numen. In this case, however, the stone pillar is simply memorializing the scene of the theophany and is accorded no inherent sanctity."[4] After the ceremony he renamed Luz *Bethel* (v. 19), which means "house of God." Bethel is today associated with the site of Beitin. Following the consecration of the place, Jacob vowed that if God continued to bless him, he would return to the land in peace, continue to worship the Lord (v. 21), and give to the Lord one tenth of his possessions (v. 22). From this statement and from Abraham's gift to Melchizedek (14:20), we can conclude that "the tenth" was given voluntarily before God made it a requirement. Unfortunately, tithing lost its real significance with the Pharisees (Matt. 23:23).

II. The Sojourn in Haran (29:1–30:43)

A. Two Marriages (29:1–30)

After a long, rugged journey requiring perhaps three weeks, Jacob reached the vicinity of Haran. The scene of a well in a field surrounded by sheep is common even today in the Near East. When Jacob greeted the shepherds as "brothers," he was using that

244

1. Derek Kidner, *Genesis*, pp. 158, 159.
2. Nahum M. Sarna, *Understanding Genesis*, p. 193.
3. See also Lev. 26:1 and Deut. 16:22.
4. Sarna, *Understanding Genesis*, p. 194.

term in its general sense. He inquired about "Laban the son of Nahor" (29:5). Laban was actually Nahor's grandson (24:15, 29), but it was not unusual to refer to a grandson as a son. Laban, a man of means and influence, was well known to the shepherds, and they provided Jacob with the necessary information (vv. 6–8). During this conversation Rachel, the daughter of Laban, appeared with her father's sheep. It was not unusual for a young lady to tend sheep, and it may have been necessary in this case because Laban had no sons. It seems strange to the Westerner that Jacob greeted Rachel with a kiss (v. 11), to say nothing of his weeping. The very fact that Rachel did not resent Jacob's conduct indicates that he had made his identity known and that she shared his feelings. She excitedly ran to her father and told him of Jacob's arrival (v. 12). Jacob was warmly welcomed into the household, much as Eliezer had been welcomed ninety-seven years earlier (24:30, 31). Romance, intrigue, and conflict followed. Verse 16

The village of Bethel (Courtesy of Matson Photo Service)

indicates that Laban had two daughters, Leah and Rachel, Leah being older. No sons are mentioned. Very little time passed before Jacob made known his desire to marry Rachel, who is described as "beautiful and well favoured" (v. 17). Leah is described as "tender [*rak*] eyed" (v. 17). *Rak* simply means "that which is weak or tender." Leah's eyes were apparently pale and lacked luster. "The Oriental likes a woman's eyes to be lively, to glow, and therefore eye make-up was used from most ancient times."[5]

The precise relationship Jacob sustained to Laban (cf. v. 15) has long been a puzzle. Since the discovery of the Nuzi documents it has been assumed that Laban adopted Jacob, and that this defined the working agreement between them. The fact that no sons are mentioned until twenty years later (31:1; cf. v. 41) seems to support this assumption. In Nuzi one man could adopt another and thus gain an heir. If, however, the first man then had a son, the inheritance situation would change and some of the laws of the first-born would apply.[6] Many scholars have argued that Jacob's was an *errubu* marriage, a type which originated in Assyria and which supposedly was common in the second millennium B.C.[7] More recently, however, John Van Seters has questioned this.[8] Even if Jacob's marriage was a specialized type, he probably was adopted by Laban. If Laban was without sons at his age, he may have been as deeply concerned about an heir as Abraham had been. It would not have been unusual, therefore, for him to adopt Jacob as his son and heir. In fact one Nuzi text records conditions under which the adopted son would receive his father's daughter in marriage.[9]

Jacob offered to serve Laban for seven years as the dowry price for Rachel (v. 18), and Laban accepted. The seven years seemed "but a few days" to Jacob, an indication of how much he loved Rachel (v. 20). Jacob fulfilled his obligation, but Laban did not. The time came for Jacob to receive Rachel, and he was made a victim

---

5. Gerhard von Rad, *Genesis*, p. 286.
6. See Cyrus H. Gordon, "Biblical Customs and the Nuzu Tablets," pp. 5ff.; Gordon, "The Story of Jacob and Laban in the Light of the Nuzu Tablets," *Bulletin of the American Schools of Oriental Research* 66 (1937): 25–27; and Roland de Vaux, "Les Patriarchs hébreux et les découvertes modernes," *Revue Biblique* 56 (1949): 33–36. For a sample text of this type of adoption see "Mesopotamian Legal Documents," in Pritchard, *ANET*, pp. 219, 220.
7. See E. A. Speiser, "New Kirkuk Documents Relating to Family Laws," pp. 1–73; and Millar Burrows, "The Complaint of Laban's Daughters," pp. 259–76.
8. "Jacob's Marriages and Ancient Near East Customs: A Re-examination," pp. 377–95.
9. "Mesopotamian Legal Documents," in Pritchard, *ANET*, pp. 219, 220.

of cunning devices much like he had employed. Instead of the beautiful Rachel, he found himself with the older Leah (v. 24). Needless to say, he was less than pleased. In an effort to vindicate himself Laban appealed to the local custom that the first-born daughter must be married before her younger sister (v. 26). He promised that if Jacob would "fulfill her week," that is, the wedding week (cf. Judg. 14:12) and serve Laban an additional seven years, he also could have Rachel. Why was Jacob willing to commit himself for such a long period? Probably he was in no position to pay the required dowry, and he knew he could not return to Canaan in the near future anyway. For Laban it meant another seven years of service from Jacob and relief from the responsibility of supporting Leah. Jacob received Rachel as his wife immediately after the wedding celebration for Leah, according to verse 28. Of course later Mosaic law prohibited concurrent marriages to sisters (Lev. 18:18). While we cannot condone Jacob's bigamy, we must recognize that God can overrule the errors of men in fulfilling His ultimate purposes (cf. Ps. 76:10). The relationship between Rachel and Leah, however, was not a happy one, and Jacob definitely gave preferential treatment to Rachel (vv. 30, 31).

B. Twelve Children (29:31–30:24)

A quick reading of the biblical text gives the impression that all twelve of Jacob's children were born in the first seven years of his marriages, and that Leah gave birth to seven of them. While it is not biologically impossible to have seven children in seven years, it is unlikely even in oriental society. Several explanations have been offered. Adam Clarke interpreted Genesis 31:38, 41 to mean that Jacob served Laban for two twenty-year periods,[10] but his handling of the pronoun *zeh* was very dubious. Another suggestion is that some of Jacob's children were born during the final six years of his stay with Laban.[11] A third solution is that Dinah was born after Jacob's first seven years of marriage to Leah;[12] while the text permits this (cf. v. 21), it does not demand it.[13]

---

10. *Clarke's Commentary*, 6 vols. (New York: Lane and Scott, 1850), 1:210.
11. Francis D. Nichol, ed., *The Seventh-Day Adventist Bible Commentary*, 1:394.
12. Charles L. Zimmerman, "The Chronology and Birth of Jacob's Children by Leah and Her Handmaid," pp. 3–12.
13. See discussion in Nichol, ed., *Bible Commentary*, 1:393, 394.

Leah had four sons in rather rapid succession, and the name of each reflected her state of mind. *Reuben* (v. 32) means "See, a son!"; Leah regarded him as a pledge of Jehovah's favor. *Simeon* (v. 33) means "hearing"; the Lord had heard how much Leah was hated. *Levi* (v. 34) means "attachment"; Leah hoped that ultimately Jacob would become attached to her. *Judah* (v. 35), which comes from a Hebrew root meaning "to praise," meant not merely "the praised one," but "the one for whom Jehovah is praised." After Judah Leah "ceased bearing" temporarily (v. 35), to keep her from becoming unduly elated by her good fortune and to keep Rachel from becoming discouraged beyond measure. From all indications Leah was a pious woman (the names of three of her first four sons referred to Jehovah) and faithful mother.

Leah's success at childbearing made Rachel envious (30:1) even though Rachel was the object of Jacob's special love. Again the oriental attitude toward childbearing is evident. Rachel's outburst, recorded in verse 2, was not well received by Jacob. She knew well that only God could remove her sterility (v. 6). Like Sarah some years earlier (16:2), she gave her handmaid, Bilhah, to her husband (v. 4), and that relationship produced Dan (v. 6) and Naphtali (v. 8). Then Leah, who was no longer bearing sons, also became concerned and gave her handmaid, Zilpah, to Jacob. To this union were born Gad and Asher (vv. 11–13).

During the wheat harvest (in May and June in upper Mesopotamia) Reuben gathered some mandrakes for Leah his mother (v. 14). The mandrake is an herb of the Belladonna family with white and reddish blossoms. Its yellow fruit is similar in size and shape to a small apple. Peoples in the ancient Near East thought mandrakes stimulated sensual desire and aided conception. It is interesting that while Rachel got the mandrakes, Leah gained another son (vv. 15–18)! She named him Issachar. Later she gave birth to a sixth son, Zebulun (v. 20), and a daughter, Dinah, whose name meant "vindications." She was not Jacob's only daughter (cf. 37:35; 46:7), but she is here mentioned in anticipation of the tragedy recorded in chapter 34.

Perhaps in answer to prayer, God remembered Rachel with a son who was named Joseph (vv. 22–24). That name has been traced to two root meanings, "to take away" and "to add."[14] If

---

14. C. F. Keil and Franz Delitzsch, *Biblical Commentary on the Old Testament*, 25 vols. (Edinburgh: T. and T. Clark, 1864–1901), 1:290.

the former is adopted, *Joseph* would signify that God had removed from Rachel the reproach of childlessness; if the latter, it would signify that the Lord would give her another son.

C. Material Prosperity (30:25–43)

After fourteen years of service, Jacob was ready to return to Canaan (vv. 25, 26). Laban, however, recognizing that Jacob was blessed of God, was not anxious to see him leave. So determined was he to keep Jacob from leaving that he was willing for Jacob to set his own conditions, a concession of no small magnitude considering Laban's previous maneuvers. Of course, the wages which Laban agreed to pay he changed ten times in six years (31:7). Laban persisted and Jacob agreed on the condition that all of Laban's white and white-spotted goats, and all of Laban's black or speckled sheep would become his. This was reasonable enough since as a rule goats were black and dark brown and sheep were white, and Laban quickly agreed. At first reading it seems that Jacob would receive all the spotted animals then in Laban's herd. But Laban and his sons separated these from the flock and took them a three-days journey away (vv. 35, 36). The agreement, therefore, must have been that Jacob would receive only the spotted animals born to the purely marked flock. The fact that Laban removed all the off-colored sheep, goats, and cattle is ample proof that he was familiar with the basic laws of heredity.

Jacob relied on the ancient superstition that the offspring were influenced by the fears or experiences of the mother during pregnancy. This process is demonstrably unscientific. Frank L. Marsh, in an excellent study, observes: "All marking of the offspring such as that which Jacob thought he was accomplishing in Laban's flocks, is completely impossible. . . . In the placenta and umbilical cord, which constitute the only connection between the mother and the fetus, there are *no nerves*. . . . Thus, absolutely no mechanism exists whereby the mother can mark her offspring in the way that Jacob thought he was accomplishing the marking."[15] The Bible records the fact that Jacob utilized a superstitious method, but it in no way attributes the results to that method. Nor is there anything unscientific about those results. William J. Tinkle writes that Laban "had indeed taken the ones which were

249

---

15. *Studies in Creationism*, pp. 368, 369. Italics are Marsh's.

visibly spotted but the rest were heterozygous for spotting—there were latent genes for that pattern—and spotted kids were the logical result. Breeding tests have shown that spotting is recessive to solid color in goats. Modern genetic studies on dominants and latency have cleared this incident, which at one time seemed to link the Bible with groundless supposition."[16] Jacob's success is attributed by the text to selective breeding (vv. 40–42) and divine intervention (31:10–12).

III. The Return to Canaan (31:1–33:20)

As we observed earlier, scholars generally agree that Laban had adopted Jacob. Thus the birth of sons to Laban (30:35; 31:1) would have changed Jacob's status as the chief heir. Perhaps this explains verse 2: " . . . Jacob beheld the countenance of Laban, and, behold, it was not toward him as before." A Nuzi tablet of adoption reads: "The tablet of adoption belonging to [Zike], the son of Akkuya: he gave his son Shennima in adoption to Shuriha-ilu, and Shuriha-ilu, with reference to Shennima, (from) all the lands . . . (and) his earnings of every sort gave to Shennima one (portion) of his property. If Shuriha-ilu should have a son of his own, as the principal (son) he shall take a double share; Shennima shall then be next in order (and) take his proper share."[17] Once a son was born to the landowner, the double portion of the inheritance went to him rather than the adopted one. Whether this, or Laban's unreliability (v. 7), or something else caused the change in Laban's attitude toward Jacob has yet to be determined.[18]

A. Separation from Laban (31:1–55)

Laban's attitude toward Jacob changed drastically, even approaching hostility. Jacob concluded that his only alternative was to leave the area immediately. He met Rachel and Leah in the fields with his flocks, where plans could be made in secret, and explained the dilemma to them. For the first time the two sisters were united in opinion. They agreed that the fortunes of Jacob, as

---

16. *Heredity*, pp. 153, 154. Also see Marsh, *Studies in Creationism*, p. 374.
17. "Mesopotamian Legal Documents," translated by Theophile J. Meek, in Pritchard, *ANET*, p. 220 (text no. 3).
18. See objections to this proposal in Van Seters, "Jacob's Marriages," pp. 377ff.

well as their own, were threatened (vv. 14–16), and that they should depart quickly. While Laban was out in the fields (v. 19), Jacob's camels were prepared, Rachel stole her father's "images" (*t^erāpîm*), and Jacob's family set out for Canaan. Not until three days later was their departure discovered (v. 22). When it was, Laban pursued them. He took seven days to overtake them (v. 23), satisfied with a leisurely pace because he knew Jacob could not move very quickly with all of his family, servants, possessions, and animals. Before Laban overtook Jacob, however, the Lord warned him in a dream to say nothing to Jacob either "good or bad" (v. 24). This expression is literally "from good to bad" and is proverbial (cf. Gen. 24:50; II Sam. 13:22). In other words, Laban was not to get Jacob to return, either by inducements or by force.

Laban's overriding concern, however, was his *t^erāpîm*, or "gods" (v. 30). He searched Jacob's camp thoroughly, but in vain. Rachel had hidden them in the camel saddle upon which she sat (v. 34). Oriental custom required children, regardless of age, to stand in the presence of their parents,[19] but Rachel did not because she claimed to be in the period of menses (v. 35). What were these images and why were they so important to Rachel? *T^erāpîm* appear a number of times in the Old Testament.[20] They were human figurines, usually small (v. 34) but sometimes quite large (cf. I Sam. 19.13–16). The majority discovered so far are figurines of female deities two to three inches in length. They were used as household gods and, when carried on the body, as personal charms.

Three reasons have been suggested for Rachel's stealing the *t^erāpîm*, and all are distinct possibilities.

First, *t^erāpîm* were thought by the ancients to guarantee fertility; a majority of *t^erāpîm* were nude goddesses whose sexual features are accentuated. Rachel, then, wanted to guarantee that she would continue to bear children.

Second, Nuzi texts reveal that household gods were an important part of the sons' inheritance. One "sale-adoption" tablet states: "If Nashwi has a son of his own, he shall divide (the estate) equally with Wullu, but the son of Nashwi shall take the gods of Nashwi. However, if Nashwi does not have a son of his own, then

---

19. Lev. 19:32; I Kings 2:19.
20. Judg. 17:5–18:30; I Sam. 15:23; 19:13–16; II Kings 23:24; Hos. 3:4; Ezek. 21:21; Zech. 10:2.

A ninth-century B.C. relief from Tell Halaf, showing a man riding a box-like camel saddle

Wullu shall take the gods of Nashwi."[21] A Kirkuk marriage contract is similar, requiring the idols to be passed on to the real son rather than the son-in-law.[22] Modern commentators generally agree that the $t^e r\bar{a}\underline{p}\hat{i}m$ symbolized inheritance rights. One writes: "Rachel was in a position to know, or at least suspect, that in conformance with local law her husband was entitled to a specific share in Laban's estate. But she also had ample reason to doubt that her father would voluntarily transfer the images as formal proof of property release; the ultimate status of Laban's daughters and their maidservants could well have been involved as well."[23] Rachel, then, sought to insure Jacob some portion of Laban's inheritance.

Moshe Greenberg suggests a third alternative. He contends that "Rachel's desire to possess the gods of Laban, if it meant anything in this connection, could mean that she wished Jacob to be recognized as paterfamilias after Laban's death—assuming, of course, that such a claim could be urged on the strength of

21. "Mesopotamian Legal Documents," translated by Meek, in Pritchard, *ANET*, pp. 219, 220 (text no. 2). Also see Gordon, "Biblical Customs," pp. 1–12; Gordon, "Jacob and Laban," pp. 25–27; and Gordon, "Parallelels nouzien aux lois et coutumes de L'Ancien Testament," *Revue Biblique* 44 (1935): 34–41.
22. C. J. Gadd, "Tablets from Kirkuk," pp. 49–161 (text no. 51).
23. Speiser, *Genesis*, p. 250. See also John Bright, *A History of Israel*, p. 71.

Terra-cotta plaques of deities from Ur, probably similar to those Rachel stole from her father (Courtesy of the British Museum)

possessing the gods. If she really meant only to insure an inheritance share for Jacob, that went too far—much too far, as we shall see."[24] Josephus provides the simplest explanation for Rachel's stealing the *t^erāpîm*, asserts Greenberg. Her reasons were religious. Since these gods afforded to their owners special protection and perhaps fertility, she deeply desired to have them. Because she was fleeing from her father, there was no normal way for her to gain access to them.[25]

These three views might not be mutually exclusive. Rachel may well have stolen her father's *t^erāpîm* to guarantee both her ability to bear children and Jacob's inheritance of some portion of Laban's wealth.

Laban finally gave up the search for his household idols and agreed to a covenant which would establish peace between the two families (v. 44). As a sign of the covenant a stone was set up for a pillar (v. 45). The terms of the agreement, which were very similar to those of other such covenants in Mesopotamia (vv. 49–52), satisfied Laban, and early in the morning, after kissing his sons and daughters and blessing them, he departed (v. 55). Thus Laban disappears from the biblical narrative. This is also the last contact between the patriarchal family and the relatives in Mesopotamia.

B. Reconciliation with Esau (32:1–33:20)

As Jacob journeyed southward, he was met by "the angels of God" (32:1). Seeing them probably encouraged Jacob and certainly reminded him of his vision at Bethel (28:11–15). He named that place *Mahanaim*, meaning "double camp," which has been interpreted as two bands of angels (one before and one behind him)[26] or another camp that matched his.[27]

After many years of separation due to Esau's bitter hatred, Jacob attempted a reconciliation between himself and his brother. Jacob sent servants to him with a humble greeting and gifts (vv. 4, 5). Esau, however, was already on his way to meet Jacob, and he had with him four hundred men. When Jacob learned of this, he was greatly distressed (vv. 6, 7). He quickly divided his flocks and possessions into two groups in order that at least one might escape

24. "Another Look at Rachel's Theft of the Teraphim," pp. 242ff.
25. Ibid., pp. 246, 247.
26. Nichol, ed., *Bible Commentary*, 1:404.
27. Kidner, *Genesis*, p. 167.

an attack, and he prayed to his God (vv. 9—12). His prayer evidenced true humility. He petitioned God for protection from Esau so that the Lord's covenant promises might be fulfilled (vv. 11, 12). Even though Jacob was trusting the Lord for protection, he took further steps toward reconciliation with Esau. As a gift to him Jacob selected more than five hundred head of sheep and cattle (vv. 14—16). The space between the various groups of animals (v. 16) may have been to guarantee organization but it also may have been to make the gift more impressive. The animals and servants crossed the Jabbok River, and Jacob and his wives followed a short distance behind (vv. 21—23). As Jacob contemplated his meeting with Esau, he became deeply concerned and anxious. He withdrew and spent time alone, which led to one of the most unusual experiences of his life.

While alone, Jacob wrestled with a man until daybreak (v. 24). This "man" is regarded by some as the preincarnate Christ[28] and by others as an angel, a special messenger from God.[29] Hosea 12:4 points toward the latter. Mary Baker Eddy's insistence that angels are nothing more than "God's thoughts" or "good thoughts"[30] has always intrigued me in light of this passage. According to Genesis the angel struck Jacob on the thigh and crippled him; this seems like a strange place to be struck with a "good thought," to say nothing of the physical consequences! In any event, Jacob ceased to struggle, and, charged with a spiritual hunger, refused to let the visitor go until he blessed him (v. 26). God honored Jacob's honest desire and changed his name from *Jacob* ("heel catcher" or "deceiver") to *Israel* ("God's fighter"[31] or "may God strive [for him]"[32]). The older derivation of *Israel* which gave it the meaning "prince of God"[33] has been largely rejected. As he had before (28:19; 32:2), Jacob memorialized his experience by giving the place a special name. He chose *Peniel* because "I have seen God face to face" (v. 30). The observation that because of Jacob's experience the children of Israel did not eat the sinew "unto this day" (v. 32) is fascinating. Even though this is mentioned nowhere

---

28. Keil and Delitzsch, *Biblical Commentary*, 1:304, 305; and Nichol, ed., *Bible Commentary*, 1:406.
29. R. Payne Smith, *Genesis*, p. 123.
30. *Science and Health with Key to the Scriptures*, p. 581.
31. Keil and Delitzsch, *Biblical Commentary*, 1:304.
32. Kidner, *Genesis*, p. 170.
33. Charles R. Erdman, *The Book of Genesis*, p. 106. Speiser, following S. R. Driver, suggests the meaning "May El persevere." *Genesis*, p. 255.

else in the Old Testament, the Jewish Talmud regarded it a sacred law. Even today Jews avoid eating the interior cord and nerve of the hind quarter of animals.

The situation was dramatic and tense. As Esau and Jacob approached each other, Jacob lined up his family so that the handmaids and their children were in front and Rachel and Joseph were last (33:1, 2). Jacob greeted Esau by bowing to the ground seven times (v. 3), reminiscent of the oriental respect reflected in the Amarna Tablets.[34] The meeting, far from being belligerent, was intensely warm and intimate (vv. 4–7). In fact Esau was a bit surprised by the great gifts from Jacob, initially declining them but finally accepting them (vv. 8–11). The two agreed to depart peacefully, Esau for the mountains of Seir (v. 14) and Jacob for the vicinity of Shechem (vv. 17–20).

IV. Life in Canaan (34:1–35:29)

A. Massacre at Shechem (34:1–31)

Jacob's residence at Shechem, rather than being another time of blessing, resulted in one of the greatest tragedies recorded in the Book of Genesis. He paid Hamor a high price for part of a field near the city of Shechem: " . . . rape, treachery, and massacre, a chain of evil that proceeded logically enough from the unequal partnership with the Canaanite community."[35] This story is often considered nothing more than a narrative from the time when the tribes of Levi and Simeon were striving to settle in central Palestine.[36] However, there is no reason to impose tribal history on a story which is eminently personal, and to do so is to reduce its moral and spiritual impact.

The age of Dinah is not given in verse 1, but since she had not been more than five or six when the family left Haran,[37] she was about fifteen or sixteen at this time. Nor is the occasion given during which Shechem, Hamor's son, seized and defiled her, but Josephus indicates that it was a special Shechemite festival.[38] Even after defiling her, Shechem wished to marry Dinah (vv. 3, 4).

---

34. "The Amarna Letters," in Pritchard, *ANET*, pp. 483–90.
35. Kidner, *Genesis*, p. 172.
36. Von Rad, *Genesis*, pp. 329, 330.
37. She was born only after Leah's sixth son was born (30:21), but the intervening events of chapters 30–33 would have taken at least eight years.
38. *Antiquities*, 1:21:1.

Two views of Shechem: *above*, from northwest of the platform in front of the Early Bronze temple; *below*, from the ruins of the east gate (Courtesy of Levant Photo Service)

Soon after hearing about Shechem's deed (v. 5), Jacob was visited by Hamor, presumably to arrange the marriage (v. 6). The bargain which Hamor tried to strike (vv. 8–10) probably reflects the Canaanites' appeal to the Israelites in later periods, such as that of the judges; whenever the Israelites responded to this appeal, they were caught up not only in Canaanite culture, but in its idolatry and immorality. The brothers of Dinah agreed to Hamor's terms only if he and his family would be circumcised (vv. 14–19). Hamor and his family accepted this condition and were circumcised (vv. 20–24). Three days later when the men were still suffering from inflammation and fever, the brothers of Dinah attacked and slew them (vv. 25–27), taking their possessions as booty and their families for slaves (vv. 28, 29). While his sons considered their deed an act of bravery and justified retribution, Jacob saw it otherwise (v. 30). Their treachery deeply troubled him, and his last words to Simeon and Levi are evidence that he never forgot their evil act (cf. 49:5–7).

B. Worship at Bethel (35:1–15)

Jacob returned to Bethel and worshiped God. Perhaps he feared reprisal from other Canaanite tribes in the vicinity. In any event, he made an altar and challenged his household to destroy their idols (35:1, 2). This included the *terāpim* which Rachel had stolen from her father (31:19) and the images carried from Mesopotamia by Jacob's servants. Earrings also were included (v. 4); they were probably cult objects. As in later days when Israel marched into Canaan, God sent fear into the hearts of the tribes round about so that they did not "pursue after the sons of Jacob" (v. 5; cf. Josh. 2:10, 11; 5:1). And the Lord again appeared to Jacob and reaffirmed His covenant with him (vv. 9–15).

C. Deaths of Rachel and Isaac (35:16–29)

From Bethel Jacob and his family went to Ephrath, or Bethlehem (v. 19), where Rachel gave birth to Benjamin. Being near death, she named him *Ben-oni*, meaning "son of my pain" or "son of my misfortune" (v. 18). Jacob, however, called him Benjamin ("son of the right hand"). Rachel died and was buried near Bethlehem. A pillar marked her grave (vv. 19, 20), and apparently it was still visible in the days of Moses (cf. v. 20).

After reviewing the sons of Jacob (vv. 22–26), the narrator

258

returns to the adventures of Jacob. From Bethlehem Jacob journeyed southward to Mamre, where he witnessed the death of his father Isaac, who was 180 years old (vv. 27–29). The fact that Esau helped Jacob bury their father might evidence further reconciliation and fellowship.

Chapter 36 consists principally of lists of the descendants of Esau and Seir the Horite, whose families had intermarried. It might seem unusual that such detail concerning the descendants of Esau be included, but the relationship between Esau and Jacob, and then between the nations of Edom and Israel, is a theme of the entire Old Testament. Moses' conclusion to this chapter is amazingly detailed and accurate. This material, however, is a parenthesis within the story of Jacob (cf. 37:2).

17

From a Pit to a Palace

Genesis 37–45

Egypt owed its survival to the Nile River. When the Nile flooded its banks regularly, even the common man was prosperous and the Nile was praised: "Praise to thee, O Nile, that issueth from the earth, and cometh to nourish Egypt. . . . That maketh barley and createth wheat, so that he may cause the temples to keep festivals. . . . When the Nile floodeth, offering is made to thee, cattle are slaughtered for thee, a great oblation is made for thee. Birds are fattened for thee, antelopes are hunted for thee in the desert. Good is recompensed unto thee."[1] Egypt was known for producing a variety of foods. Successful crops, of course, were always attributed to the blessing of the gods. The ancient Egyptian took great pride in the land's fertility and high productivity. He often measured the value and glory of a city by its agricultural wealth. A model letter which school boys copied reflects very vividly their pride in the new city called House-of-Rameses: "Its field is full of all good things, and it hath provisions and sustenance every day. Its ponds (?) are full of fishes, and its lakes of

---

1. "To the Nile," in Adolf Erman, ed., *The Ancient Egyptians*, pp. 146–48.

birds. . . . Its granaries are full of barley and wheat, and they reach unto the sky. . . . Provisions and sustenance are in it daily. One rejoiceth when one dwelleth in it, and none saith unto it, 'Would that!' The small in it are like unto the great."[2] There were times of crop failure and tragedy, however. The ancient prophet Ipu-Wer described such a time, and his sentiments probably reflect those of Egyptians during the seven-year famine recorded in Genesis: "Nay, but corn hath perished everywhere. People are stripped of clothing, perfume, and oil. Every one saith: 'There is no more.' The storehouse is bare, and he that kept it lieth stretched out on the ground. . . . Would that I had lifted up my voice at that moment, that it might have saved me from the pain in which I am!"[3]

The story of Joseph is regarded as among the best short stories of the world because of its "dramatic movement, its brilliant color, its play of all the elemental passions, and its abiding human interest. . . ."[4] Apart from the episode involving Judah and Tamar (chapter 38) and Jacob's farewell blessing (chapter 49), the rest of Genesis is devoted to Joseph's life. The material is unique in Genesis for its detailed report of the customs, practices, and conditions of a non-Israelite people. It is a masterpiece of historical narration, including character delineation, tension, and suspense. Equally brilliant are Moses' incidental insights into the various deeds of the principal characters.

Modern critical source analysis usually sees in the Joseph story two sources, J and E, combined by a redactor into their present form.[5] Of course, the redactor did not include all available material, and this explains some of the textual problems in the narrative.[6] Von Rad, though, does not agree that the story of Joseph was based on tribal traditions. He argues instead that, even in its earlier version, it was a special kind of novel which could not have been composed prior to the monarchy.[7] However ingenious these two approaches, the soundest—from the standpoint of cultural background, literary style, and general content—is to see Moses as

---

2. "In Praise of the New City Called House-of-Ramesses," in Erman, ed., *The Ancient Egyptians*, p. 206.
3. "The Admonitions of a Prophet," in Erman, ed., *The Ancient Egyptians*, p. 99.
4. Charles R. Erdman, *The Book of Genesis*, p. 112.
5. Gerhard von Rad, *Genesis*, p. 343.
6. See R. N. Whybray, "The Joseph Story and Pentateuchal Criticism," p. 522.
7. *Genesis*, p. 542. See also Whybray, "The Joseph Story," p. 526.

the author. He was reared and trained in the royal court, and was fully capable of recording accurately the kind of cultural detail so characteristic of the Joseph story.

I. Joseph Entering Slavery (37:1–36)

A. His Brothers' Jealousy (37:1–11)

From "the generations of Esau" (36:1) the writer returns to "the generations of Jacob" (37:2). The center of attention is seventeen-year-old Joseph. Commentators differ widely in their view of young Joseph. One writes that Joseph "commands none of our sympathies," and that the narrative depicts "a father's favoritism, tittle-tattle, sibling jealousies, egotistic boyish dreams—all the unlovely elements of a family situation containing the infallible ingredients of explosive tragedy. . . ."[8] In contrast to this, Erdman writes: "However naive or even self-conscous he may appear as he relates his dreams to his brothers, this was not a sign of childish vanity or pride; it was an exhibition of faith. Joseph regarded his visions as the veritable voice of God."[9]

Joseph was tending sheep with his brothers. The text says without elaboration that he "brought unto his father their evil report" (37:2). It is difficult to judge whether Joseph did this on his own initiative or was required to do it by his father (cf. Lev. 5:1). The fact that "Israel loved Joseph more than all his children" (v. 3) indicates that he had learned nothing from his earlier experiences of favoritism. In fact, similar jealousies and hatred resulted (v. 4). His gift to Joseph of a "coat of many colours" (*keṯoneṯ passîm*), a further evidence of his preference for Joseph, caused the brothers to hate Joseph even more. The expression *keṯoneṯ passîm* has been translated three principal ways: "a coat of many colors," "a long-sleeved robe," and "an ornamented tunic." The word *passîm* also appears in II Samuel 13:18, 19 where it describes the dress of Tamar, King David's daughter. Some cuneiform documents discovered in Mesopotamia list and describe various garments, one of which is called *kitû* (or *kutinnū*) *pišannu.* This was normally a ceremonial robe draped around the statue of a goddess and decorated distinctively with gold orna-

263

---

8. Nahum M. Sarna, *Understanding Genesis*, p. 212.
9. *The Book of Genesis*, p. 113. For another study of this problem see John Peck, "Note on Genesis 37:2 and Joseph's Character," pp. 342, 343.

ments sewn to it.[10] Speiser contends that "the Hebrew phrase
. . . *passim* would be an adaptation of Akk. *pišannu*, a technical
term denoting appliqué ornaments on costly vests and bodices."[11]

The dreams of Joseph, like those of Abimelech (20:3), Jacob
(28:12ff.; 31:11), and Laban (31:24), were divinely inspired, but
unlike them his was filled with symbolism. So were those of the
baker, the butler, and Pharaoh. In Joseph's first dream (v. 7) he
and his brothers were binding sheaves in the field, and his
brothers' sheaves "made obeisance" to Joseph's. The meaning of
the dream was obvious to Joseph's brothers (v. 8). In his second
dream the personification of natural elements is extended to the
sun and moon. They, too, bowed down to Joseph, making him
supreme even over his parents (v. 9). When his father heard the
dreams, he was astonished and rebuked Joseph (v. 10). His brothers reacted even more strongly (v. 11).

B. His Sale into Slavery (37:12–35)

Having exhausted the grazing areas in the south, Joseph's brothers herded their father's flocks some eighty miles north to Dothan.
Shepherds could move freely through the central hill country
during the Middle Bronze age because it was only sparsely occupied. On the south side of the mound of Dothan is a fine well
which still provides the water needed for the flocks and the fields
below the tell. Excavations conducted at Tell Dothan by Joseph P.
Free, director of the Wheaton Archaeological Expedition, have
confirmed that Dothan was occupied in the time of Jacob. In
1953, the first year of excavation, a significant quantity of Middle
Bronze pottery was discovered both inside and outside the large
city wall, which was built in the Early Bronze age. One discovery
of particular interest, from level IV inside the city wall, was the
remains of a one- or two-year-old child buried under a wall made
of large stones. By the child's mouth was a small Middle Bronze
jar, by its right hand a juglet, and by its feet a double-handled
Middle Bronze jug. The child was probably a "foundation-
sacrifice."[12] Beginning as early as the Early Bronze age,[13] the site

10. A. Leo Oppenheim, "The Golden Garments of the Gods," p. 177.
11. *Genesis*, p. 290.
12. Joseph P. Free, "The First Season of Excavation at Dothan," pp. 16–18.
13. Free, "The Second Season at Dothan," p. 14 (n. 3). For additional
information on Dothan, see Free's other articles: "The Third Season at

had a long occupation, due largely to its strategic location. Dothan is twelve miles north of Samaria in the direction of Esdraelon, and is on the great caravan road from the north to Egypt.

When Joseph visited his brothers in Dothan, he received a less than warm reception. His brothers plotted to slay him and then report to their father that a wild animal had devoured him (v. 20). Presumably this would prevent the fulfillment of Joseph's dreams. When Reuben, who had not been in on the plot, heard about it, he was unenthusiastic. As the eldest son he felt a special responsibility for his brother and attempted to thwart the evil plan by suggesting that they merely throw Joseph into an empty cistern ("pit"), from which Reuben hoped to rescue him later (v. 22). The vindictive brothers followed Reuben's suggestion after stripping from Joseph his coat (v. 23). Possibly they intended him to die a horrible death by starvation. It should not be concluded that the brothers merely hated Joseph as a brother. They were rebelling "against the matter contained in the dreams, [and] against the divine power itself . . . who had given the dreams."[14]

While the brothers were eating, they saw a company of Ishmaelite tradesmen on their way from Gilead to Egypt (v. 25). They agreed to sell Joseph as a slave to the Ishmaelites and thereby avoid responsibility for his death. The terms *Ishmaelite* and *Midianite* are used interchangeably in verse 28, as they are in Judges 8:22, 24. *Ishmaelite* may not be an ethnic designation here, but simply an appellative for nomadic merchants. The purchase price for Joseph was twenty pieces, or shekels, of silver, which probably was about average;[15] the price of a slave varied with the circumstances and the slave's sex, age, and condition. In the late third millennium B.C. the average price in Mesopotamia was ten to fifteen shekels of silver.[16] Reuben, who was absent when the transaction took place, returned to the pit and, to his distress, found it empty. He apparently helped his brothers stain Joseph's coat with the blood of a goat (v. 31). When the coat was shown to Jacob, he immediately went into mourning for his son, thinking he

Dothan"; "Dothan, 1954"; "The Excavation of Dothan"; "The Fourth Season at Dothan"; "Radiocarbon Date of Iron Age Level at Dothan"; "The Sixth Season at Dothan"; and "The Seventh Season at Dothan."
14. Von Rad, *Genesis*, p. 348.
15. However, on the basis of Exod. 21:32, some feel that it was below average.
16. Kenneth A. Kitchen, "Slave," in J. D. Douglas, ed., *New Bible Dictionary*, p. 1196.

had been killed by a wild animal (vv. 32–35). There is a touch of irony here: Jacob, who had deceived his father with a goat's skin, was deceived by his sons with goat's blood.

Archaeology has shed a great deal of light on the slave trade between Egypt and its neighbors to the north. Egypt's chief source of supply for slaves was its prisoners of war, but peaceful slave trading was also common.[17] Two documents in particular nicely illustrate this. The first is the last will and testament of King Amenemhet III, in which he disposed of four Asiatic slaves received as a gift from his brother.[18] The second is a papyrus from the late Middle Kingdom[19] which lists seventy-seven slaves, forty-eight of which are Asiatics. They include men, women, and children who were capable of being sold to others.[20] The women served as weavers, the men and children as domestics, cooks, brewers, and warehouse keepers. These and other documents demonstrate the amazing accuracy of the Joseph story. Continued studies in these areas, coupled with expanded archaeological expeditions, presumably will shed even more light on these narratives.

C. His Arrival in Egypt (37:36)

Dating Joseph's entrance into Egypt (v. 36) and his rise to power is difficult, in part because the pharaoh of the Joseph narratives is not named. H. H. Rowley and Gordon place Joseph's arrival in Egypt after 1400 B.C.;[21] the majority of scholars place it in the Hyksos period (ca. 1730–1570 B.C.);[22] and some place it in the 1800s B.C. during the Middle Kingdom period,[23] and specifically during the reign of Sesostris III (Senusert III, Twelfth

---

17. J. Vergote, *Joseph en Égypte*, pp. 16–20.
18. "Middle Kingdom Egyptian Contacts with Asia," in Pritchard, *ANET*, p. 229.
19. See William C. Hayes, *A Papyrus of the Late Middle Kingdom in the Brooklyn Museum*.
20. Georges Posener, "Les Asiatiques en Egypte sous les XIIe et XIIIe dynasties," *Syria* 34 (1957): 145–63.
21. *From Joseph to Joshua*, pp. 116–20; *Introduction to Old Testament Times*, pp. 102ff.
22. William F. Albright, *The Biblical Period from Abraham to Ezra*, p. 11.
23. Merrill F. Unger, *Archaeology and the Old Testament* (Grand Rapids: Zondervan Publishing House, 1954), p. 134; John J. Davis, *Moses and the Gods of Egypt*, pp. 45–51; and Davis, *Mummies, Men and Madness*, pp. 94–96.

Dynasty).[24] The third view is most compatible with scriptural data. According to I Kings 6:1 the exodus from Egypt took place 480 years before the fourth year of Solomon. The fourth year of Solomon is usually regarded as about 966 B.C., meaning that the exodus occurred approximately 1446–45 B.C. The Egyptian sojourn was 430 years long (Exod. 12:40), so it began approximately 1875 B.C. This synchronizes with the dates normally accepted for the reign of Sesostris III: 1878–43 B.C.[25] Evidence is abundant that Middle Kingdom pharaohs had interests in the Delta region.[26] Sesostris' capital, for example, was It-towy (Lisht), which is near the Delta.[27] James R. Battenfield suggests that the Joseph story explains why Sesostris attempted to abolish feudalism: "Sesostris III bought out the landed nomarchs not because of some sort of social revolution, but because of an economic disaster, a severe food shortage."[28] Genesis 47:20 indicates that Joseph bought all the land of Egypt for Pharaoh. If this marked the cessation of feudalism, as Battenfield suggests, "it would seem that Joseph could not have lived 215 years later in the fifteenth dynasty, Hyksos-dominated Egypt, because at that time (1674–1570) feudalism was being reinstituted and not abolished."[29] Many other internal evidences for associating Joseph with a Middle Kingdom pharaoh will be considered as we come to them.

II. Tamar Deceiving Judah (38:1–30)

The interruption of Joseph's story with Judah's family difficulties might seem unnecessary and trivial, but the information supplied in this chapter settles the problem of seniority in the tribe of Judah and supplies important information for the royal

---

24. This proposal is discussed in detail in James R. Battenfield, "A Consideration of the Identity of the Pharaoh of Genesis 47," pp. 77–85.
25. Studies of Gen. 15:13–16, Acts 7:6, and Exod. 12:40 are Battenfield, "The Pharaoh of Genesis 47," pp. 78–80; Jack R. Riggs, "The Length of Israel's Sojourn in Egypt," pp. 18–35; Davis, *Moses and the Gods of Egypt*, pp. 148–50; Harold W. Hoehner, "The Duration of the Egyptian Bondage," pp. 309–12; Gleason Archer, *A Survey of Old Testament Introduction*, pp. 211, 212.
26. E. P. Uphill, "Pithom and Raamses: Their Location and Significance," pp. 305, 308, 313; John Van Seters, *The Hyksos*, pp. 95, 96.
27. Alan Gardiner, *Egypt of the Pharaohs*, p. 127.
28. "The Pharaoh of Genesis 47," p. 85.
29. Ibid., pp. 83, 84.

genealogy (Matt. 1:3; Luke 3:33). The heart of the story is Tamar's desire to bear Judah's heir and her various deceptions to achieve that end.

Judah married an unnamed daughter of Shua, an Adullamite living south of Jerusalem. By her he had three sons: Er, Onan, and Shelah (vv. 3–5). Er, who married Tamar, was killed by God because of his wickedness (vv. 6, 7). The nature of his evil activity is not described, but it must have been very serious to merit such a judgment. Er left no heir, so according to the law of levirate marriage, his brother Onan was to marry the childless widow and give Er an heir. This is the first mention in the Bible of levirate marriage, but it was common in ancient Near Eastern law codes.[30] Onan, however, forsook his levirate responsibility, and God killed him, also (vv. 9, 10). "The enormity of Onan's sin is in its studied outrage against the family, against his brother's widow and against his own body."[31] The death of Judah's two older sons soon after marrying Tamar made Judah hesitate to give his third son, but Judah promised that when Shelah reached marriageable age, he would give him to Tamar (v. 11).

When the time came, Judah failed to make good his promise. Tamar, feeling deeply responsible to produce an heir for Judah's eldest son, resorted to the prevailing Hittite and Assyrian custom of having the duty of levirate marriage performed by the father of the deceased. Hearing that Judah was shearing his sheep (vv. 12, 13), which was often a time for licentious and unrestrained behavior, she disguised herself as a harlot, or more specifically, a temple prostitute. When Judah first saw her, he identified her as a common "harlot," a *zônâ* (v. 15). Verses 21 and 22, however, make it clear that she dressed and acted like a Canaanite temple prostitute (*keḏēšâ*). Tamar required from Judah a pledge until he could pay in full for her services (vv. 17, 18). So he gave her a "signet" (v. 18) which probably was a cylinder seal carried around the neck on a cord; "bracelets," which is better rendered "cord" (RV, RSV); and a staff, which probably had distinctive, identifying marks carved into it.

When Judah later attempted to make payment, he was unable to find Tamar. Not until three months later did word reach him

---

30. Millar Burrows, "The Ancient Oriental Background of Hebrew Levirate Marriage," pp. 2–15; George W. Coats, "Widow's Rights: A Crux in the Structure of Genesis 38," pp. 461–66.
31. Derek Kidner, *Genesis*, p. 188.

that Tamar was pregnant because of harlotry (v. 24). His initial
reaction was that she should be burned, an unusual punishment
for harlotry. In the later Mosaic law stoning was the usual punishment (Deut. 22:20—24); only priests' daughters or women guilty of
certain forms of incest were burned (Lev. 20:14; 21:9).[32] When
Tamar was brought before him, however, Judah found himself
incapable of punishing her at all because he discovered that he
himself had made her pregnant (v. 25). Furthermore, he was
forced to admit that she was more righteous than he because he had
consciously neglected to give her Shelah as a husband (v. 26).
Tamar gave birth to twins, Perez and Zerah (vv. 27—30). Even
though the midwife did not consider Perez the first-born, he was
placed before Zerah in all genealogical lists (cf. Gen. 46:12; Num.
26:20). According to Ruth 4:18—22 he was the ancestor of King
David and ultimately of the Messiah (Matt. 1:3—16).

III. Joseph Serving Potiphar (39:1—23)

Once in Egypt Joseph was sold to Potiphar, an "officer [*sārîs*]
of Pharaoh" and a "captain of the guard" (*sar haṭṭabbāhîm*). *Sārîs*
usually means "eunuch," but Potiphar was married, so here it has
the derived meaning of "prominent court official."[33] *Sar
haṭṭabbāhîm* is also used of Nebuzaradan, the servant of Nebu-
chadnezzar, in II Kings 25:8 and Jeremiah 39:9, 10.[34] From its use
in II Kings and Jeremiah, one would conclude that Potiphar's
position involved protecting the Pharaoh himself; perhaps
Potiphar was the commanding officer of the royal body guard.
Even though Joseph was in Egypt and far from his family, the
Lord was with him (39:2) and he became a trusted servant of
Potiphar (v. 4). Perhaps his elevation to positions of responsibility
were providential preparation for his later career. One must be
reminded that regardless of what genius Joseph possessed, his
successes were made possible by the Lord (cf. v. 5).

One cannot help but be impressed by Joseph's courage and
determination. Despite his treatment at his brothers' hands, he
sought no sympathy, solicited no pity. On the contrary, he ener-

---

32. Burning was also a punishment in Mesopotamia. "The Code of Hammurabi," in Pritchard, *ANET*, pp. 167 (paragraph 25), 170 (paragraph 110).
33. H. C. Leupold, *Exposition of Genesis*, 2:993.
34. The titles "leader of the palace guard" and "lord of the palace guard"
occur in Egyptian texts. See W. A. Ward, "Egyptian Titles in Genesis 39—50,"
p. 41.

getically committed himself to whatever task was laid before him. The handsome young man's (v. 6) consummate skill in organization and leadership made him valuable not only to his father but to Potiphar as well. Potiphar made Joseph his comptroller (*mer-per*), which meant being a personal attendant to his master and overseeing his entire estate.[35]

With a measure of success often comes an even greater measure of temptation. The indiscreet and immoral advances of Potiphar's wife powerfully challenged Joseph's moral and spiritual integrity. His reaction contrasts sharply with Reuben's (35:22) and Judah's (38:16): first Joseph refused her (v. 8), and finally he retreated from her (v. 12; cf. II Tim. 2:22). Unfortunately, many believers flee temptation only to wait around the corner for it to catch up

35. Vergote, *Joseph en Égypte*, pp. 24, 25.

A wall painting from the tomb of Nakht (Eighteenth Dynasty), showing, *above*, men cutting and loading grain, and, *below*, the owner of the tomb watching his workers cut a tree and prepare the soil (Courtesy of the Egyptian Expedition, the Metropolitan Museum of Art)

to them! Joseph's reasons for refusing Potiphar's wife were two: he wished to be faithful to his master, who had helped him (v. 8); and, even more important, he wished to be faithful to God (v. 9). In spite of her persistent approaches (v. 10), Joseph remained free from the great stain and tragedy that later plagued David (II Sam. 11). Joseph probably had calculated the risk. By succumbing, he would have opportunity for further advancement and recognition—if, of course, the affair could be successfully concealed from Potiphar. By refusing he would incur the wrath of a woman without moral standard. And that he did. She had other servants of the household seize Joseph on the pretext that he had attacked her (vv. 13—15). She told a similar lie to her husband, blaming him for ever bringing "the Hebrew servant" to the household (v. 17). Potiphar believed his wife's story and cast Joseph into the king's prison. The Genesis account tells of no physical torture or punishment inflicted there, but there is little doubt that Joseph's initial experiences were difficult. The psalmist says of Joseph that his "feet they hurt with fetters; he was laid in iron" (105:18).

The motif of a married woman making improper proposals, being rejected, and then falsely accusing the man of having attempted to dishonor her, is common in ancient Near Eastern literature.[36] One example is the Egyptian "Story of Two Brothers," usually dated in the late thirteenth century B.C.[37] Current literary critics of the Old Testament see parallels in structure and content between such stories and the one of Joseph in Potiphar's house, and conclude that the latter is generically related to the former. Such a conclusion is tenuous, to say the least. Even though it is widely adopted in Old Testament study, it would be laughed out of court in other disciplines.

While Joseph possessed a high degree of courage and personal integrity, the source of his victory was the Lord Himself (v. 21). The Lord not only strengthened Joseph to resist temptation in Potiphar's house, but put him in another very responsible position in the prison (vv. 21—23). His honesty and forthrightness made the keeper of the prison trust him completely. It seems God was preparing Joseph for his future governmental career no matter where he resided. The early years of Joseph, therefore, provide a sparkling example of unblemished fidelity to his master and to his God.

271

---

36. Ibid., pp. 22—25.
37. In Pritchard, *ANET*, pp. 23—25.

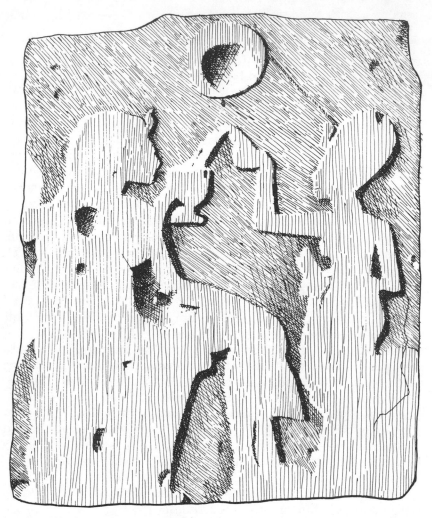

Smenkhkare performs the duties of a butler for Akhenaton in a relief dated in the fourteenth century B.C.

IV. Joseph Interpreting Dreams (40:1—41:36)

A. The Butler's and Baker's Dreams (40:1—23)

While incarcerated, Joseph came in contact with important people who had fallen into disfavor with Pharaoh. Two of these were the Pharaoh's "butler" (*mašqēh melek*) and "baker" (v. 1), later called his "chief butler" (v. 9) and "chief baker" (v. 16). The translation "butler" for *mašqēh melek* is unfortunate. The phrase literally means "cupbearer of the king." Egyptian inscriptions include a number of titles for those who served either wine or beer to the pharaoh and his guests.[38] It might seem strange for a baker to be important in the royal court, but his responsibility to prepare food not only for the living pharaoh, but for his mortuary temple and priesthood perhaps was what exalted him: "To insure the happiness of the deceased there was a constant flow of offerings into the temples and mortuary priesthoods. This was partially in the form of food. One of the staples of Egyptian economy at all levels of the social scale was bread. Included in this category were pastries, cakes, and fruit-breads of all sizes, shapes, and ingredients. The Onomasticon of Amenope, for instance, lists over twenty kinds of baked goods and the Harris Papyrus gives at least thirty, the latter being all in lists of temple offerings. . . ."[39] The baker's chore apparently was not an easy one. In some rather humorous exhortations and warnings to schoolboys, dating from the Nineteenth Dynasty, the occupation of a scribe is compared favorably to any other—including that of a baker: "When the baker standeth and baketh and layeth bread on the fire, his head is inside the oven, and his son holdest fast his feet. Cometh it to pass that he slippeth from his sons' hand, he falleth into the blaze. But the scribe, he directeth every work that is in this land."[40] Of course it is doubtful that the chief baker in the royal court faced any such danger!

The two imprisoned court officials had dreams which deeply perplexed them (vv. 5–7). Since dreams were considered significant in ancient Egypt, the two men sought an interpretation, but they were unsuccessful until Joseph happened on the scene (v. 8). It is interesting that Joseph's dreams, although symbolic, were immediately comprehensible to himself and his brothers. This was not the case with the dreams of the cup bearer and baker. Nahum M. Sarna makes the significant observation that, although "Israel shared with its pagan neighbors a belief in the reality of dreams as a medium of divine communication, it never developed, as in Egypt and Mesopotamia, a class of professional interpreters or a dream litiger. In the entire Bible, only two Israelites engage in the interpretation of dreams—Joseph and Daniel—and significantly enough, each serves a pagan monarch, the one in Egypt, the other in Mesopotamia, precisely the lands in which oneiromancy flour-

38. Ward, "Egyptian Titles," pp. 43, 44.
39. Ibid., pp. 44, 45.
40. In Erman, ed., *The Ancient Egyptians*, p. 197.

ished. Moreover, in each case, the Israelite is careful to disclaim any innate ability, attributing all to God."[41] After the cup bearer's dream was interpreted by Joseph to mean that the cup bearer would be restored to his former position (vv. 9–15), the chief baker related to Joseph his dream. However, to the chief baker's dismay, his dream meant the opposite (vv. 16–19). Joseph's interpretations proved valid. During a royal celebration Pharaoh "lifted up the head" of both the cup bearer and the chief baker (v. 20)—restoring the cup bearer and hanging the chief baker (vv. 21, 22)![42]

B. The Pharaoh's Dreams (41:1–36)

Two years passed. This time Pharaoh himself had a dream. Standing by "the river" (v. 1)—a clear reference to the Nile—he witnessed seven healthy, attractive cows come up out of the water, and after them seven malnourished, ugly cows. When the latter devoured the former, his dream ended (vv. 2–4). (Pharaohs evidently went to the river regularly [cf. Exod. 7:15; 8:20]. Sometimes the occasion was formal worship at one of the numerous, great, temple estates, most of which were associated in one way or

---

41. *Understanding Genesis*, pp. 218, 219.
42. For a brief discussion of a possible parallel to the story of the cup bearer and baker see Francis D. Nichol, ed., *The Seventh-Day Adventist Bible Commentary*, 1:442. Also worthy of note is the excellent treatment of the various grades of prison staff by Kitchen, "A Recently published Egyptian Papyrus and Its Bearing on the Joseph Story," pp. 1, 2.

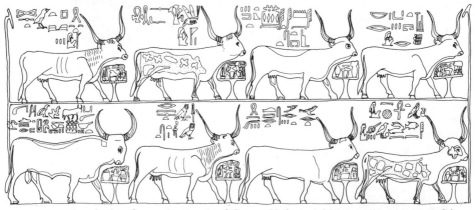

A painting from the tomb of Queen Nefertari (thirteenth century B.C.) shows Egyptian cattle

another with the sacred Nile.) His second dream was analogous to the first but with different symbolism (vv. 5–7). He called for professional interpreters of dreams, "magicians" (*harṭummîm*) and wise men (v. 8). *Harṭummîm* appears to be another Egyptian loan-word. It appears outside the Pentateuch only in Daniel (1:20; 2:2). Wise men and magicians were summoned by Pharaoh in Moses' time, too (Exod. 7:11). In all probability the magicians were the chief "lector-priests," who had learned the sacred writings, rituals, and spells at special temple schools.[43] In spite of their expertise, they were incapable of interpreting Pharaoh's dreams. Remembering Joseph's unusual skill in interpretation, the chief baker told Pharaoh, and Pharaoh summoned Joseph. The fact that Joseph shaved before presenting himself (v. 14) is significant. Had Pharaoh been a Hyksos king, shaving would have been unimportant. But native Egyptians were clean-shaven, making it eminently important.

Joseph first explained to Pharaoh that he could not interpret his dreams, but God could (v. 16). After Pharaoh recounted his dreams, Joseph interpreted them by God's power. The two dreams were one, and in them God was revealing the immediate future. The next seven years would be years of great abundance, the seven years after that, years of famine. Seven-year famines were not unknown in Egypt. A later Egyptian text tells of such a famine during King Djoser's reign, showing how tragic such a famine is and how the Egyptians reacted to it: "I was in distress on the Great Throne, and those who are in the palace were in heart's affliction from a very great evil, since the Nile had not come in my time for a space of seven years. Grain was scant, fruits were dried up, and everything which they eat was short. Every man robbed his companion. They moved without going (ahead). The infant was wailing; the youth was waiting; the heart of the old men was in sorrow, their legs were bent, crouching on the ground, their arms were folded."[44] Joseph not only interpreted the dream, but advised Pharaoh how to meet the impending disaster (vv. 33–36). Pharaoh was so impressed with Joseph, "in whom the spirit of God is" (v. 38), that he elevated him to a position second only to his own (v. 40).

---

43. Vergote, *Joseph en Égypte*, pp. 66–94; Kitchen, "Egyptian Magic," in Douglas, ed., *New Bible Dictionary*, p. 769.
44. "The Tradition of Seven Lean Years in Egypt," translated by John A. Wilson, in Pritchard, *ANET*, p. 31.

V. Joseph Governing Egypt (41:37–57)

A. His Installation (41:37–46)

There is some question as to the exact position that Joseph held in the royal court. He appears to have been vizier (prime minister). [45] Pharaoh said that "only in the throne will I be greater than thou" (v. 40) and made Joseph ride "in the second chariot" (v. 43). Pharaoh gave Joseph jurisdiction over "all the land of Egypt" (v. 41), a fact which is repeated many times (cf. 41:43, 44, 46, 55; 42:6; 45:8). Thutmose III gave his newly-appointed vizier the same when he charged him: "Look thou to this office of vizier. Be vigilant over everything that is done in it. Behold, it is the support of the entire land. Behold, as to the vizierate, behold, it is not sweet at all, behold, it is bitter as gall. . . ."[46] Finally, Pharaoh gave Joseph the royal seal (v. 42), with which Joseph could transact affairs of state in the name and with the authority of the crown. Joseph's clothing and jewelry (v. 43) accord well with numerous Egyptian paintings. His "vestures of fine linen" must have been similar to the clothes worn by Rekh-mi-Re when he was appointed vizier: "I was a noble, the second of the king and the fourth of him who judged the Pair. . . . It was the first occasion of my being summoned. All my brothers were in the outer office. I went forth . . . clad in fine linen. . . ."[47] W. A. Ward has suggested that Joseph was not vizier but merely an important official with considerable power. He contends that of the six titles attributed to Joseph, only half were working titles; the other half were strictly honorific.[48] The combination of titles and powers given Joseph, however, seems to put him above a mere elevated noble with honorific titles.

The fact that Joseph ruled the entire land of Egypt virtually rules out the possibility that this was the Hyksos period because the Hyksos controlled both upper and lower Egypt for only a very brief time. In spite of this, the mention of chariots in the narrative has caused many to conclude that this was the Hyksos period. Wheeled vehicles and horses (mentioned specifically in 47:17) were not introduced in Egypt until this period, they argue. It is

45. G. Ernest Wright, *Biblical Archaeology*, pp. 54, 55; Rowley, *From Joseph to Joshua*, p. 120; Speiser, *Genesis*, p. 316.
46. "The Vizier of Egypt," translated by Wilson, in Pritchard, *ANET*, p. 213.
47. Ibid.
48. "The Egyptian Office of Joseph," pp. 145–50.

true that the earliest representation of a horse discovered so far—a wooden figure of a black mare striped with white chalk and mounted by a groom—has been tentatively dated at 1550 B.C.[49] However, because no earlier representation has been discovered is no reason to assume that horses did not exist in Egypt prior to then. We know that Twelfth-Dynasty pharaohs sent merchants and royal couriers as far north as Ugarit, and that in Asia Minor and Syria horses were coming into use for military purposes as early as 1900 B.C.[50] Horses and chariots also were used to varying degrees in Mesopotamia by that time.[51]

Pharaoh ordered Egyptians to "bow the knee" to Joseph (v. 43), a custom reflected in Egyptian drawings.[52] He gave Joseph an Egyptian name, *Zaphenath-paneah* (v. 45), and the practice of giving foreigners an Egyptian name is equally well attested. One example is the list of Asiatic slaves referred to above.[53] What Joseph's new name meant is not clear. Kitchen points out that with one small change it could mean "Joseph, who is called 'Ip ankh.'"[54] Joseph married Asenath ("she belongs to Neith") the daughter of Poti-phera ("he whom Ra has given"). Both names are Egyptian. The father's name probably indicates that he was in the service of the sun god Ra, an important Egyptian deity as early as the Fifth Dynasty.[55] Joseph was thirty years old when he assumed his new duties (v. 46). Since he was sold into slavery at the age of seventeen (37:2), we can conclude that he spent thirteen years in servitude.

B. His Administration (41:47–57)

In accordance with his plan, Joseph gathered food during the seven years of abundant harvest (vv. 47–49). He was also blessed

49. Dorothy W. Phillips, *Ancient Egyptian Animals*, rev. ed. (New York: The Metropolitan Museum of Art, 1948), p. 22 (fig. 38).
50. See the important discussion of this matter by Albright, "New Light on the History of Western Asia in the Second Millennium B.C.," *Bulletin of the American Schools of Oriental Research* 77 (1940): 31.
51. See Henry Field, *The Track of Man*, pp. 168ff.; M. E. L. Mallowan, "Excavations at Brak and Chagar Bazar," p. 216; Speiser, *Excavations at Tepe Gawra*, 1:68–72, 162, 163; and Leon Legrain, "Horseback Riding in Mesopotamia in the Third Millennium B.C.," pp. 27–33.
52. Kidner, *Genesis*, p. 197.
53. Albright, "Northwest Semitic Names in a List of Egyptian Slaves from the Eighteenth Century B.C.," p. 223.
54. "Zaphnath-paaneah," in Douglas, ed., *New Bible Dictionary*, p. 1353.
55. Ward, "Egyptian Titles in Genesis 39–50," p. 51.

A model, taken from an Egyptian tomb dated ca. 2050 B.C., of a granary (Courtesy of the British Museum)

with two sons, Manasseh and Ephraim (vv. 51, 52). As his interpretation of Pharaoh's dream had indicated, the seven years of plenty were followed by seven years of famine (v. 57). It might surprise some that Joseph "sold" grain to the Egyptians during this period (v. 56). But we should remember that they had been warned of the impending disaster, and that having to pay for food would encourage them to draw on the limited supply sparingly. One cannot help but be impressed by Joseph's ingenious administration, to say nothing of the boundless energy with which he traveled throughout the land while preparing for the famine (v. 45).

VI. Joseph Dealing with His Brothers (42:1–45:28)

A. Their First Visit (42:1–38)

The famine extended to Canaan, and Jacob became somewhat upset with his sons' lack of initiative; they just sat around looking at one another helplessly (42:1). Word had reached him that grain

A Bedouin family on the move, using donkeys (see Gen. 42:26) as beasts of burden (Courtesy of Matson Photo Service)

was still available in Egypt, and he wanted ten of his sons to go there and buy some (vv. 2–5). (Benjamin was kept back not because he was too young—he was more than twenty years old—but because he was Rachel's only remaining child and in that respect had taken Joseph's place.) An Egyptian text reflects a similar situation: a frontier official reported that he admitted "the Bedouin tribes of Edom" into the eastern Delta "to keep them alive and to keep their cattle alive." The document also notes that such peoples were admitted only on specified days.[56]

The account of the brothers' descent into Egypt and their encounter with Joseph is historical narration par excellence. Dramatic and emotional tension build as the brothers appear and reappear before Joseph, and the climax, of course, is a warm and intimate reunion. Determining Joseph's real motive in testing his brothers is most difficult. Most scholars have felt that Joseph was not being vindictive but was engaged merely in official probing and testing.[57] However, Joseph's manner, coupled with the numerous tests through which he put his brothers, gives the distinct impression that he was humbling his previously arrogant brothers (vv. 6–14).

When they came to him to buy food, he recognized them but they failed to recognize him (v. 7). He accused them of spying (v. 9), a serious charge punishable by death. To test their claim of innocence, Joseph demanded that they bring to him their youngest brother (vv. 15, 16). Then he imprisoned them for three days, underscoring his power and insuring their obedience (v. 17). The inconvenience of three days in prison was small in comparison to three years.

279

56. Wilson, *The Culture of Ancient Egypt*, p. 258.
57. Kidner, *Genesis*, p. 199; Nichol, ed., *Bible Commentary*, 1:452.

Their difficult situation caused Joseph's brothers to reflect, perhaps for the first time, upon their moral conduct in years past, and they candidly admitted their guilt concerning Joseph (vv. 21, 22). It could be that this was the response that Joseph's tests were designed to elicit. Of course, underlying all of his demands was a deep desire to see his younger brother Benjamin and his father Jacob. That Joseph was not merely testing his brothers out of vengefulness is more than proven by the fact that, when he spoke with them a second time, he had to weep, although he was careful not to weep in their presence (v. 24). A hard man of hate is incapable of such tender emotion. Joseph had his brothers' sacks filled with the grain they had bought, but he also put in them the money with which they had paid for the grain. Not until they had left for Canaan did one of them discover his money, and they became very concerned (vv. 27, 28).

Only nine of the brothers made the trip back to Canaan; Joseph had kept Simeon as a hostage in order to guarantee that the rest would return to Egypt and bring Benjamin with them. Explaining this to Jacob was not easy. He had already lost Joseph and now Simeon was missing. Furthermore, as they emptied their sacks each man found the money with which he had paid for his grain, and as might be expected, they were greatly afraid (v. 35). Jacob's response to his sons' request was rather pessimistic, and with good reason (v. 36). Reuben apparently was convinced of the governor's honesty, for he guaranteed Benjamin's safety with the lives of his own two sons (v. 37). While Reuben's offer represented a great sacrifice, it was also rash. In any event, Jacob was not impressed (v. 38).

B. Their Second Visit (43:1–45:28)

Just how long it took for Jacob and his family to exhaust the supplies they had purchased in Egypt is unknown. But it was before the seven-year famine ended, for Jacob requested his sons to return to Egypt (vv. 1, 2). When Judah reminded his father that to return without Benjamin would be fruitless and perhaps disastrous, Jacob expressed his bitterness concerning his sons' failure to procure food the first time without incident: Why had they revealed to the Egyptian governor that they had one more brother? (v. 6). After Judah guaranteed Benjamin's safe return (vv. 8, 9), Jacob finally consented, but not without a final expression of his pessimism (v. 14). The brothers packed presents for the

280

governor—balm, honey, spices, myrrh, nuts, and almonds—and took "double money" in order to pay for their original purchase of grain as well as a new purchase (vv. 11–13).

1. Their interview with Joseph (43:16–34). The question has often been asked, Why did the brothers not secure their grain from an official other than Joseph? They probably guessed that all officials were under orders to bring them to Joseph should they return. Joseph probably kept careful record of the sale of grain to foreigners, and this would have required a number of border officials to check on those entering Egypt. When Joseph's servant brought his brothers to the royal palace, they were greatly afraid because of the money which had been returned to their sacks on the previous visit. Joseph, however, quickly dispelled their fears, brought Simeon to them from prison, and provided them with the best oriental hospitality of the day (vv. 23–26). The fact that they "bowed themselves to him to the earth" (v. 26; cf. 42:6) is a clear fulfillment of Joseph's earlier prophecy (37:8–11, 19, 20).

While Joseph maintained his composure through most of the introductions, he eventually fled to his chamber and wept (v. 30). Here is the master touch of Moses, whose brush strokes of historical reflection delineate the smallest details. In the banquet that followed, the Egyptians did not eat with the Hebrews (v. 32). That would have been "an abomination unto the Egyptians" (v. 32), presumably because the Egyptians had a deep hatred for Asiatic shepherds (cf. 46:34; Exod. 8:26). This discrimination toward the Hebrews is another reason to associate Joseph with a native Egyptian pharaoh, for it seems inconceivable that a Hyksos king would have demanded such discrimination. Joseph's arrangement of the brothers according to birthright must have startled them (v. 33).

2. Benjamin's arrest (44:1–17). One would expect Joseph to identify himself on this occasion, but he was a master at manipulating circumstances and continued his charade. He sent his brothers home, but in order to guarantee Jacob the opportunity to come to Egypt, he had his servant put his personal silver cup in the sack of Benjamin (44:1, 2). Soldiers then pursued the brothers, searched their sacks, and discovered the cup in Benjamin's. All the brothers were required to return to Joseph's residence to explain the matter (vv. 1–14). Joseph immediately challenged their motives and heightened the tension by pointing out that the cup they

281

had taken was no ordinary cup (v. 15). Joseph implied that it was a divining cup, and this is something of a problem since no other records attest the use of such a cup this early.[58] However, it has been suggested that two Middle Kingdom statuettes, each kneeling in front of a cup, might represent cup divination in this period. [59] It is also possible that the practice of hydromancy was not common to Egypt but was invoked by Joseph to give his scheme an air of authentication.

3. **Judah's intercession (44:18−34).** Judah's plea to Joseph was in marked contrast to his earlier bitterness (37:26, 27). As spokesman for the brothers, he interceded before this unknown vizier. The discovery of the incriminating evidence had made this ruler's mercy the brothers' only hope. It is possible that Joseph's schemes had been intended to probe his brothers' attitude toward each other and toward their father. He also wanted to test the sincerity of their repentance. Were they willing to break the heart of Jacob again as they had many years ago when they showed him Joseph's bloodstained robe? Judah's expression of deep concern and tender sympathy for Jacob more than answered the question. It must have been extremely difficult for Joseph to maintain composure through Judah's entire speech, but the text seems to imply that he did. Judah's speech was impressive for its dignity and organization: "This noble appeal does not rely on pathos: it has the cumulative weight of factual reminder (19−23), graphic portraiture (20, 24−29, 30b) and a selfless concern proved to the hilt in the plea not for mercy but for leave to suffer vicariously (30−34)."[60] It became clear to Joseph that his brothers' attitudes had undergone profound change.

4. **Their acceptance (45:1−28).** There is little question that the eloquence and emotion of Judah's speech impressed Joseph. Judah's obvious love for Jacob was more than he could overlook. Unable to control his emotions much longer, he demanded that all except his family leave the room. Then he revealed his identity and wept (vv. 1, 2). His brothers found his revelation so incredible that they were unable even to respond (v. 3). He told them again

58. Kidner, *Genesis*, p. 205.
59. J. S. Wright, "Divination," in Douglas, ed., *New Bible Dictionary*, p. 321 (fig. 69).
60. Kidner, *Genesis*, p. 206.

A limestone stele, dated between 2475 and 2000 B.C., showing an Egyptian official and his wife (Courtesy of the Metropolitan Museum of Art, Rogers Fund, 1925)

who he was and reminded them that they had sold him into Egypt (v. 4). His brothers probably expected bitter resentment, but instead he recognized in what they had done the workings of divine providence. They had been agents in getting Joseph to Egypt, but God prepared the way (v. 5). Joseph's testimony to God's role in his life and that of his family is an eloquent one (vv. 6–9).

He offered his brothers some of the best land in Egypt in which to settle (v. 10). The name *Goshen* has not yet been attested in Egyptian documents, but scholars generally agree that it was the area around the Wadi Tumilat in the eastern part of the Nile Delta. The main valley extends for approximately forty miles and is usually dry except in the rainy season. This accords well with the text, which indicates that Goshen was "near" the royal court (45:10). Joseph was concerned, however, not only for his brothers but for his father as well. He desired his father, too, to come to

284

A terra-cotta model wagon (see Gen. 45:19) found at Tepe Gawra and dated in the third millennium B.C.

Egypt and benefit from the providential blessings of God (v. 13).

When Pharaoh received word of the presence of Joseph's brothers, he was pleased and more than willing to offer Joseph's family the best that Egypt had to offer (vv. 16—18). Pharaoh's approval of Joseph's proposed residence for his family is no surprise since Joseph had endeared himself to the king, probably rescuing him from a great embarrassment during the famine years. The brothers were sent back to Canaan with abundant gifts for their families and their father. These would completely confirm their story of what had happened. When Jacob heard it, he found it as unbelievable as they had at first (v. 26). But the many gifts convinced him of his sons' veracity, and he agreed to visit Joseph before he died (vv. 27, 28).

Joseph's attitude and actions provide an outstanding illustration of genuine love and forgiveness. Humanly speaking, he could have been vindictive toward his helpless brothers; unregenerate society would have considered vindictiveness justified. However, the sensitive man of God does not take advantage of such opportunities for vindictiveness, but seeks to provide the best for those whom he has forgiven.

18

The Last Days of Jacob

Genesis 46–50

One can only guess what thoughts dominated the mind of Jacob as he anticipated his trip to Egypt. Mingled with the joy and excitement of seeing Joseph after a long separation were apprehensions. If his sons had deceived him once, was it impossible that they should do it again? Could the Egyptians be trusted, or was their generosity a mere ploy to attract foreigners to them? Of course we shall never know if Jacob fought such a battle within himself, but we do know that he went to Egypt; that is a matter of biblical and historical record. That step of faith in God made possible the growth of the twelve tribes into the nation of Israel.

I. Jacob's Arrival in Egypt (46:1–47:31)

A. His Journey (46:1–27)

Jacob probably lived at Hebron for a number of years before journeying to Egypt (cf. 35:27; 37:14). On his way he stopped at Beersheba, long a favorite place of worship for the patriarchs. Abraham (21:33) and Isaac (26:25) had both erected altars there. It is possible that the sight of his ancestors' altars was what moved Jacob to offer sacrifices to the God whom he loved (46:1, 2). His grandfather's and father's experiences relating to Egypt—Abraham suffered great humiliation there (12:10–20) and Isaac was forbidden to go there (26:2)—must have caused Jacob deep concern. However, what God had forbidden Isaac He encouraged Jacob to do, not because Egypt had become any less idolatrous but because God had providentially prepared the way for the growth of the nation of Israel. Jacob knew about God's revelation to Abraham that his descendants would spend a four-hundred-year sojourn in a strange land (15:13–17). The Lord promised to be with Jacob and his family in Egypt and ultimately to bring them out (vv. 3, 4). The long journey took Jacob and his sons southwest through the wilderness of Shur.

It is important to observe that Jacob took with him to Egypt all of his sons except Simeon and Joseph, who were already there. Scholars have, on occasion, argued that the exodus from Egypt involved only a few of the tribes, some having already left Egypt and some having never left Canaan.[1] The register in verses 8–26 includes essentially those who went to Egypt at this time, although Simeon and Joseph and his sons are also listed. It gives the names of "the children of Israel," which is the first time that Moses referred to the family as a whole in this way. The descendants of Leah and her handmaid, Zilpah, are listed before those of Rachel and Bilhah. According to verse 15 the progeny of Leah totaled thirty-three. This number either excluded Er and Onan (who had died in Canaan) and included Jacob and Dinah, or vice versa. The former is more likely. According to verse 22 Rachel's progeny totaled fourteen—two sons and twelve grandsons. Bilhah's totaled seven—two sons and five grandsons (v. 25). The grand total was sixty-six (v. 26), to which Moses added Jacob, Joseph, and Joseph's two sons to make seventy. This agrees with Deuteronomy 10:22 and the Hebrew text of Exodus 1:5. Exodus 1:5 in the Septuagint, however, reads seventy-five, which Stephen apparently quoted in his sermon (Acts 7:14) and which the Dead Sea Scrolls support. The number seventy-five probably includes five later descendants of Joseph.

B. His Audience with Pharaoh (46:28–47:12)

288   When Jacob finally reached Goshen in the eastern Delta, he sent Judah to inform Joseph of the family's arrival. Joseph immedi-

1. This matter is discussed further in John J. Davis, *Moses and the Gods of Egypt*, p. 44.

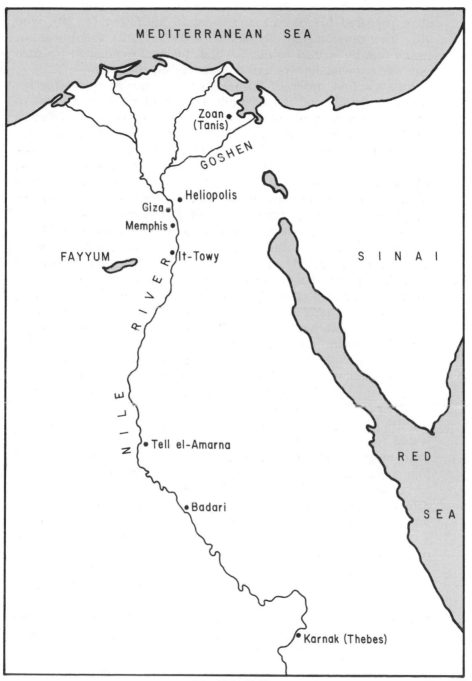

The Nile Valley

ately prepared his chariot and went to his father (v. 29), who after their reunion said, "Now let me die" (v. 30). Jacob was not saying that he wished to die but that seeing Joseph with his own eyes and knowing he was well completely satisfied him.

Joseph's first order of business was to arrange a meeting between his family and the Pharaoh. He considered it important to properly introduce his brothers and their occupation to Pharaoh (vv. 31, 32). Joseph warned them that shepherds were an abomination to the Egyptians (v. 34) and encouraged them to deemphasize their sheep and emphasize their cattle (vv. 32–34). This is additional evidence that Joseph served a native Egyptian king. The Hyksos kings would have cared nothing for the feelings of the Egyptians in such a matter.[2] Rowley observes: "The Biblical statement that the susceptibilities of the Egyptians were studied in assigning a district to the Israelites does not suggest the Hyksos. The depth of hatred they inspired in the Egyptians does not naturally accord with such an attitude of studied consideration."[3] Joseph was not trying to deceive Pharaoh—which of course would have been impossible. He only wanted his brothers to appear in the best possible light and quickly gain Pharaoh's favor. Joseph desired for them immediate and free access to Goshen. This land was ideal because it was well suited for flocks and herds; it was near the capital, so Joseph could contact his family easily (45:10); and it was isolated from the Egyptians, permitting the Hebrews to live their own lives and practice their own culture.

First to appear before Pharaoh were five of Joseph's brothers whom he selected (47:2), and their negotiations with Pharaoh were magnificently forthright and honest. The king first asked their occupation, and they answered that they, like their ancestors, were shepherds (v. 3). They added that the famine had eliminated pasture in Canaan and requested the privilege of dwelling in Goshen (v. 4). Evidently satisfied, the king called for Joseph's father and the rest of his brothers and informed them all of his decision (vv. 5, 6). Jacob, overwhelmed with Pharaoh's generosity, blessed him (v. 7). Then the king, showing genuine personal concern, asked Jacob his age. Jacob responded, "The days of my pilgrimage are an hundred and thirty years" (v. 9). His description of his life as a pilgrimage is significant. He, like Abraham and Isaac, did not actually possess Canaan but was

2. See Josephus, *Antiquities*, 2:7:5; and Herodotus, 2:47:164.
3. *From Joseph to Joshua*, p. 26.

obliged to wander from place to place. Jacob's 130 years seemed to him "few" by comparison with Abraham's 175 and Isaac's 180; his years seemed "evil" in that he had been constantly confronted by distress, anger, tribulation, and anguish.

The mention of "the land of Rameses" in verse 11 has long been a problem for commentators since the first king of the Ramesside dynasty did not reign until approximately 1319 B.C. The expression is usually regarded either an anachronism[4] or "a modernization of an obsolete place-name by some later scribe."[5] Harris writes: "Jacob's settlement in Egypt would be before King Rameses on anybody's chronology, and at that time he says he put them in the land of Rameses. Possibly the famous King Rameses chose his name from the land Rameses. Or there could have been another King Rameses. It is also possible that Genesis 47:11 is an anachronism. It may be that some later scribe, finding here a name that nobody knew any more and being very much concerned to have a Bible that even the high school student could understand, inserted this new form of the name. This city of Ra-amses was earlier known as Tanis and, before that, Avaris. It is not impossible that the name Rameses was a name brought up to date in Genesis 47:11."[6] The contention of many that the name *Rameses* did not occur earlier than the Nineteenth Dynasty has been disproved recently. That name is clearly referred to in a burial painting from the reign of Amenhotep III, who was part of the Eighteenth Dynasty.[7] This precedes the reign of Rameses I by at least sixty years. Forthcoming research may discover even earlier uses of the name.

C. Joseph's Economic Policy (47:13–27)

With Joseph's family settled in the land of Goshen, the narrative returns to Joseph and the great famine. Apparently Joseph put all the money paid for the grain into the royal treasury (v. 14). As money became scarce, Joseph permitted the grain to be bartered for such things as cattle, horses, and flocks (vv. 16, 17), so the

---

4. E. A. Speiser, *Genesis*, p. 351.
5. Merrill F. Unger, *Archaeology and the Old Testament* (Grand Rapids: Zondervan Publishing House, 1954), p. 149.
6. "Problem Periods in Old Testament History," p. 11.
7. Benjamin Mazar, ed., *The World of the Bible*, 5 vols. (Yonkers, N.Y.: Educational Heritage, 1964), 3:118 (9th col. from right). I am indebted to Gleason Archer for calling this to my attention.

people of Egypt could secure enough bread to survive. In all probability, the animals which became the property of Pharaoh were left in the care of their owners, making the terms less severe than they initially appear. The cattle probably were near starvation, and their owners were close to losing their entire investment. Now the owners could at least profit from the milk the revived cattle produced. The famine became so bad that in desperation the people offered to exchange their very land for bread (v. 19). Thus Joseph secured for the Pharaoh all land except that which belonged to the priests (v. 22), who were extremely powerful and owned much. Very few pharaohs ever successfully challenged the power and holdings of the priesthood, so Joseph was wise not to try. Joseph moved large numbers of people to major cities in order to facilitate the distribution of food (v. 21). While they were without money and cattle, they did not live merely on handouts. Joseph provided them with seed and everything necessary for agriculture, requiring only that one-fifth of their crops be given to Pharaoh (vv. 24–26). The people responded favorably, considering the arrangement fully equitable.

This narrative gives us some insight into Joseph's genius for leadership. Like Solomon he was probably blessed with special wisdom from the Lord in this situation.

D. Joseph's Promise to Jacob (47:28–31)

While residing in the beautiful eastern Delta region, Jacob's family multiplied and grew (v. 27). Jacob called his son Joseph to his side and required him to take an oath. Joseph put his hand under Jacob's thigh (v. 29), a solemn symbol that the oath was binding even after Jacob's death (cf. Gen. 24:2–4). Joseph swore to bury Jacob in Canaan, his homeland. Jacob's desire to be buried there clearly indicated his explicit faith in the covenant promises of God. He realized that the sojourn of his family in Egypt was temporary, and that God would redeem them and return them to the promised land. According to verse 31 Israel (Jacob) bowed himself upon the head of his *mṭṭh*, a word which is pointed *miṭṭâ* ("bed") in the traditional Hebrew text and *maṭṭeh* ("staff") in the Septuagint. The latter, which is followed by Hebrews 11:21, would be as appropriate as the former since the aged and infirm Jacob could have been leaning on a staff while talking to Joseph. Both versions, however, use *bed* in 48:2. Speiser considers both translations unacceptable because both probably take "the

292

The Nile Valley

Hebrew stem too literally." He suggests that the term "to bow low" need not signify anything more than a gesture of appreciation on the part of a bedridden man near the point of death.[8]

II. Jacob's Blessings (48:1—49:33)

A. Of Joseph's Sons (48:1—22)

It is of interest that the writer of Hebrews chose Jacob's blessing of Joseph's sons, Manasseh and Ephraim, as his outstanding act of faith (Heb. 11:21). One need not search intensively to discover why. The whole narrative gives unequivocal evidence of Jacob's clear faith in God's covenant promises and his sensitivity to the leadership of the Holy Spirit.

It was no accident that Moses referred to Jacob as Israel in the latter part of verse 2. As *Israel* he was the bearer of the covenant promises of God; as *Jacob* he was only a human warrior, feeble with age and near death. Israel began by reminding Joseph that "God Almighty" had appeared to him in Canaan and assured him of future blessing (vv. 3, 4).

293

8. *Genesis*, p. 357.

When Ephraim and Manasseh were brought before him, Jacob formally adopted them as his own sons (v. 5). There is a slight touch of irony here: Jacob had secured Isaac's blessing by guile and deceit, while Joseph is securing the blessing for his sons by honesty and forthrightness. The aged Jacob, unable to recognize his grandsons, had them identified (vv. 8–11). Then Jacob deliberately placed his right hand upon the younger Ephraim for the first-born blessing and his left hand upon Manasseh (v. 14). This is the first mention of the imposition of hands as a symbol of blessing. A similar procedure was later employed to dedicate priests (Num. 27:18, 23; Deut. 34:9) and still later to ordain church officers (Acts 6:6; 8:17; I Tim. 4:14; II Tim. 1:6). When Jacob blessed Ephraim as the first-born, he somewhat startled Joseph (v. 18), but he assured Joseph that he had made no mistake and that Manasseh would also be a great nation. The attitude and words of Jacob clearly prove his spiritual sensitivity. There is no question that Jacob gave complete priority to God's will in the whole matter. God's blessing in his life was sufficient reason to follow the Lord's will implicitly. Jacob's blessing on Ephraim began to realize fulfillment during the time of the judges. The tribe of Ephraim had increased in number and power to the point that it exercised leadership among the northern ten tribes.[9]

Jacob concluded with a promise that Joseph would ultimately return to Canaan (v. 21) and occupy a "portion" ($š^e\underline{k}em$) of land "which I took out of the hand of the Amorite with my sword and with my bow" (v. 22). Verse 22 is somewhat difficult to interpret. $Š^e\underline{k}em$ literally means "shoulder" or "ridge," thus the Revised Standard Version's translation, "mountain slope." $Š^e\underline{k}em$ is also the name of the city Shechem, which is dominated by Mt. Gerizim. But we have no record of a conquest of Shechem by Jacob, or later by Joseph or even Joshua. It is not impossible that the property which Jacob owned at Shechem was taken away by the Amorites after he left the region (cf. 35:4, 5) and that he eventually returned and repossessed it by force of arms.

B. Of His Sons (49:1–33)

A large segment of Old Testament scholars consistently reject the idea of predictive prophecy. They are forced to reduce seem-

---

9. On the importance of the name *Ephraim*, which became equal to the name *Israel*, see Isa. 7:2; Hos. 4:17; 13:1.

ingly predictive texts like Genesis 49 to mere historical notices written after the fact. "To those who cannot accept prediction, the oracles of this chapter are *vaticinia ex eventibus*, prophecies fabricated from the events they appear to foresee; and because the events are widely separated the speech then must be broken down into a string of sayings uttered over the centuries. But taken as the genuine vision of Jacob, its variable range presents no difficulty: there is no reason why the curtain should fall at the same point for all the tribes, every reason why it should not."[10] There has been widespread discussion and debate regarding this chapter's origin, language, and significance.[11] Much of the debate centers around some obscure words and phrases in the text.

The whole prophecy is introduced by the important phrase, "in the last days" (*'ahᵃrît hayyāmîm*). This indicates that the forthcoming utterances concern that which will befall the tribes "in

10. Derek Kidner, *Genesis*, p. 215.
11. For example, Edwin M. Good, "The 'Blessing' of Judah, Gen. 49: 8–12," pp. 427–32; Bruce Vawter, "The Canaanite Background of Genesis 49," pp. 1–18; W. L. Moran, "Genesis 49:10 and Its Use in Ezekiel 21:32," pp. 405–23; and John H. Bennetch, "The Prophecy of Jacob," pp. 417–35.

A seventeenth-century B.C. Babylonian contract between several heirs (Courtesy of the Harvard Semitic Museum)

days to come." This Hebrew expression often signifies the last days in prophetic literature (Isa. 2:2; Ezek. 38:16), and sometimes bears the more general sense of "in the latter days" (Deut. 4:30; 31:29). This prophecy is beautiful poetry which follows the normal parallelistic pattern.

1. Reuben (49:3, 4). The prophecy concerning Reuben is a type of reversed climax. Jacob began with a feeling of great joy, remembering that Reuben was the first-born and "the excellency of dignity, and the excellency of power." Then Jacob recalled Reuben's fornication with Bilhah, his father's concubine (35:22), which disqualified him for the first-born blessing. Jacob described his character as "unstable as water" (v. 4). The word translated "unstable" literally means "a boiling over of water," a vivid metaphor of unstable emotions. In Judges 9:4 and Zephaniah 3:4 another form of the same root describes frivolity and pride. With the rights of the first-born went the leadership of Israel, and history demonstrates that Reuben's tribe never significantly influenced the nation. Not one prominent personality descended from Reuben. In fact even though Israelite kings had constant contact with the peoples of Transjordan, nothing significant is ever said of Reuben. The tribe had become so insignificant by the time of Isaiah that when he lamented for the land east of the Jordan, he mentioned only Moab (Isa. 15).

2. Simeon and Levi (49:5–7). The wicked violence of Simeon and Levi against the inhabitants of Shechem (34:25) was never forgotten by Jacob. He addressed his second and third sons together since they were full brothers and their natures were identical. Jacob's anger at their unrestrained treachery in Shechem is "a moral judgment on a story told earlier without comment." [12] Jacob prophesied that both tribes would experience division and dispersion. This prediction was at least partially fulfilled by the time Israel was about to enter Canaan under Joshua. When Moses numbered Israel the second time, Simeon was the weakest tribe (Num. 26:14), and when Moses blessed the tribes, he omitted Simeon (cf. Deut. 33:8). By God's grace and providence, however, Levi received forty-eight cities scattered throughout the lands allotted other tribes (Josh. 21:1–42). While in the wilderness, Levi's descendants alone had stood for that which was right (Exod. 32:26). By Mosaic appointment they were scattered

296

---

12. Kidner, *Genesis*, p. 216.

through the tribes as teachers and instructors in the law. In spite of the division and dispersion of Simeon and Levi, both will enter the Messianic kingdom, according to Ezekiel 44 and Revelation 7.

3. Judah (49:8–12). The blessing of Judah is longer and more eloquent than any except Joseph's. It contains some obscure expressions, and the word *Shiloh* continues to be hotly debated. Judah, it will be remembered, had engineered the sale of Joseph into slavery and wronged his daughter-in-law, Tamar. However, by this time both sins had been expiated. Jacob left little doubt that Judah would become one of the most prominent tribes and one "whom thy brethren shall praise" (v. 8). The phrase "his hand would be upon the neck of the enemies" indicated that Judah's tribe would succeed in warfare, and its success is a matter of record (cf. Num. 2:9; 10:14; Judg. 1, 2).

The heart of Jacob's prophecy was the promise that "the scepter shall not depart from Judah, nor a lawgiver from between his feet, until Shiloh come; and unto him shall the gathering of the people be" (v. 10). The scepter, of course, was the symbol of royal power and in its earliest form was a long staff which the king held in his hand when speaking to public assemblies. Jacob was not saying that Judah's rule would end when Shiloh came: "It is not meant, therefore, that Judah will wield the sceptre until Shiloh come, only to lose it at his appearance. On the contrary, this term denotes the turning-point to which the superiority of Judah will continue,—not then to cease, but at that time to be enlarged so as to embrace all the nations."[13] The term *Shiloh* has been variously translated "tribute to him,"[14] "ruler or counselor,"[15] and "that which belongs to him."[16] John H. Bennetch writes: "Perhaps the safest view of the passage . . . is [that] . . . Shiloh is a proper name, the name of a Palestinian town which Jacob appropriated for use in his prophecy. Since the word connotes place of rest, it would designate Judah, if not Messiah himself, as the one characterized by rest (cf. the preceding verse of the forecast). Both the

13. Bennetch, "The Prophecy of Jacob," p. 424. See also C. F. Keil and Franz Delitzsch, *Biblical Commentary on the Old Testament*, 25 vols. (Edinburgh: T. and T. Clark, 1864–1901), 1:393.
14. Moran, "Genesis 49:10," p. 412. This view divides the consonantal text into *šy lh*, vocalized *šay lôh*, "tribute to him." The whole clause is translated, then, "until tribute is brought to him and his is the obedience of the peoples."
15. Kidner, *Genesis*, p. 218 (n. 2); and Gerhard von Rad, *Genesis*, p. 420.
16. Von Rad, *Genesis*, p. 420. This view is based on the use of *šellō* in Ezek. 21:32.

A.V. and the R.V. take Shiloh as a reference to a person."[17] With all the possibilities in view, the best seems to be that *Shiloh* is a proper name for the coming Messiah. This is the traditional interpretation of both Jewish and Christian writers; ancient writers did not agree, however, on the term's etymological significance. Applying Messianic connotations to the term seems appropriate in light of the fact that "the latter days" of verse 1 could well extend beyond the conquest and settlement period in Israel's history. The scepter's association with the tribe of Judah seems to conform to other Messianic promises (cf. Num. 24:14–17; Heb. 7:14; Matt. 2:5). Its fullest context, therefore, requires that *Shiloh* refer to "the lion that is of the tribe of Judah" (Rev. 5:5).

Many have seen in the language of verse 10 an anticipation of the triumphal entry of Jesus into Jerusalem (Matt. 21:7). Asses (v. 11) were often used by persons of superior rank (Judg. 1:14; 10:4; 12:14; II Sam. 19:27). Verses 11 and 12 seem to describe peace, prosperity, and abundance in the land[18] resulting from the presence of the Messiah.[19] It has often been pointed out that no Judean would tie his ass to a vine because asses are herbivorous and vines are very tasty to them.[20] But the problem quickly disappears if we understand the language to be metaphorical and not literal. As von Rad puts it, "In spite of many open questions, one must hold to the Messianic interpretation of the saying."[21] Edwin M. Good disagrees, however, seeing the whole series of metaphorical expressions as "an ironic reflection on Judah's misdeeds in two earlier incidents, and that in its turn casts a certain irony over the laudatory word play of verse 8."[22] In spite of Good's ingenious analysis, the Messianic application of the metaphors is eminently appropriate to this passage, especially in the light of Isaiah 11:1–9, Ezekiel 34:23–31, and Amos 9:11–15.

4. Zebulun (49:13). Even though Jacob indicated that Zebulun would dwell "at the haven of the sea," it is clear from Joshua 19:10–16 that his tribe's border never reached the Mediterranean or touched Sidon directly. The territory of Zebulun lay between the Sea of Galilee and the Mediterranean, very close to

---

17. "The Prophecy of Jacob," p. 426. Also see Keil and Delitzsch, *Biblical Commentary*, 1:392–401.
18. Keil and Delitzsch, *Biblical Commentary*, 1:402.
19. Kidner, *Genesis*, p. 219.
20. Good, "The 'Blessing' of Judah," pp. 430, 431; and von Rad, *Genesis*, p. 420.
21. *Genesis*, p. 420.
22. "The 'Blessing' of Judah," p. 432.

both but separated from the former by Naphtali and from the latter by Asher. Even though the tribe of Zebulun never controlled any Mediterranean coastline, it was in a position to benefit from sea trade and commerce. Martin Noth makes the following interesting suggestion: ". . . the dwelling places of this tribe that are known to us did not lie on the coast at all or even anywhere near it; and there is no reason to assume that Zebulun had lived by the sea at some previous time, since all the inhabitable places on the coast had been occupied long before the tribes of Israel appeared. It is more likely that this reference to Zebulun, which was probably intended as a criticism, means that the Zebulunites had to perform certain compulsory tasks, above all in the harbours of the northern coastal plain."[23] Noth's suggestion may be supported by Judges 5:17, which says that the tribe of Asher "continued on the seashore" even though it lived not on the coast but in the mountainous hinterland of the northern coastal plain. In any event, we do know that the great caravan route from the east passed through Zebulun (cf. Deut. 33:18, 19), thereby providing this tribe with important contacts from both north and south.

5. **Issachar (49:14, 15).** Zebulun and Issachar, like Simeon and Levi, had the same mother, but their natures were different so they received different prophecies. While Zebulun would enjoy contacts with the outside world, Issachar would be limited to domestic responsibility. The comparison of Issachar to a bony and strongly built ass indicated that tribe would devote itself more to agriculture and material goods than to political power. The tribe of Issachar would be robust and hardy. It would receive pleasant country that would produce an abundance of food. This prophecy was fulfilled when Joshua allotted to this tribe the territory of lower Galilee, including the beautiful tableland of Jezreel. The tribe distinguished itself for heroic bravery and military commitment (Judg. 5:14, 15, 18) and as late as the time of David was supplying warriors to the royal army. That both Zebulun and Issachar were industrious by nature is implied by the blessing of Moses (Deut. 33).

6. **Dan (49:16–18).** Jacob prophesied that Dan, the first-born son of Rachel's maid, Bilhah, would judge "his people." In Deuteronomy 33:7 "his people" refers to the whole nation, so Jacob was

299

---

23. *The History of Israel,* 2nd ed. (New York: Harper and Row Publishers, 1960), p. 79.

saying that the tribe of Dan would occupy an important judicial position in the future state of Israel. This was partially fulfilled when Israel was judged for twenty years by Samson, a Danite (Judg. 13:2). While this tribe never became great in numbers, it did become very influential in Israel. When the tribe was unable to conquer the territory allotted to it, six hundred families moved to Laish in the north and there encouraged idolatry among the people (Judg. 18). This total lack of moral commitment and spiritual stability is what Jacob meant when he described the tribe as "a serpent by the way." It is no accident that Dan is the only one of the twelve tribes omitted from Revelation 7.

7. Gad (49:19). Jacob said very little about the tribe of Gad, but he did indicate that it would be constantly attacked and harassed, and that it would ultimately triumph. The tribe's decision to live in the Transjordan exposed it to the constant threat of invasion.

8. Asher (49:20). Jacob predicted that Asher would occupy a fertile and highly productive land. This was fulfilled when Joshua gave that tribe the lowlands of Carmel, west to the Mediterranean and north to the territory of Tyre. Moses also alluded to the rich produce of the western Galilean hill country (Deut. 33:24). This tribe might well have produced the wheat and oil which Solomon gave the household of King Hiram (I Kings 5:11).

9. Naphtali (49:21). According to Jacob, Naphtali would possess mountainous land and would display the gift of sophisticated speech. Since we have little subsequent information about the tribe of Naphtali, it is difficult to determine to what extent it enjoyed "beautiful words" (v. 21). Barak apparently came from Naphtali (Judg. 4:6), and Naphtali, along with Zebulun, was recognized for heroism in the great conflict with the Canaanite general, Sisera (Judg. 5:18).

10. Joseph (49:22–26). The blessing of the aged saint Jacob on Joseph flows with special eloquence and the fullness of paternal love. It is without a doubt the most comprehensive of the individual prophecies, including that of Judah. A number of obscure expressions, however, make the Hebrew text of this section rather difficult to interpret. The traditional interpretation of verse 22, reflected in the Authorized, Revised, and Revised Standard versions, moves from Joseph's present glory and fruitfulness back to his difficult past. The picture of the fruit tree denotes Joseph's

300

depth of character and width of influence.[24] On the basis of Ugaritic parallels, Bruce Vawter suggests that the metaphors may refer to animals rather than plants.[25] While his suggestion is intriguing, it is far from proven. In any event the imagery of Jacob's prediction portrayed growth and prosperity. It is also clear that the descendants of Joseph would experience hostility and military conflict, probably because of their success, and that they would triumph and continue to grow.

11. Benjamin (49:27). There is little doubt that Jacob compared Benjamin to the wolf because of the tribe's warlike character. History confirms this description. At one point this tribe stood against all the others in defense of its wickedness in Gibeah (Judg. 20, 21). The Benjamites distinguished themselves as archers and slingers (Judg. 20:16; I Chron. 8:40; 12:2; II Chron. 14:8; 17:17). The judge Ehud (Judg. 3:15), King Saul (I Sam. 9:1; II Sam. 1:19—27) and Jonathan were Benjamites. So was the apostle Paul (Rom. 11:1), which probably indicates that tribal identities survived into the New Testament period. This is important because some maintain that certain tribes were "lost" and that they migrated to western Europe and North America. There is abundant evidence to the contrary.

III. Jacob's Death and Burial (49:28—50:13)

With consummate grace and skill Moses narrates the last moments of Jacob's life. In addition to tender admonitions, Jacob requested that he be buried in the cave that Abraham had purchased from Ephron the Hittite (vv. 29, 30), where Abraham, Sarah, Isaac, Rebekah, and Leah (v. 31) were already buried. Jacob died peacefully, completely satisfied with God's grace to him. According to Genesis 47:27 he died at the age of 147.

Joseph's tender affection for his father is expressed in the words, "Joseph fell upon his father's face, and wept upon him, and kissed him" (50:1). He immediately commanded his servants to secure "physicians" (*hārōpe'îm*) to embalm Jacob's body, and this was done (v. 2). *Hārōpe'îm* comes from the verbal root *rāpā'*, meaning "to heal." This common word elsewhere refers to physi-

301

24. Kidner, *Genesis*, p. 221.
25. Vawter, "Genesis 49," pp. 7—12.

cians who were concerned with healing diseases. Why, then, did Joseph employ this term for embalmers? There are two possibilities. First, he may have used the term in its broadest sense of one who worked with the human body. However, it is clear that in ancient Egypt embalmers and physicians were members of distinct professions. Second, Joseph may have called for physicians to embalm Jacob's body in order to avoid the magic and mysticism of the embalmers and priests. Physicians would have been fully capable of embalming.

The mention of forty days in verse 3 seems to imply that Jacob's body was mummified. The process of mummification is generally well known today as a result of Herodotus' writings and Egyptian tomb paintings and inscriptions. The process was governed by a specific religious ritual. A period of seventy days was usually allowed for the preparation of the mummy and for mourning. After death the body was taken to an embalmer's shop, which was either a permanent structure associated with a temple or a temporary booth erected for that purpose. With the body on a wooden table, the embalmer made an incision in the left flank and removed all organs except the heart, and at times the kidneys. The brain was removed through the nostrils with various metal probes and hooks, a method which fragmented the brain and made it difficult to preserve. Rarely are the remains of brain material associated with the mummies. Some contend that this material was often discarded. The liver, lungs, stomach, and intestines, on the other hand, were each preserved in a substance known as natron. These later were placed in four canopic jars, each of which was dedicated to one of the four genies of the underworld.

After the viscera of the body were carefully prepared, the body itself was packed in dry natron. Natron is a mixture of sodium carbonate and sodium bicarbonate, with sodium choloride and sodium sulfate as impurities. It is found in several places in Egypt on the ground or near the surface and results from evaporation. It made possible a rapid dehydration of the body, thereby preventing decomposition. Of course the dry, warm atmosphere of Egypt also contributed to this process. After the body moisture had been absorbed by the natron, the packs of natron were removed and the corpse was sponged with water and perfumes. The skin was then anointed with resins and the body packed with linen soaked in the same material. Once the body was wrapped, the embalmers cleaned the shop and placed in jars, for storage in the tomb, all the embalming materials that had touched the body.

According to verse 3 the total period for the embalming and

302

mourning was seventy days. The period which the embalming process required varies from one Egyptian document to another. For example, in one the embalming took 16 days, the bandaging 35, and the burial 70, which is a total of 121 days. In another the embalming took 66 days, special preparations for burial 4, and the burial itself 26, which is a total of 96 days.[26] Herodotus suggested that the body was soaked in natron for 70 days. It appears that a number of possibilities existed for the duration of mummification and burial. There is good objective evidence that one possibility was the 70 days mentioned in Genesis 50:3. In all probability these 70 days included the 40 allowed to the embalmers. In other words there was a 70-day period between death and the completion of burial rites. At least five Egyptian texts reflect the same. One from the Ptolemaic period reads: " . . . he had a goodly burial after the seventy days of his embalming had been fulfilled."[27] The 70-day period was recognized as early as the Eighteenth Dynasty, according to two texts dating from that period. One is from the reign of Queen Hatshepsut, the other from that of her successor, Thutmose III.[28]

Jacob was buried shortly after the embalming was completed. A large group of servants, mourners, and elders of his household, as well as representatives from the land of Egypt, made the journey to Canaan. Following a seven day mourning period at the threshing floor of Atad (v. 10), the body of Jacob was placed in the cave of Machpelah (v. 13).

IV. Joseph's Last Days (50:14–26)

With Jacob dead, Joseph's brothers feared that Joseph's congenial attitude toward them might change. They had, however, underestimated the genuineness of Joseph's affection. Not only had Jacob forgiven them, as indicated by his lack of reference to their sin in his last testament, but Joseph had as well. He told his brothers: "But as for you, ye thought evil against me; but God meant it for good. . . ." (v. 20). This is one of the clearest declarations of divine providence anywhere in Scripture. It serves as an important reminder that while the evil of men may appear to be to

---

26. See E. A. Wallis Budge, *The Mummy* (New York: Biblo and Tannen, 1964), p. 179.
27. *An Egyptian Mummy* (Melbourne: The Australian Institute of Archaeology, n.d.), p. 7.
28. Ibid. For a full discussion of the Egyptian concept of death and mummification, see Davis, *Mummies, Men and Madness.*

the disadvantage of the saints, the purposes and plans of God will ultimately prevail.

Joseph died at age 110, which the Egyptians considered an ideal age. The instructions of the vizier Ptah-Hotep seem to reflect this: "What I have done on earth is not inconsiderable. I attained one hundred and ten years of life which the king gave me, with favour foremost among the ancestors, through doing right for the king up to the point of veneration."[29] No less than twenty-seven such references have been discovered in Egyptian texts.[30] Some have speculated that Joseph was willing to be buried in Egypt because a change in political conditions late in his life made immediate burial in Canaan impossible.[31] But once God fulfilled His promise to deliver His people from the land and give them possession of Canaan, Joseph wished to be reburied in Canaan (vv. 23–25). Joseph, like Jacob, was embalmed and put in a "coffin" (*'ārôn*). *'Ārôn*, meaning "a chest or ark," is the same word for the ark of the covenant in the Old Testament.

For his faith in God's promises to return His people to Canaan, Joseph is called in Hebrews 11:22 a great man of faith. It is doubtful that Joseph would have permitted all the ceremonial acts associated with mummification since these acts were oriented toward polytheism. The very possibility that Jacob and Joseph were mummified makes it a distinct possibility that their bodies are in an excellent state of preservation and can be recovered. Such intriguing prospects as this keep the archaeologist going.

The Book of Genesis began with the brightness and glory of God's original creation. All that He did was pronounced good, and the earliest earth was a divine masterpiece. However, sin entered the picture, and the book ends not with man in a beautiful garden but with the bones of Joseph in a coffin. His coffin is a grim reminder of the effects of sin and depravity. But just as Joseph was hopeful and optimistic when he died, so we rejoice in the redemption which God has provided. While our bones may rest in the wilderness of a cursed earth, they will one day be resurrected, and there will be a new heaven and a new earth.

---

29. Translated by John A. Wilson, in Pritchard, *ANET*, p. 414. Also see n. 33.
30. See J. M. A. Janssen, "On the Ideal Lifetime of the Egyptian," *Oudheidkundige Mededeelingen vit het Rijksmuseum van Oudheden te Leiden* 31 (1950): 33, 34; and J. Vergote, *Joseph en Égypte*, pp. 200, 201.
31. See Pierre Montet, *Egypt and the Bible*, p. 13.

Bibliography

I. Books

Aalders, G. Ch. *De Exegese van Gen. 2 en 3 en de beslissing der Synode van Assen.* Uitgave van J. H. Kok te Kampen., n.d.

Aharoni, Yohanan, and Avi-Yonah, Michael. *The Macmillan Bible Atlas.* New York: The Macmillan Co., 1968.

Albright, William F. *Archaeology, Historical Analogy and Early Biblical Tradition.* Baton Rouge: Louisiana State University Press, 1966.

_____. *The Biblical Period from Abraham to Ezra.* New York: Harper and Row Publishers, 1949.

Allis, Oswald T. *The Five Books of Moses.* Philadelphia: The Presbyterian and Reformed Publishing Co., 1949.

_____. *God Spake by Moses.* Philadelphia: The Presbyterian and Reformed Publishing Co., 1951.

Anati, Emmanuel. *Palestine Before the Hebrews.* New York: Alfred A. Knopf, 1963.

Anderson, Bernhard W. *The Beginning of History.* Nashville: Abingdon Press, 1963.

Anderson, Sir Robert. *Bible and Modern Criticism.* New York: Fleming H. Revell, 1905.

Archer, Gleason. *A Survey of Old Testament Introduction.* Chicago: Moody Press, 1964.

Bacon, Benjamin W. *The Genesis of Genesis.* Hartford: The Student Publishing Co., 1893.

Baney, Ralph E. *Search for Sodom and Gomorrah.* Kansas City: CAM Press, 1962.

Barnhouse, Donald G. *Genesis.* 2 vols. Grand Rapids: Zondervan Publishing House, 1971.

_____. *The Invisible War.* Grand Rapids: Zondervan Publishing House, 1965.

Barth, Karl. *The Doctrine of Creation.* 4 pts. Church Dogmatics, edited by G. W. Bromiley and T. F. Torrance, vol. 3. Edinburgh: T. and T. Clark, 1960.

Barton, George A. *Archaeology and the Bible.* Philadelphia: American Sunday School Union, 1916.

Baxter, J. Sidlow. *Explore the Book.* Vol. 1. Grand Rapids: Zondervan Publishing House, 1960.

Bennett, W. H. *Genesis.* The New Century Bible, edited by Walter F. Adeney. New York: Henry Frowde, n.d.

Benson, John. *Benson's Commentary.* Vol. 1. New York: Carlton and Porter, 1815.

Berkouwer, G. C. *Man: The Image of God.* Grand Rapids: Wm. B. Eerdmans Co., 1962.

Blenkinsopp, Joseph. *From Adam to Abraham.* Glen Rock, N.J.: Paulist Press, 1965.

Boardman, G. D. *Studies in the Creative Week.* New York: Appleton and Co., 1878.

Body, C. W. E. *The Permanent Value of the Book of Genesis.* New York: Longmans, Green and Co., 1894.

Bonhoeffer, Dietrich. *Creation and Temptation.* London: SCM Press, 1966.

306

Bright, John. *A History of Israel.* Philadelphia: The Westminster Press, 1959.

Brooks, Keith L. *The Riches of Genesis.* Los Angeles: Brooks Publishers, 1936.

Brown, Francis; Driver, S. R.; and Briggs, Charles. *A Hebrew and English Lexicon of the Old Testament.* Corrected impression. Oxford: The Clarendon Press, 1952.

Bruce, F. F. *The Hittites and the Old Testament.* London: Tyndale Press, 1948.

Budde, Karl. *Die Biblische Urgeschichte* (Gen. 1–12). Giessen: J. Ricker'sche Buchhandlung, 1883.

Burrows, Millar. *More Light on the Dead Sea Scrolls.* New York: The Viking Press, 1958.

Bush, George. *Notes on the Book of Genesis.* 2 vols. Boston: Henry A. Young and Co., 1870.

Cadiou, René. *La Migration D'Abraham.* Paris: Tour-Mauboval, 1957.

Candlish, Robert S. *The Book of Genesis.* 2 vols. Edinburgh: Adam and Charles Black, 1868.

Carroll, B. H. *Studies in Genesis.* Nashville: Broadman Press, 1937.

Charles, R. H., ed. *The Apocrypha and Pseudepigrapha of the Old Testament.* 2 vols. Oxford: The Clarendon Press, 1913.

Cheyne, T. K. *Traditions and Beliefs of Ancient Israel.* London: Adam and Charles Black, 1907.

Chivers, Keith. *Does Genesis Make Sense?* London: S.P.C.K., 1951.

Clark, Harold W. *Genesis and Science.* Nashville: Southern Publishing Association, 1967.

Clay, Albert T. *The Origin of Biblical Traditions.* New Haven: Yale University Press, 1923.

Clements, R. E. *Abraham and David.* Naperville, Ill.: Alec R. Allenson, 1967.

Cole, Glen G. *Creation and Science.* Cincinnati: Standard Publishing Co., 1927.

307

Conant, Thomas J. *The Book of Genesis.* New York: American Bible Union, 1868.

Cramer, Karl. *Genesis 1–11: Urgeschichte?* Tübingen: J. C. B. Mohr, 1959.

Cummings, Violet M. *Noah's Ark: Fact or Fable?* San Diego: Creation-Science Research Center, 1972.

Custance, Arthur C. *Without Form and Void.* Brockville, Canada: Arthur C. Custance, 1970.

Danielou, Jean. *In The Beginning . . . Genesis I–III.* Translated by Julien L. Randolf. Baltimore: Helicon Press, 1965.

Davidson, Robert. *Genesis 1–11.* The Cambridge Bible Commentary, edited by P. R. Ackroyd; A. R. C. Leaney; and J. W. Packer; vol. 1. Cambridge: The University Press, 1973.

Davies, G. Henton. *Genesis.* The Broadman Bible Commentary, edited by Clifton J. Allen, vol. 1. Nashville: Broadman Press, 1969.

Davis, John J. *Biblical Numerology.* Grand Rapids: Baker Book House, 1968.

_____. *Conquest and Crisis.* Grand Rapids: Baker Book House, 1969.

_____. *Contemporary Counterfeits.* Winona Lake, Ind.: BMH Books, 1973.

_____. *Moses and the Gods of Egypt.* Grand Rapids: Baker Book House, 1971.

_____. *Mummies, Men and Madness.* Winona Lake, Ind.: BMH Books, 1972.

DeHaan, M. R. *Genesis and Evolution.* Grand Rapids: Zondervan Publishing House, 1962.

_____. *Portraits of Christ in Genesis.* Grand Rapids: Zondervan Publishing House, 1966.

Delitzsch, Franz. *A New Commentary on Genesis.* 5th ed. 2 vols. Translated by Sophia Taylor. Edinburgh: T. and T. Clark, 1888.

De Vaux, Roland. *Ancient Israel.* Translated by John McHugh. London: Darton, Longman and Todd, 1961.

308

_____. *The Bible and the Ancient Near East*. New York: Doubleday and Co., 1971.

Dexinger, Ferdinand. *Sturz der Göttersöhne oder Engel vor der Sintflut?* Wien: Herder and Co., 1966.

Dillmann, A. *Genesis.* 2 vols. Translated by Wm. B. Stevenson. Edinburgh: T. and T. Clark, 1897.

Douglas, J. D., ed. *New Bible Dictionary*. Grand Rapids: Wm. B. Eerdmans Co., 1962.

Driver, G. R. *Canaanite Myths and Legends*. Edinburgh: T. and T. Clark, 1956.

Driver, S. R. *The Book of Genesis*. Westminster Commentaries, edited by Walter Lock, vol. 1. London: Methuen and Co., 1906.

_____. *Hebrew Tenses.* Oxford: Oxford University Press, 1892.

Eddy, Mary Baker. *Science and Health with Key to the Scriptures.* Boston: Trustees under the will of Mary B. G. Eddy, 1934.

Edwards, I. E. S.; Gadd, C. J.; and Hammond, N. G. L.: eds. *The Cambridge Ancient History.* 3rd ed. Vol. 1, pt. 2. Cambridge: The University Press, 1971.

Edward, I. E. S.; Gadd, C. J.; Hammond, N. G. L.; and Sollberger, E.: eds. *The Cambridge Ancient History.* 3rd ed. Vol. 2, pt. 1. Cambridge: The University Press, 1973.

Ehrich, R. W. *Chronologies in Old World Archaeology.* Chicago: University of Chicago Press, 1966.

Elliott, Ralph H. *The Message of Genesis*. Nashville: Broadman Press, 1961.

Engell, Ivan. *Studies in Divine Kingship in the Ancient Near East.* 2nd ed. Oxford: Basil Blackwell, 1967.

Erdman, Charles R. *The Book of Genesis*. New York: Fleming H. Revell, 1950.

Erman, Adolf, ed. *The Ancient Egyptians*. New York: Harper and Row Publishers, 1966.

Evans, William. *Genesis.* New York: Fleming H. Revell, 1916.

Falk, Ze'ev W. *Hebrew Law in Biblical Times*. Jerusalem: Wahrmann Books, 1964.

Field, Henry. *The Track of Man.* Garden City, N.Y.: Doubleday and Co., 1953.

Filby, Frederick A. *Creation Revealed: A Study of Genesis 1 in the Light of Modern Science.* Westwood, N.J.: Fleming H. Revell, 1964.

_____. *The Flood Reconsidered.* Grand Rapids: Zondervan Publishing House, 1970.

Finegan, Jack. *Handbook of Biblical Chronology.* Princeton: Princeton University Press, 1964.

_____. *Light from the Ancient Past.* Princeton: Princeton University Press, 1959.

Finn, A. H. *The Author of the Pentateuch.* London: The Bible League, n.d.

Fishman, Isidore. *From Sabbath to Sabbath.* London: Vallentine, Mitchell and Co., 1965.

Free, Joseph P. *Archaeology and Bible History.* Wheaton: Van Kampen Press, 1950.

Fretheim, Terence E. *Creation, Fall and Flood.* Minneapolis: Augsburg Publishing Co., 1969.

Fritsch, Charles T. *Genesis.* The Layman's Bible Commentary, edited by Balmer H. Kelly, vol. 2. Richmond: John Knox Press, 1959.

Gardiner, Alan. *Egypt of the Pharaohs.* Oxford: The Clarendon Press, 1966.

Garstang, John. *The Hittite Empire.* London: Constable, 1929.

Gaubert, Henri. *Abraham Loved by God.* New York: Hastings House, 1968.

Gibson, John M. *The Ages Before Moses.* New York: Anson D. F. Randolf and Co., 1879.

Ginzberg, Louis. *The Legends of the Jews.* 7 vols. Philadelphia: The Jewish Publication Society of America, 1909–38.

Girdlestone, Henry. *Genesis: Its Authenticity and Authority Discussed.* London: James Nisbet and Co., 1864.

Glueck, Nelson. *Rivers in the Desert.* New York: Farrar, Straus and Cudahy, 1959.

Gonzalez, Angel. *Abraham, Father of Believers.* London: Burns and Oates/Herder and Herder, 1968.

Gordon, Alex R. *The Early Traditions of Genesis.* Edinburgh: T. and T. Clark, 1907.

Gordon, Cyrus H. *The Ancient Near East.* New York: W. W. Norton and Co., 1965.

_____. *Introduction to Old Testament Times.* Ventnor, N.J.: Ventnor Publishers, 1953.

Grant, F. W. *Genesis in the Light of the New Testament.* Swengel, Pa.: Bible Truth Depot, n.d.

Graves, Robert, and Patai, Raphael. *Hebrew Myths: The Book of Genesis.* London: Cassell and Co., 1963.

Gray, James M. *Great Epochs of Sacred History.* New York: Fleming H. Revell, 1910.

Green, William H. *The Unity of the Book of Genesis.* New York: Charles Scribner's Sons, 1897.

Greenwood, George. *The Book of Genesis.* 2 vols. London: The Church Printing Co., 1899.

Gressmann, Hugo. *The Tower of Babel.* New York. Jewish Institute of Religion Press, 1928.

Griffith-Jones, E., and Welch, A. C. *Genesis.* New York: Doubleday, Doran and Co., n.d.

Gruber, L. Franklin. *The Six Creative Days.* Burlington, Iowa: Lutheran Literary Board, 1941.

Gunkel, Hermann. *The Legends of Genesis.* Translated by H. W. Carruth. New York: Schocken Books, 1964.

Gurney, O. R. *The Hittites.* Rev. ed. Baltimore: Penguin Books, 1961.

Haldar, Alfred. *Who Were the Amorites?* Leiden: E. J. Brill, 1971.

Harris, R. Laird. *Man: God's Eternal Creation.* Chicago: Moody Press, 1971.

Harrison, R. K. *Introduction to the Old Testament.* Grand Rapids: Wm. B. Eerdmans Co., 1969.

Hayes, William C. *A Papyrus of the Late Middle Kingdom in the Brooklyn Museum.* Brooklyn: Brooklyn Museum, 1955.

Hedge, Frederic H. *The Primeval World*. Boston: Roberts Brothers, 1870.

Heidel, Alexander. *The Babylonian Genesis*. Chicago: University of Chicago Press, 1942.

Heiligstedt, August. *(Praeparation zur) Genesis*. Halle: Edvard Anton, 1883.

Herbert, A. S. *Genesis 12–50: Abraham and His Heirs*. London: SCM Press, 1962.

Hershon, Paul I. *Genesis: With a Talmudical Commentary*. London: Samuel Bagster and Sons, 1883.

Hill, Dorothy B. *Abraham, His Heritage and Ours*. Boston: Beacon Press, 1957.

Hindson, Edward E. *The Philistines and the Old Testament*. Grand Rapids: Baker Book House, 1971.

Honeycutt, Roy L., Jr. *Exodus*. The Broadman Bible Commentary, edited by Clifton J. Allen, vol. 2. Nashville: Broadman Press, 1969.

Hopkins, Garland E. *The Mighty Beginnings*. St. Louis: The Bethany Press, 1956.

Howard, Henry E. J. *The Book of Genesis, According to the Version of the LXX*. Cambridge: Macmillan and Co., 1855.

Hvidberg, Flemming F. *Weeping and Laughter in the Old Testament*. Leiden: E. J. Brill, 1962.

Jacobus, Melancthon W. *Notes, Critical and Explanatory on the Book of Genesis*. New York: Robert Carter and Brothers, 1866.

Johnson, Marshall D. *The Purpose of the Biblical Genealogies*. Cambridge: The University Press, 1969.

Jones, F. A. *The Dates of Genesis*. London: The Kingsgate Press, 1909.

Jukes, Andrew. *The Names of God*. London: Longmans, Green and Co., 1892.

Kaiser, Walter C., ed. *Classical Evangelical Essays in Old Testament Interpretation*. Grand Rapids: Baker Book House, 1972.

Kalisch, M. M. *Genesis*. London: Longman, Brown, Green, Longmans and Roberts, 1858.

Kenyon, Kathleen. *Amorites and Canaanites.* New York: Oxford University Press, 1966.

_____. *Archaeology in the Holy Land.* 2nd ed. London: University Paperbacks, 1965.

_____. *Digging Up Jericho.* London: Ernest Benn, 1957.

Kidner, Derek. *Genesis.* Downers Grove, Ill.: Inter-Varsity Press, 1967.

Kitchen, Kenneth A. *Ancient Orient and Old Testament.* Chicago: Inter-Varsity Press, 1966.

Kluger, Rivkah. *Satan in the Old Testament.* Translated by Hildegard Nagel. Evanston: Northwestern University Press, 1967.

Koch, Robert. *Erlösungstheologie, Genesis 1–11.* Frankfurt: Verlag Gerhard Kaffke, 1965.

Koehler, L., and Baumgartner, W., eds. *Lexicon in Veteris Testamenti Libros.* Leiden: E. J. Brill, 1958.

Kramer, Samuel N. *History Begins at Sumer.* New York: Doubleday and Co., 1959.

_____. *The Sumerians.* Chicago: University of Chicago Press, 1963.

Külling, Samuel R. *Zur Datierung der "Genesis-P-Stücke" Namentlich des Kapitels Genesis XVII.* Kampen: J. H. Kok, 1964.

Kyle, Melvin G. *Creation of Inanimate Things.* St. Louis: Bibliotheca Sacra, 1929.

Lammerts, Walter E., ed. *Scientific Studies in Special Creation.* Philadelphia: The Presbyterian and Reformed Publishing Co., 1971.

_____. *Why Not Creation?* Grand Rapids: Baker Book House, 1970.

Lange, John P. *Genesis.* Translated by T. Lewis and A. Gosman. New York: Charles Scribner and Co., 1868.

LaSor, William S. *Amazing Dead Sea Scrolls and the Christian Faith.* Chicago: Moody Press, 1959.

Lenormant, Francois. *The Book of Genesis: A Translation from the Hebrew.* London: Longmans, Green and Co., 1886.

Lenzen, H. *Die Sumerer.* Berlin: Gebr. Mann, 1948.

313

Leupold, H. C. *Exposition of Genesis.* 2 vols. Grand Rapids: Baker Book House, 1958.

Lever, Jan. *Creation and Evolution.* Grand Rapids: Grand Rapids International Publications, 1958.

Lewis, Jack P. *A Study of the Interpretation of Noah and the Flood in Jewish and Christian Literature.* Leiden: E. J. Brill, 1968.

Lillegard, George O. *From Eden to Egypt.* Milwaukee: Northwestern Publishing House, 1956.

Luther, Martin. *Luther's Commentary on Genesis.* Translated by J. T. Mueller. Grand Rapids: Zondervan Publishing House, 1958.

Lüthi, Walter. *Abraham.* Basel: Friedrich Reinhardt Verlag Basel, 1967.

_____. *Adam.* Basel: Druck und Einband, 1965.

McClain, Alva J. *The Greatness of the Kingdom.* Grand Rapids: Zondervan Publishing House, 1959.

Mackintosh, C. H. *Notes on the Book of Genesis.* New York: Loizeaux Brothers, 1880.

Marsh, Frank L. *Life, Man and Time.* Escondido, Calif.: Outdoor Pictures, 1967.

_____. *Studies in Creationism.* Washington, D.C.: Review and Herald Publishing Association, 1950.

Meek, Theophile J. *Hebrew Origins.* New York: Harper and Row Publishers, 1960.

Mercer, Samuel A. B. *The Book of Genesis.* London: A. R. Mowbray and Co., 1919.

Mitchell, H. G. *The World Before Abraham.* New York: Houghton, Mifflin and Co., 1901.

Montet, Pierre. *Egypt and the Bible.* Translated by Leslie R. Keylock. Philadelphia: Fortress Press, 1968.

Montgomery, John W. *The Quest for Noah's Ark.* Minneapolis: Bethany Christian Fellowship, 1972.

Morgan, G. Campbell. *Genesis.* The Analyzed Bible, vol. 1. New York: Fleming H. Revell, 1911.

Morgenstern, Julian. *The Book of Genesis.* New York: Schocken Books, 1965.

Morris, Henry M. *Biblical Cosmology and Modern Science.* Grand Rapids: Baker Book House, 1970.

_____. *Evolution and the Modern Christian.* Philadelphia: The Presbyterian and Reformed Publishing Co., 1967.

Murphy, James G. *The Book of Genesis.* Boston: Estes and Lauriat, 1873.

Murray, John. *Principles of Conduct.* Grand Rapids: Wm. B. Eerdmans Co., 1957.

Newman, Jacob. *The Commentary of Nahmanides on Genesis Chapters 1–6.* Leiden: E. J. Brill, 1960.

Nichol, Francis D., ed. *The Seventh-Day Adventist Bible Commentary.* Vol. 1. Washington, D. C.: Review and Herald Publishing Association, 1953.

Niles, D. T. *Studies on Genesis.* Philadelphia: The Westminster Press, 1958.

Nüchtern, Philipp. *Die Urgeschichten.* Stuttgart: Ehrenfied Klotz Verlag, 1967.

Ockenga, Harold J. *Women Who Made Bible History.* Grand Rapids: Zondervan Publishing House, 1962.

Owen, G. Frederick. *Archaeology and the Bible.* Westwood, N.Y.: Fleming H. Revell, 1961.

Page, Thornton and Lou W., eds. *The Origin of the Solar System.* New York: The Macmillan Co., 1966.

Parker, C. F. *Introduction to Genesis.* London: The Covenant Publishing Co., 1936.

Parker, Joseph. *Adam, Noah and Abraham.* New York: Macmillan and Co., 1880.

Parrot, André. *Abraham and His Times.* Translated by James H. Farley. Philadelphia: Fortress Press, 1968.

_____. *The Tower of Babel.* Translated by Edwin Hudson. London: SCM Press, 1955.

315

Patten, Donald W. *The Biblical Flood and the Ice Age Epoch.* Seattle: Pacific Meridian Publishing Co., 1966.

Paul, William. *The Book of Genesis.* Edinburgh: William Blackwood and Sons, 1870.

Payne, D. F. *Genesis One Reconsidered.* Carol Stream, Ill.: Tyndale House, 1964.

Payne, J. Barton, ed. *New Perspectives on the Old Testament.* Waco, Tex.: Word Books, 1970.

Pember, George H. *Earth's Earliest Ages.* London: Hodder and Stoughton, 1907.

Pentecost, J. Dwight. *Things to Come.* Findlay, Ohio: Dunham Publishing Co., 1958.

Petrie, Sir Flinders. *Palestine and Israel.* London: S.P.C.K., 1934.

Pfeiffer, Charles F., ed. *The Biblical World.* Grand Rapids: Baker Book House, 1958.

_____. *The Book of Genesis.* Grand Rapids: Baker Book House, 1958.

_____. *The Patriarchal Age.* Grand Rapids: Baker Book House, 1961.

Pieters, Albertus. *Notes on Genesis.* Grand Rapids: Wm. B. Eerdmans Co., 1947.

Pink, Arthur W. *Gleanings in Genesis.* Chicago: Moody Press, 1922.

Politeyan, J. *Biblical Archaeology and the Hebrew Vocation.* London: Elliot Stock, 1930.

Pratt, H. B. *Studies on the Book of Genesis.* New York: The American Tract Society, 1906.

Prenter, Regin. *Creation and Redemption.* Translated by Theodor I. Jensen. Philadelphia: Fortress Press, 1967.

Price, George M. *Genesis Vindicated.* Washington, D.C.: Review and Herald Publishing Association, 1941.

Pritchard, James B., ed. *The Ancient Near East in Pictures.* Princeton: Princeton University Press, 1969.

Procksch, Otto. *Die Genesis*. Leipzig: A. Deichertsche Verlags-buchhandlung, 1913.

Ramm, Bernard. *The Christian View of Science and Scripture*. Grand Rapids: Wm. B. Eerdmans Co., 1954.

Rand, Howard B. *Primogenesis*. Haverhill, Mass.: Destiny Publishers, 1953.

Redlich, E. Basil. *The Early Traditions of Genesis*. London: Gerald Duckworth and Co., 1950.

Renckens, Henricus. *Israel's Concept of the Beginning*. New York: Herder and Herder, 1964.

Reventlow, Henning G. *Opfere deinen Sohn*. Neukirchener Verlag des Erziehungsvereins Gmbht., 1968.

Richardson, Alan. *Genesis I—XI*. London: SCM Press, 1953.

Riley, W. B. *Genesis*. The Bible of the Expositor and Evangelist, vol. 1. Cleveland: Union Gospel Press, 1926.

Roberton, Eric S. *The Bible's Prose Epic of Eve and Her Sons*. London: Williams and Norgate, 1916.

Robertson, Frederick W. *Notes on Genesis*. London: Harry S. King and Co., 1877.

Routley, Erik. *Beginning the Old Testament*. Philadelphia: Muhlenberg Press, 1962.

Rowley, H. H. *From Joseph to Joshua*. London: Oxford University Press, 1950.

Ryle, Herbert E. *The Book of Genesis*. The Cambridge Bible for Schools and Colleges: The Old Testament, edited by A.F. Kirkpatrick, vol. 1. Cambridge: The University Press, 1914.

_____. *The Early Narratives of Genesis*. London: Macmillan and Co., 1892.

Sarna, Nahum M. *Understanding Genesis*. New York: Schocken Books, 1970.

Sauer, Erich. *King of the Earth: The Nobility of Man According to the Bible and Science*. Grand Rapids: Wm. B. Eerdmans Co., 1962.

Sayce, A. H. *Patriarchal Palestine*. London: S.P.C.K., 1895.

Schaeffer, Francis A. *Genesis in Space and Time*. Downers Grove, Ill.: Inter-Varsity Press, 1972.

Schwarze, C. Theodore. *The Marvel of Earth's Canopies*. Westchester, Ill.: Christian Readers Club, 1957.

Shuckford, Samuel. *The Sacred and Profane History of the World*. London: William Tegg and Co., 1858.

Simpson, Cuthbert A., and Bowie, Walter R. *The Book of Genesis*. The Interpreter's Bible, edited by George A. Buttrick, vol. 1. Nashville: Abingdon Press, 1952.

Skinner, John. *A Critical and Exegetical Commentary on Genesis*. The International Critical Commentary on the Holy Scriptures of the Old and New Testaments, edited by S. R. Driver; Alfred Plummer; and C. A. Briggs: vol. 1. New York: Charles Scribner's Sons, 1910.

――――. *The Divine Names in Genesis*. London: Hodder and Stoughton, 1914.

Skoss, Solomon L. *The Arabic Commentary of 'Ali Ben Suleimān the Karaite on the Book of Genesis*. Philadelphia: The Dropsie College for Hebrew and Cognate Learning, 1928.

Slusher, Harold S. *Critique of Radiometric Dating*. San Diego: Institute for Creation Research, 1973.

Smick, Elmer B. *Archaeology of the Jordan Valley*. Grand Rapids: Baker Book House, 1973.

Smith, R. Payne. *Genesis*. London: Cassell and Co., n.d.

Snaith, Norman H. *Notes on the Hebrew Text of Genesis I-VIII*. London: The Epworth Press, 1947.

Speiser, E. A. *Excavations at Tepe Gawra*. Vol. 1. Philadelphia: University of Pennsylvania Press, 1935.

――――. *Genesis*. The Anchor Bible, edited by William F. Albright and David N. Freedman, vol. 1. New York: Doubleday and Co., 1964.

――――. *Mesopotamian Origins*. Philadelphia: University of Pennsylvania Press, 1930.

Spurrell, G. J. *Notes on the Text of the Book of Genesis*. Oxford: The Clarendon Press, 1896.

318

Strahan, James. *Hebrew Ideals.* Edinburgh: T. and T. Clark, 1902.

Strong, Augustus H. *Systematic Theology.* 3 vols. Philadelphia: The Griffith and Rowland Press, 1907.

Thiele, Edwin R. *The Mysterious Numbers of the Hebrew Kings.* Rev. ed. Grand Rapids: Wm. B. Eerdmans Co., 1965.

Thielicke, Helmut. *Theological Ethics: Foundations.* Edited by William H. Lazareth. Philadelphia: Fortress Press, 1966.

Thomas, D. Winton, ed. *Archaeology and Old Testament Study.* Oxford: The Clarendon Press, 1967.

Tinkle, William J. *Heredity.* Grand Rapids: Zondervan Publishing House, 1970.

Turner, Samuel H. *A Companion to the Book of Genesis.* London: Wiley and Putnam, 1841.

Unger, Merrill F. *Biblical Demonology.* Chicago: Scripture Press, 1952.

Urquhart, John. *The Bible: Its Structure and Purpose.* Vol. 1. New York: Gospel Publishing House, 1904.

Van Seters, John. *The Hyksos.* New Haven: Yale University Press, 1966.

Van der Ziel, Albert. *Genesis and Scientific Inquiry.* Minneapolis: T. S. Denison and Co., 1965.

Vawter, Bruce. *A Path Through Genesis.* New York: Sheed and Ward, 1956.

Velikovsky, Immanuel. *Earth in Upheavel.* New York: Doubleday and Co., 1955.

Vergote, J. *Joseph en Égypte. Genèse Chap. 37–50 à la lumière des études égyptologiques récentes.* Louvain: Publications Universitaires, 1959.

Von Rad, Gerhard. *Genesis.* Translated by John Marks. Philadelphia: The Westminster Press, 1961.

Vos, Howard F. *Genesis and Archaeology.* Chicago: Moody Press, 1963.

Walker, Rollin H. *A Study of Genesis and Exodus.* New York: The Methodist Book Concern, 1923.

Watts, J. Wash. *A Distinctive Translation of Genesis.* Grand Rapids: Wm. B. Eerdmans Co., 1963.

Whitcomb, John C. *The Early Earth.* Winona Lake, Ind.: BMH Books, 1972.

Whitcomb, John C., and Morris, Henry M. *The Genesis Flood.* Philadelphia: The Presbyterian and Reformed Publishing Co., 1961.

White, Reginald E. O. *They Teach Us to Pray.* New York: Harper and Row Publishers, 1957.

Whitelaw, Thomas. *Genesis.* The Pulpit Commentary, edited by H. D. M. Spence, vol. 1. New York: Funk and Wagnalls, 1888.

_____. *The Patriarchal Times.* London: James Nisbet and Co., 1887.

Wilder-Smith, A. E. *Man's Origin, Man's Destiny.* Wheaton: Harold Shaw Publishers, 1968.

Wilson, John A. *The Culture of Ancient Egypt.* Chicago: University of Chicago Press, 1951.

Wiseman, P. J. *Creation Revealed in Six Days.* London: Marshall, Morgan and Scott, 1949.

_____. *New Discoveries in Babylonia About Genesis.* London: Marshall, Morgan and Scott, 1936.

Wolff, Richard. *A Commentary on the Epistle of Jude.* Grand Rapids: Zondervan Publishing House, 1960.

Woolley, Sir Leonard. *The Sumerians.* Oxford: The Clarendon Press, 1929.

Worcester, Elwood. *The Book of Genesis in the Light of Modern Knowledge.* New York: McClure, Phillips and Co., 1901.

Wright, G. Ernest, ed. *The Bible and the Ancient Near East.* New York: Doubleday and Co., 1961.

_____. *Biblical Archaeology.* Philadelphia: The Westminster Press, 1957.

320 _____. *Shechem.* New York: McGraw-Hill, 1965.

Wright, G. Frederick. *Origin and Antiquity of Man.* Oberlin, Ohio: Bibliotheca Sacra, 1912.

Yates, Kyle M. *Genesis.* The Wycliffe Bible Commentary, edited by Charles F. Pfeiffer and Everett F. Harrison. Chicago: Moody Press, 1962.

Young, E. J. *Genesis 3.* London: The Banner of Truth Trust, 1966.

_____. *Studies in Genesis One.* Philadelphia: The Presbyterian and Reformed Publishing Co., 1964.

Zobel, Hans-Jürgen. *Stammesspruch und Geschichte.* Berlin: Verlag Alfred Töpelmann, 1965.

II. Articles

Acrey, D. O. "Problems in Absolute Age Determination." *Creation Research Society Quarterly* 1 (1965).

Aharoni, Yohanan. "Excavations at Tel Beer-Sheba." *The Biblical Archaeologist* 35 (1972).

_____. "The Land of Gerar." *Israel Exploration Journal* 6 (1956).

_____. "Tamar and the Roads to Elath." *Israel Exploration Journal* 13 (1963)

Albright, William F. "Abraham and the Caravan Trade." *Bulletin of the American Schools of Oriental Research* 163 (1961).

_____. "Abram the Hebrew: A New Archaeological Interpretation." *Bulletin of the American Schools of Oriental Research* 163 (1961).

_____. "The Archaeological Results of an Expedition to Moab and the Dead Sea." *Bulletin of the American Schools of Oriental Research* 14 (1924).

_____. "The Babylonian Matter in the Predeuteronomic Primeval History (JE) in Gen. 1–11." *Journal of Biblical Literature* 58 (1939).

_____. "Bronze Age Mounds of Northern Palestine and the Hauran." *Bulletin of the American Schools of Oriental Research* 19 (1925).

_____. "Cuneiform Material for Egyptian Prosopography." *Journal of Near Eastern Studies* 5 (1946).

———. "Early-Bronze Pottery from Bab ed-Dra' in Moab." *Bulletin of the American Schools of Oriental Research* 95 (1944).

———. "The Egyptian Empire in Asia in the Twenty-first Century B.C." *Journal of the Palestine Oriental Society* 8 (1928).

———. "The Hebrew Expression for 'Making a Covenant' in Pre-Israelite Documents." *Bulletin of the American Schools of Oriental Research* 121 (1951).

———. "The Historical Background of Genesis XIV." *Journal of the Society for Oriental Research* 10 (1926).

———. "The Names *Shaddai* and *Abram*." *Journal of Biblical Literature* 54 (1935).

———. "New Egyptian Data on Palestine in the Patriarchal Age." *Bulletin of the American Schools of Oriental Research* 81 (1941).

———. "New Light on the Early History of Phoenician Colonization." *Bulletin of the American Schools of Oriental Research* 83 (1941).

———. "Northwest Semitic Names in a List of Egyptian Slaves from the Eighteenth Century B.C." *Journal of the American Oriental Society* 74 (1954).

———. Review of *Hebrew Union College Annual*, vol. 16, *Journal of Biblical Literature* 64 (1945).

———. "Some Remarks on the Meaning of the Verb *SHR* in Genesis." *Bulletin of the American Schools of Oriental Research* 164 1961).

———. "Two Little Understood Amarna Letters from the Middle Jordan Valley." *Bulletin of the American Schools of Oriental Research* 89 (1943).

———. "Was the Patriarch Terah a Canaanite Moon-god?" *Bulletin of the American Schools of Oriental Research* 71 (1938).

Alexander, P. S. "The Targumim and Early Exegesis of 'Sons of God' in Genesis 6." *Journal of Jewish Studies* 23 (1972).

Allen, Roy M. "The Evaluation of Radioactive Evidence on the Age of the Earth." *Journal of the American Scientific Affiliation* 4 (1952).

322

Alonso, Schökel L. "Motives Sapien Ciales y de alianza en Gn. 2–3." *Biblica* 43 (1926).

Anderson, F. I. "Note on Genesis 30:8." *Journal of Biblical Literature* 88 (1969).

Armerding, Carl. "The God of Nahor." *Bibliotheca Sacra* 106 (1949).

Astour, Michael C. "Tamar the Hierodule: An Essay in the Method of Vestigal Motifs." *Journal of Biblical Literature* 85 (1966).

Baab, Otto J. "A Theory of Two Translators for the Greek Genesis." *Journal of Biblical Literature* 52 (1933).

Bailey, J. A. "Initiation and the Primal Woman in Gilgamesh and Genesis 2–3." *Journal of Biblical Literature* 89 (1970).

Baker, Aelred. "Parallelism: England's Contribution to Biblical Studies." *The Catholic Biblical Quarterly* 35 (1973).

Baldwin, Joyce. "How To Make a Woman." *His* 33 (1973).

Baqir, T., and Francis, B. "The Babylonian Story of Creation." *Sumer* 5 (1949).

Bar-Deroma, H. "Kadesh-Barne'a." *The Palestine Exploration Quarterly* 96 (1964)

Barrows, E. P. "The Mosaic Six Days and Geology." *Bibliotheca Sacra* 14 (1857).

Bartlett, J. R. "The Rise and Fall of the Kingdom of Edom." *The Palestine Exploration Quarterly* 104 (1972).

Basset, F. W. "Noah's Nakedness and the Curse of Canaan: A Case of Incest?" *Vetus Testamentum* 21 (1971).

Battenfield, James R. "A Consideration of the Identity of the Pharaoh of Genesis 47." *Journal of the Evangelical Theological Society* 15 (1972).

Bennetch, John H. "Genesis: An Apologetic." *Bibliotheca Sacra* 106 (1949).

_____. "The Prophecy of Jacob." *Bibliotheca Sacra* 95 (1938).

Birney, Leroy. "An Exegetical Study of Genesis 6:1–4." *Journal of the Evangelical Theological Society* 13 (1970).

323

Blythin, Islwyn. "A Note on Genesis 1:2." *Vetus Testamentum* 12 (1962).

_____. "The Patriarchs and the Promise." *Scottish Journal of Theology* 21 (1968).

Bonfante, G. "Who Were the Philistines?" *American Journal of Archaeology* 50 (1946).

Boyd, Jesse L., Jr. "The Sacrifice of Isaac." *Biblical Viewpoint* 2 (1968).

Bradley, L. Richard. "The Curse of Canaan and the American Negro." *Concordia Theological Monthly* 42 (1971).

Braidwood, Robert J. "Asiatic Prehistory and the Origin of Man." *Journal of Near Eastern Studies* 11 (1947).

Brow, Robert. "The Late-Date Genesis Man." *Christianity Today* 16 (Sept. 15, 1972).

Bruce, F. F. "And the Earth Was Without Form and Void: An Enquiry into the Exact Meaning of Genesis 1:2." *Journal of the Transactions of the Victoria Institute* 78 (1946).

Brueggemann, Walter. "From Dust to Kingship." *Zeitschrift für die Alttestamentliche Wissenschaft* 84 (1972).

_____. "Of the Same Flesh and Bone (Gn. 2, 23a)." *The Catholic Biblical Quarterly* 32 (1970).

_____. "Weariness, Exile and Chaos." *The Catholic Biblical Quarterly* 24 (1972).

Bruns, J. E. "Depth-Psychology and the Fall." *The Catholic Biblical Quarterly* 21 (1959).

Burns, Everett H. "Genesis Chapter Three." *Presbyterian Journal* 29 (1970).

Burrows, Millar. "The Ancient Oriental Background of Hebrew Levirate Marriage." *Bulletin of the American Schools of Oriental Research* 77 (1940).

_____. "The Complaint of Laban's Daughters." *Journal of the American Oriental Society* 57 (1937).

Burtness, J. M. "What Does It Mean To 'Have Dominion over the Earth?'" *Dialog* 10 (1971).

Buswell, James O. "Adam and Neolithic Man." *Eternity* 18 (1967).

———. "Genesis, the Neolithic Age, and the Antiquity of Adam." *Faith and Thought* 96 (1967).

Callaway, Joseph A. "Burials in Ancient Palestine from the Stone Age to Abraham." *The Biblical Archaeologist* 26 (1963).

Campbell, E. F. "The Amarna Letters and the Amarna Period." *The Biblical Archaeologist* 23 (1960).

———. "In Search of the Philistines." *The Biblical Archaeologist* 26 (1963).

Camping, Harold. "The Biblical Calendar of History." *Journal of the American Scientific Affiliation* 22 (1970).

Carmichael, C. M. "Some Sayings in Genesis 49." *Journal of Biblical Literature* 88 (1969).

Castellino, G. R. "Genesis IV:7." *Vetus Testamentum* 10 (1960).

Cazelles, Henri. "Connexions et structure de Genesis, XV." *Revue Biblique* 69 (1962).

Clark, Gordon. "The Image of God in Man." *Journal of the Evangelical Theological Society* 12 (1969).

Clark, Harold W. "When Was the Earth Created?" *Creation Research Society Quarterly* 1 (1964).

Clark, Robert E. D. "The Black Sea and Noah's Flood." *Faith and Thought* 100 (1972–73).

Clark, W. M. "The Animal Series in the Primeval History." *Vetus Testamentum* 18 (1968).

———. "The Flood and the Structure of Pre-patriarchal History." *Zeitschrift für die Alttestamentliche Wissenschaft* 83 (1971).

———. "The Righteousness of Noah." *Vetus Testamentum* 21 (1971).

Clines, D. J. A. "The Image of God in Man." *Tyndale Bulletin* 19 (1968).

———. "The Theology of the Flood Narrative." *Faith and Thought* 100 (1972–73).

Coats, George W. "Widow's Rights: A Crux in the Structure of Genesis 38." *The Catholic Biblical Quarterly* 34 (1972).

Cohen, Gary G. "Hermeneutical Principles and Creation Theories." *Grace Journal* 5 (1964).

Comiskey, J. P. "The Order of Melchizedek." *Bible Today* 27 (1966).

Cook, Melvin A. "Radiological Dating and Some Pertinent Applications of Historical Interest." *Creation Research Society Quarterly* 5 (1968).

Cross, Frank M., Jr. "The Discovery of the Samaria Papyri." *The Biblical Archaeologist* 26 (1963).

Custance, Arthur C. "The Flood Traditions and the Bible." *Bibliotheca Sacra* 96 (1939).

Custer, Stewart. "New Testament Quotations from Genesis." *Biblical Viewpoint* 2 (1968).

_____. "The Sons of God and the Daughters of Men." *Biblical Viewpoint* 2 (1968).

Dahood, M. "Is 'Eben Yisrā'ēl' a Divine Title? (Gen. 49:24)." *Biblica* 40 (1959).

Davies, L. M. "The Present State of Teleology." *Transactions of the Victoria Institute* 79 (1947).

Davis, John J. "The Patriarch's Knowledge of Jehovah." *Grace Journal* 3 (1963).

Davis, Leon. "Adam Names the Animals, Genesis 2:18–23." *Biola Broadcaster* 1 (1971).

Della Vida, G. L. "El 'Elion in Genesis 14:18–20." *Journal of Biblical Literature* 63 (1944).

Dilling, David R. "The Atonement and Human Sacrifice." *Grace Journal* 5 (1964).

Dougherty, J. J. "The World of the Hebrew Patriarchs." *Scripture* 3 (1948).

Dyson, R. A. "Apropos of a New Study of Genesis." *Biblica* 35 (1934).

Eissfeldt, Otto. "The Alphabetical Cuneiform Texts from Ras

Shamra Published in 'Le Palais Royal D'Ugarit.' " *Journal of Semitic Studies* 5 (1960).

Emerton, J. A. "The Riddle of Genesis 14." *Vetus Testamentum* 21 (1971).

———. "Some False Clues in the Study of Genesis XIV." *Vetus Testamentum* 21 (1971).

Erpenstein, O. M. "Could There Be Life on Other Planets of the Solar System?" *Creation Research Society Quarterly* 9 (1972).

Feinberg, Charles. "The Image of God." *Bibliotheca Sacra* 129 (1972).

Ferguson, Albert B. "New Explanation for Peleg." *Bible Science Newsletter* 10 (1972).

Ferguson, Paul. "Are the Enuma Elish Creation Tablets the Literary Source of Genesis One?" *Science and Scripture* 2 (1972).

Ferrin, Howard W. "All Israel Shall Be Saved." *Bibliotheca Sacra* 112 (1955).

Filby, Frederick A. "Noah's Flood: Approaches to Reconciliation." *Faith and Thought* 100 (1972–73).

Fisher, Eugene. "Gilgamesh and Genesis: The Flood Story in Context." *The Catholic Biblical Quarterly* 32 (1970).

Fisher, Loren R. "Abraham and His Priest-King." *Journal of Biblical Literature* 81 (1962).

Free, Joseph P. "Abraham's Camels." *Journal of Near Eastern Studies* 4 (1944).

———. "Dothan, 1954." *Annual of the Department of Antiquities, Jordan* 3 (1956).

———. "The Excavation of Dothan." *The Biblical Archaeologist* 19 (1956).

———. "The Fifth Season at Dothan." *Bulletin of the American Schools of Oriental Research* 152 (1958).

———. "The First Season of Excavation at Dothan." *Bulletin of the American Schools of Oriental Research* 131 (1953).

———. "The Fourth Season at Dothan." *Bulletin of the American Schools of Oriental Research* 143 (1956).

327

_____. "Radiocarbon Date of Iron Age Level at Dothan." *Bulletin of the American Schools of Oriental Research* 147 (1956).

_____. "The Second Season at Dothan." *Bulletin of the American Schools of Oriental Research* 135 (1954).

_____. "The Seventh Season at Dothan." *Bulletin of the American Schools of Oriental Research* 160 (1960).

_____. "The Sixth Season at Dothan." *Bulletin of the American Schools of Oriental Research* 156 (1959).

_____. "The Third Season at Dothan." *Bulletin of the American Schools of Oriental Research* 139 (1955).

Gabriel, J. "Die Kainitengenealogie (Gen. 4:17–24)." *Biblica* 40 (1959).

Gadd, C. J. "Tablets from Kirkuk." *Revue d'Assyriologie* 23 (1926).

Gammie, John G. "Loci of the Melchizedek Tradition of Genesis 14:18–20." *Journal of Biblical Literature* 90 (1971).

Gehman, H. S. "Hebraisms of the Old Greek Version of Genesis." *Vetus Testamentum* 3 (1953).

Gentry, Robert V. "Cosmological Implications of Extinct Radioactivity from Pleochroic Halos." *Creation Research Society Quarterly* 3 (1966).

Gevirtz, S. "Abraham's 318." *Israel Exploration Journal* 19 (1969).

_____. "The Reprimand of Reuben." *Journal of Near Eastern Studies* 30 (1971).

Gibson, J. C. L. "Light from Mari on the Patriarchs." *Journal of Semitic Studies* 7 (1962).

Ginsberg, H. L. "Abram's 'Damascene' Steward." *Bulletin of the American Schools of Oriental Research* 200 (1970).

Glueck, Nelson. "An Aerial Reconnaissance in Southern Transjordan." *Bulletin of the American Schools of Oriental Research* 67 (1937).

_____. "The Age of Abraham in the Negev." *The Biblical Archaeologist* 18 (1955).

_____. "Archaeological Exploration of the Negev in 1959," *Bulletin of the American Schools of Oriental Research* 159 (1960).

_____. "Explorations in Eastern Palestine, II." *Annual of the American Schools of Oriental Research* 15 (1934–35).

_____. "Further Explorations in Eastern Palestine." *Bulletin of the American Schools of Oriental Research* 86 (1942).

Goetze, Albrecht. "Remarks on the Ration Lists from Alalakh VII." *Journal of Cuneiform Studies* 13 (1959)

Good, Edwin M. "The 'Blessing' of Judah, Gen. 49:8–12." *Journal of Biblical Literature* 82 (1963).

Goodman, Marvin L. "Non-Literal Interpretations of Genesis Creation." *Grace Journal* 14 (1973).

Gordon, Cyrus H. "Abraham and the Merchants of Ura." *Journal of Near Eastern Studies* 17 (1958).

_____. "Biblical Customs and the Nuzu Tablets." *The Biblical Archaeologist* 3 (1940).

_____. "The Patriarchal Narratives." *Journal of Near Eastern Studies* 13 (1954).

_____. "The Role of the Philistines." *Antiquity* 30 (1956).

Greenberg, Moshe. "Another Look at Rachel's Theft of the Teraphim." *Journal of Biblical Literature* 81 (1962).

Gressmann, Hugo. "Sage und Geschichte in den Patriarchenerzählungen." *Zeitschrift für die Alttestamentliche Wissenschaft* 30 (1910).

Grieve, Jerry A. "The Origin of Languages." *Ashland Theological Bulletin* 3 (1970).

Groningen, Van. "Interpretation of Genesis." *Journal of the Evangelical Theological Society* 13 (1970).

Grossfeld, Bernard. "Targum Onkelos and Rabbinic Interpretation to Genesis 2:1, 2." *Journal of Jewish Studies* 24 (1973).

Gruenthaner, M. J. "The Date of Abraham." *The Catholic Biblical Quarterly* 4 (1942), 5 (1943).

Habel, N. C. "Gospel Promise to Abraham." *Concordia Theological Monthly* 40 (1969).

329

Haggai, Waddy A. "The God Who Is Enough." *Sunday School Times and Gospel Herald* 71 (1973).

Harland, J. Penrose. "Sodom and Gomorrah." In *The Biblical Archaeologist Reader*, edited by G. Ernest Wright and D. N. Freedman. New York: Doubleday and Co., 1961.

Harris, R. Laird. "The Bible and Cosmology." *Bulletin of the Evangelical Theological Society* 5 (1962).

_____. "Problem Periods in Old Testament History." *The Seminary Review* 16 (1969).

Hartman, Thomas C. "Some Thoughts on the Sumerian King List and Genesis 5 and 11B." *Journal of Biblical Literature* 91 (1972).

Hasel, Gerhard F. "Recent Translations of Genesis 1:1: A Critical Look." *The Bible Translator* 22 (1971).

_____. "The Significance of the Cosmology in Genesis 1 in Relation to Ancient Near Eastern Parallels." *Andrews University Seminary Studies* 10 (1972).

Haugen, Einar. "The Curse of Babel." *Daedalus* 102 (1973).

Hodgson, L. "Exegesis and Exposition." *Canadian Journal of Theology* 13 (1967).

Hoehner, Harold W. "The Duration of the Egyptian Bondage." *Bibliotheca Sacra* 125 (1969).

Horn, Siegfried H. "Shechem in the Light of Archaeological Evidence." *Asbury Seminarian* 23 (1969).

Huntress, Erminie. " 'Son of God' in Jewish Writings Prior to the Christian Era." *Journal of Biblical Literature* 54 (1935).

Hvidberg, Flemming F. "The Canaanite Background of Genesis I-III." *Vetus Testamentum* 10 (1960).

Hyatt, J. Philip. "Yahweh as 'The God of My Father.' " *Vetus Testamentum* 2 (1955).

Isserlin, B. S. J. "On Some Possible Early Occurrences of the Camel in Palestine." *The Palestine Exploration Quarterly* 82 (1950).

James, E. D. "The Conception of Creation in Cosmology." *Liber Amicorum: Studies in Honor of C. J. Bleeker.* Supplement to *Numen* 12 (1969).

Jirku, A. "Zum historischen Stil von Gen. 14." *Zeitschrift für die Alttestamentliche Wissenschaft* 39 (1921).

Johnston, J. O. D. "The Problems of Radiocarbon Dating." *The Palestine Exploration Quarterly* (1973).

Jones, Arthur J. "Boundaries of the *Min:* An Analysis of the Mosaic Lists of Clean and Unclean Animals." *Creation Research Society Quarterly* 9 (1972).

_____. "A General Analysis of the Biblical 'Kind' (*Min*)." *Creation Research Society Quarterly* 9 (1972).

Jones, Gwilym H. "Abraham and Cyrus: Type and Anti-type?" *Vetus Testamentum* 22 (1972).

Kardimon, S. "Adoption as a Remedy for Infertility in the Period of the Patriarchs." *Journal of Semitic Studies* 3 (1958).

Kelso, James L. "Excavations at Bethel." *The Biblical Archaeologist* 19 (1956).

_____. "The Third Campaign at Bethel." *Bulletin of the American Schools of Oriental Research* 51 (1958).

Kelso, James L., and Horley, J. P. "Early Bronze Pottery from Bâb ed-Drâ' in Moab." *Bulletin of the American Schools of Oriental Research* 95 (1944).

Kitchen, Kenneth A. "A Recently Published Egyptian Papyrus and Its Bearing on the Joseph Story." *Tyndale House Bulletin* (1956–57).

Kofahl, Robert E. "Entropy Prior to the Fall." *Creation Research Society Quarterly* 10 (1973).

Korfmann, Manfred. "The Sling as a Weapon." *Scientific American* 229 (1973).

Kornfield, William J. "The Early-Date Genesis Man." *Christianity Today* 17 (June 8, 1973).

Kraeling, E. G. "Calneh, Genesis 10:10." *Journal of Biblical Literature* 54 (1935).

331

———. "The Earliest Hebrew Flood Story." *Journal of Biblical Literature* 66 (1947).

———. "The Interpretation of the Name Noah in Genesis 5:29." *Journal of Biblical Literature* 48 (1929).

———. "The Origin of the Name 'Hebrews.'" *American Journal of Semitic Languages and Literatures* 58 (1941).

———. "The Significance and Origin of Genesis 6:1–4." *Journal of Near Eastern Studies* 6 (1947).

———. "The Tower of Babel." *Journal of the American Oriental Society* 40 (1920).

———. "Xisouthros, Deucalion and the Flood Traditions." *Journal of the American Oriental Society* 67 (1947).

Kramer, Samuel N. "The Epic of Gilgamesh and Its Sumerian Sources." *Journal of the American Oriental Society* 64 (1944).

———. "Man's Golden Age: A Sumerian Parallel to Genesis XI:1." *Journal of the American Oriental Society* 63 (1943).

Kselman, John S. "A Note on Genesis 7:11." *The Catholic Biblical Quarterly* 35 (1973).

Külling, Samuel R. "The Dating of the So-Called 'P-Sections' in Genesis." *Journal of the Evangelical Theological Society* 15 (1972).

Lambdin, T. O. "Egyptian Loan Words in the Old Testament." *Journal of the American Oriental Society* 73 (1953).

Lambert, Maurice. "La période présargonique: Essai d'une histoire sumérienne." *Sumer* 8 (1952).

———. "A Study of the First Chapter of Genesis." *Hebrew Union College Annual* 1 (1924).

Lambert, W. G. "The Domesticated Camel in the Second Millennium—Evidence from Alalakh and Ugarit." *Bulletin of the American Schools of Oriental Research* 160 (1960).

Lane, William R. "The Initiation of Creation." *Vetus Testamentum* 13 (1963).

Lang, G. H. "Melchizedek." *Evangelical Quarterly* 31 (1959).

Lapp, Paul W. "Bâb edh-Dhrâ' Tomb A 76 and Early Bronze I in

Palestine." *Bulletin of the American Schools of Oriental Research* 189 (1968).

_____. "The Cemetery at Bâb edh-Dhrâ`." *Archaeology* 19 (1966).

Legrain, Leon. "Horseback Riding in Mesopotamia in the Third Millennium B.C." *University Museum Bulletin* 11 (1946).

Lehmann, Manfred R. "Abraham's Purchase of Machpelah and Hittite Law." *Bulletin of the American Schools of Oriental Research* 129 (1953).

Livingston, David. "Location of Biblical Bethel and Ai Reconsidered." *The Westminster Theological Journal* 33 (1970).

Los, F. J. "The Table of Peoples of the Tenth Chapter of Genesis." *Mankind Quarterly* 7 (1967).

Lowe, William G. "Discovering the Calendar of the Creation." *Science and Scripture* 1 (1971).

MacRae, Allan A. "Abraham and the Stars." *Bulletin of the Evangelical Theological Society* 8 (1965).

_____. "The Scientific Approach to the Old Testament (Part II)." *Bibliotheca Sacra* 110 (1953).

Malamat, A. "Man and the Bible: Some Patterns of Tribal Organization and Distribution." *Journal of the American Oriental Society* 82 (1962).

_____. "Mari." *The Biblical Archaeologist* 34 (1971).

Mallowan, M. E. L. "Excavations at Brak and Chagar Bazar." *Iraq* 9 (1947).

Martin, John. "A Famine Element in the Flood Story." *Journal of Biblical Literature* 45 (1926).

May, Herbert G. "The Creation of Light in Genesis 1:3–5." *Journal of Biblical Literature* 58 (1939).

_____. "The Patriarchal Idea of God." *Journal of Biblical Literature* 60 (1941).

Mayes, A. D. H. "Israel in the Pre-Monarchy Period." *Vetus Testamentum* 23 (1973).

Mazar, Benjamin. "The Historical Background of the Book of Genesis." *Journal of Near Eastern Studies* 28 (1969).

333

Mendelsohn, I. "The Family in the Ancient Near East." *The Biblical Archaeologist* 11 (1948).

―――. "On the Preferential Status of the Eldest Son." *Bulletin of the American Schools of Oriental Research* 156 (1959).

Mendenhall, George E. "Puppy and Lettuce in Northwest-Semitic Covenant Making." *Bulletin of the American Schools of Oriental Research* 133 (1954).

Meyers, Eric M. "Secondary Burials in Palestine." *The Biblical Archaeologist* 33 (1970).

Miller, J. Maxwell. "In the 'Image' and 'Likeness' of God." *Journal of Biblical Literature* 91 (1972).

Mixter, Russell L. "Man in Creation." *Christian Life* 23 (1961).

Moore, James R. "Charles Lyell and the Noachian Deluge." *Evangelical Quarterly* 45 (1973).

Moore, L. Paul, Jr. "Prayer in the Pentateuch." *Bibliotheca Sacra* 98 (1941).

Moran, W. L. "Genesis 49:10 and Its Use in Ezekiel 21:32." *Biblica* 39 (1958).

Morgenstern, Julian. "A Note on Genesis 5:29." *Journal of Biblical Literature* 49 (1930).

Morris, Henry M. "The Chronology of Genesis 1–11 and Geologic Time." *Biblical Viewpoint* 2 (1968).

Neal, Marshall. "The Messianic Hope in Genesis." *Biblical Viewpoint* 2 (1968).

Neff, Robert W. "The Annunciation in the Birth Narrative of Ishmael." *Biblical Research* 17 (1972).

―――. "The Birth and Election of Isaac in the Priestly Tradition." *Biblical Research* 15 (1970).

Nielsen, Eduard. "Creation and the Fall of Man: A Cross-Disciplinary Investigation." *Hebrew Union College Annual* 43 (1972).

Olson, W. S. "Has Science Dated the Biblical Flood?" *Zygon* 2 (1967).

Oppenheim, A. Leo. "The Golden Garments of the Gods." *Journal of Near Eastern Studies* 8 (1949).

Orlinsky, Harry M. "The Plain Meaning of $R\hat{u}^a\underline{h}$ in Genesis 1:2." *The Jewish Quarterly Review* 48 (1957).

Panosian, Edward M. "Genesis: 'This Beginning of Miracles.'" *Biblical Viewpoint* 2 (1968).

Payne, J. Barton. "The Concept of 'Kinds' in Scripture." *Journal of the American Scientific Affiliation* 10 (1958).

———. "Theistic Evolution and the Hebrew of Genesis 1–2." *Bulletin of the Evangelical Theological Society* 8 (1965).

Peck, John. "Note on Genesis 37:2 and Joseph's Character." *Expository Times* 82 (1971).

Poebel, A. "The Assyrian King List from Khorsabad." *Journal of Near Eastern Studies* 1 (1942).

Porten, Bezalel, and Rappaport, Uriel. "Poetic Structure in Genesis 9:7." *Vetus Testamentum* 21 (1971).

Rainey, Anson F. "Bethel Is Still Beitin." *The Westminister Theological Journal* 33 (1971).

Redford, D.B. "A Study of the Biblical Story of Joseph (Gen. 37–50)." Supplement to *Vetus Testamentum* 20 (1970).

Reicke, Bo. "The Knowledge Hidden in the Tree of Paradise." *Journal of Semitic Studies* 1 (1956).

Reymond, Robert L. "Practical Principles from the Patriarchs." *Biblical Viewpoint* 2 (1968).

Rice, G. "Cosmological Ideas and Religious Truth in Genesis 1." *Journal of Religious Thought* 23 (1966).

———. "The Curse That Never Was." *Journal of Religious Thought* 29 (1972).

Riemann, Paul A. "Am I My Brother's Keeper?" *Interpretation* 24 (1970).

Riggs, Jack R. "The Length of Israel's Sojourn in Egypt." *Grace Journal* 12 (1971).

Rist, Martin. "The God of Abraham, Isaac, and Jacob. A Liturgical and Magical Formula." *Journal of Biblical Literature* 57 (1938).

Rodd, C. S. "Shall Not the Judge of All the Earth Do What Is Just? (Gen. 18:25)." *Expository Times* 83 (1972).

Romanoff, Paul. "A Third Version of the Flood Narrative." *Journal of Biblical Literature* 50 (1931).

Roth, Wolfgang M. W. "The Wooing of Rebekah." *The Catholic Biblical Quarterly* 34 (1972).

Rowe, M. "Genesis and the Natural Order." *Cross and Crown* 23 (1971).

Ruprecht, Eberhard. "Die Frage nach den vorliterarischen Überlieferungen in der Genesisforschung des ausgehenden." *Zeitschrift für die Alttestamentliche Wissenschaft* 84 (1972).

Russell, Colin. "Noah and the Neptunists." *Faith and Thought* 100 (1972–73).

Saggs, H. W. F. "Ur of the Chaldees: A Problem of Identification." *Iraq* 22 (1960).

Sasson, Jack M. "Circumcision in the Ancient Near East." *Journal of Biblical Literature* 85 (1966).

Sayce, A. H. "The Tenth Chapter of Genesis." *Journal of Biblical Literature* 44 (1925).

Schmidt, Nathaniel. "The Numen of Penuel (Gen. 32:24–31)." *Journal of Biblical Literature* 45 (1926)

Schultz, Samuel J. "The Unity of the Human Race." *Bibliotheca Sacra* 113 (1956).

Seebass, H. "Zum Text von Gen. XVI:13b." *Vetus Testamentum* 21 (1971).

Seely, Paul. "Adam and Anthropology: A Proposed Solution." *Journal of the American Scientific Affiliation* 22 (1970).

―――. "The Three Storied Universe." *Journal of the American Scientific Affiliation* 21 (1969).

Simpson, George G. "The Nonprevalence of Humanoids." *Science* 143 (1964).

Speiser, E. A. " 'Coming' and 'Going' at the City Gate." *Bulletin of the American Schools of Oriental Research* 144 (1956).

―――. " '*Ed* in the Story of Creation." *Bulletin of American Schools of Oriental Research* 140 (1955).

―――. "The Ethnic Divisions of Man." In *The Interpreter's Dic-*

tionary of the Bible, edited by George A. Buttrick, vol. 2. New York: Abingdon Press, 1962.

_____. "Ethnic Movements in the Near East in the Second Millennium B.C." *Annual of the American Schools of Oriental Research* 13 (1933).

_____. " 'I Know Not the Day of My Death.' " *Journal of Biblical Literature* 74 (1955).

_____. "New Kirkuk Documents Relating to Family Laws." *Annual of the American Schools of Oriental Research* 10 (1930).

_____. "Word Plays in the Creation Epic's Version of the Founding of Babylon." *Orientalia* 25 (1956).

Steenstra, P. H. "Theology of Moses." *Journal of Biblical Literature* 14 (1895).

Stern, Harold S. "The Knowledge of Good and Evil." *Vetus Testamentum* 8 (1958).

Strickling, James E. "A Quantitative Analysis of the Life Spans of the Genesis Patriarchs." *Creation Research Society Quarterly* 10 (1973).

Tanner, William F. "Geology and the Days of Genesis." *Journal of the American Scientific Affiliation* 16 (1964).

Thompson, John A. "Samaritan Evidence for 'All of Them in the Land of Shinar' (Gen. 10:10)." *Journal of Biblical Literature* 90 (1971).

Thompson, P. E. S. "The Yahwist Creation Story." *Vetus Testamentum* 21 (1971).

Thornton, C. G. "Trees, Gibbets, and Crosses." *Journal of the Evangelical Theological Society* 23 (1972).

Tribe, Phyllis. "Eve and Adam: Genesis 2–3 Reread." *Andover Newton Quarterly* 13 (1973)

Tucker, G. M. "The Legal Background of Genesis 23." *Journal of Biblical Literature* 85 (1966).

Unger, Merrill F. "Archaeology and Genesis 3–4." *Bibliotheca Sacra* 110 (1953).

_____. "The Babylonian and Biblical Accounts of Creation." *Bibliotheca Sacra* 103 (1952).

337

Uphill, E. P. "Pithom and Raamses: Their Location and Significance." *Journal of Near Eastern Studies* 27 (1968).

Van Dyken, Peter L. "Was God's Covenant with Abraham Ever Abolished?" *Torch and Trumpet* (1961).

Van Seters, John. "Jacob's Marriages and Ancient Near East Customs: A Re-examination." *Harvard Theological Review* 62 (1969).

Vawter, Bruce. "The Canaanite Background of Genesis 49." *The Catholic Biblical Quarterly* 17 (1955).

Walvoord, John F. "The Fulfillment of the Abrahamic Covenant." *Bibliotheca Sacra* 102 (1945).

Ward, W. A. "The Egyptian Office of Joseph." *Journal of Semitic Studies* 5 (1960).

_____. "Egyptian Titles in Genesis 39–50." *Bibliotheca Sacra* 114 (1957).

Waterman, L. "Jacob the Forgotten Supplanter." *American Journal of Semitic Languages and Literatures* 4 (1938).

Weir, C. Mullo. "The Alleged Hurrian Wife-Sister Motif in Genesis." *Glasgow University Oriental Society Transactions* 22 (1970).

Whitley, C. F. "The Pattern of Creation in Genesis 1." *Journal of Near Eastern Studies* 17 (1958).

Whybray, R. N. "The Joseph Story and Pentateuchal Criticism." *Vetus Testamentum* 18 (1968).

Wilson, Clifford A. "The Problem of Childlessness in Near Eastern Law." *Buried History* 5 (1969).

Winnett, F. V. "The Founding of Hebron." *Bulletin of the Canadian Society of Biblical Studies* 3 (1937).

Winter, W. "Biblical and Archaeological Data on Ai Reappraised." *The Seminary Review* 16 (1970).

Wiseman, D. J. "Genesis 10: Some Archaeological Considerations." *Journal of the Transactions of the Victoria Institute* 87 (1955).

Woltzer, H. R. "The Age of the Earth." *Free University Quarterly* 3 (1955).

Wood, Robert W. "The Age of Man." *Creation Research Society Quarterly* 2 (1966).

Woudstra, Marten H. "Recent Translations of Genesis 3:15." *Calvin Theological Journal* 6 (1971).

Wright, G. Ernest. "The Ark Again?" *Newsletter: American Schools of Oriental Research* 3 (1970).

———. "The Chronology of Palestinian Pottery in Middle Bronze I." *Bulletin of the American Schools of Oriental Research* (1938).

———. "History and the Patriarchs." *Expository Times* 71 (1959–60).

———. "The Samaritans at Shechem." *Harvard Theological Review* 55 (1962).

Yaron, Reuven. "Aramaic Marriage Contracts." *Journal of Semitic Studies* 5 (1960).

Yoder, John H. "Capital Punishment and the Bible." *Christianity Today* 4 (Feb. 1, 1960).

Young, G. Douglas. "Further Light on the Translation of Genesis 1:1." *Journal of the American Scientific Affiliation* 10 (1958).

———. "The Relevance of Scientific Thought to Scriptural Interpretation." *Bulletin of the Evangelical Theological Society* 4 (1961).

Zimmerman, Charles L. "The Chronology and Birth of Jacob's Children by Leah and Her Handmaid." *Grace Journal* 13 (1972).

Zimmermann, Frank. "Some Textual Studies in Genesis." *Journal of Biblical Literature* 73 (1954).

Indexes

I. Index of Authors

342

343

352

353

354

355